The Leisure Industries

Also by Ken Roberts

Leisure

Strike at Pilkingtons (with T Lane)

From School to Work: A Study of the Youth Employment Service

The Character Training Industry (with G White and H J Parker)

The Fragmentary Class Structure (with F G Cook, S C Clark and E Semeonoff)

The Working Class

Contemporary Society and The Growth of Leisure

Youth and Leisure

School-leavers and their Prospects

Leisure and Lifestyle: A Comparative Analysis of Free Time (with A Olszewska)

Trends in Sports: A Multinational Perspective (with T J Kamphorst)

Youth and Work: The Transition into Employment in England and Germany (with J Bynner)

Careers and Identities (with M Banks, I Bates, G Breakwell, J Bynner, N Emler and L Jamieson)

Black Youth in Liverpool (with M Connolly, G Ben-Tovim and P Torkington)

Inner-City Sport: Who Plays and What are the Benefits? (with D A Brodie)

Youth and Employment in Modern Britain

Leisure and Social Stratification

Leisure in Contemporary Society

Surviving Post-Communism: Young People in the Former Soviet Union (with S C Clark, C Fagan and J Tholen)

Class in Modern Britain

The Leisure Industries

KEN ROBERTS

First published 2004 by
PALGRAVE MACMILLAN
Houndmills, Basingstoke, Hampshire RG21 6XS and
175 Fifth Avenue, New York, N.Y. 10010
Companies and representatives throughout the world

PALGRAVE MACMILLAN is the global academic imprint of the Palgrave
Macmillan division of St. Martin's Press, LLC and of Palgrave Macmillan Ltd.
Macmillan is a registered trademark in the United States, United Kingdom
and other countries. Palgrave is a registered trademark in the European
Union and other countries.

ISBN 1–4039–0411–1 hardback
ISBN 1–4039–0412–X paperback

This book is printed on paper suitable for recycling and
made from fully managed and sustained forest sources.

A catalogue record for this book is available from the British Library.

Library of Congress Cataloging-in-Publication Data
Roberts, Kenneth, 1940–
    p. cm.
  Includes bibliographical references and index.
  ISBN 0–4039–0411–1 (cloth) — ISBN 1–4039–0412–X (paper)
  1. Leisure industry. I. Title.
  GV188R63 2004
  790.1–dc22   2003069647

10   9   8   7   6   5   4   3   2   1
13 12 11 10 09 08 07 06 05 04

Printed in China

Contents

PART II   PROVISIONS

List of Tables and Boxes

Tables

Boxes

1 Introduction

Why study leisure providers?

> ... more people work in film and TV than in the car industry – let alone shipbuilding. The overseas earnings of British rock music exceed those generated by the steel industry. (Tony Blair, 'Britain can remake it', *Guardian*, 22 July 1997)

Most present-day politicians are aware of leisure's economic importance, but confronting the facts can still provoke culture shock elsewhere. During Britain's 2001 foot-and-mouth outbreak, many people were surprised to learn that tourism now far outstrips agriculture in importance in Britain's rural economy. Even today, tabloid newspapers, probably for want of better headlines, occasionally mock recreation management, sport, tourism and media studies as joke subjects, and evidence of dumbing-down in higher education. All such talk is grotesquely out of date. Nowadays leisure studies is more likely to prove vocational – leading on to a job – than preparation for a career in science-based manufacturing. Tourism alone accounts for almost 5 per cent of UK Gross Domestic Product (GDP). It employs over 2 million people, around 7 per cent of the country's workforce, more than either transport or construction. Sport accounts for around 3 per cent of GDP in economically advanced countries (Henry and Gratton, 2001). Households spend more on leisure goods and services than on either housing or food and non-alcoholic drinks (see Table 2.1, p. 19).

The reasons why leisure's economic importance has been, and is still, growing have been explained clearly by Jonathan Gershuny (2000). As technological advances are introduced, and as workers become more skilled, they become more productive. This enables them to take home higher pay, and sometimes to reduce their hours of work. The proportion of income devoted to basic needs declines. More is spent on satisfying 'luxurious' wants. Thus demand for leisure goods and services increases, creating more and more employment in these fields. Between

1

1971 and 1996 total consumer spending in Britain rose by roughly 75 per cent, but spending on leisure goods and services increased by approximately 100 per cent. The proportion of all spending devoted to leisure goods and services rose from 22 per cent to 26 per cent, or from 33 per cent to 38 per cent if the boundaries of leisure are set wider (Martin and Mason, 1998). Leisure has blurred edges. Spending on holidays and admissions to cinemas is clearly 'in', but it is less clear what proportions of all spending on meals-out and transport should be classified as leisure. Yet no matter where the boundaries are drawn, the spending graphs slope upwards.

Leisure's role in people's lives is not purely economic. Leisure has important social, psychological and cultural dimensions. As leisure's share of the economy grows, so does its role in people's everyday lives. So the balance tilts from life being work- and production-centred to becoming leisure- or consumption-centred. Leisure becomes an alternative or complementary source of identities (who people think they are, and how others see them). It is not leisure goods, activities or services themselves which confer identities. They come from the meanings which become associated with them in the course of all the marketing, embellishment in media coverage, and in everyday social intercourse. The leisure industries do not supply just goods and services. They also market desires, and enable consumers to be recognised as – and to feel like – particular kinds of people as a result of what they wear, eat, drink, what they listen to and watch, and where they are seen and who they are seen with. The leisure industries do not create social class, age, gender, ethnic or national divisions, but they can sharpen, deepen or diminish these divisions, and characterise the relevant groups. They do this by deciding which market is most appropriate for a given activity, good or service, along with the associated identity. Without this necessarily being anyone's conscious intention, it has been argued that collectively the leisure industries convey an impression that black people are particularly talented in sport and entertainment (Cashmore, 1982). In a similar way, tourism has been accused of stereotyping third world people as 'happy servants' of consumers from richer countries (Morgan and Pritchard, 1998). The tourism, sport, entertainment and hospitality industries have all been criticised for casting women in a 'beauty role' (Richards and Milestone, 2000). It is possible for those concerned to 'fight back'; to challenge and emancipate themselves from the roles and characteristics with which they are typecast. So women may use sport to demonstrate that they can be competitive, assertive, even aggressive (see Talbot, 1990), but this is easier if one is a consumer rather than a worker in the leisure industries. In other words, money talks. But even with money there can be personal discomfort and social costs in defying other's expectations.

We will encounter the social and cultural dimensions of leisure throughout this book. Much more is involved than leisure's economic importance, yet that alone would be sufficient justification for a book on the leisure industries. Even so, thinking in purely theoretical terms, the principal reason for examining leisure providers must be that they are thoroughly implicated in actually creating modern leisure. Any individual business, government department or voluntary organisation, at any particular moment in time, has to address a leisure market that already exists

– people with so much time and money to spend, and tastes to satisfy. But historically the providers have helped to create the kind of leisure that is now experienced in the Western world, and increasingly in all other parts of the world. Leisure, as we know it today, arises when three conditions are met:

- First, work must be modernised, meaning that it must be compartmentalised – separated from the rest of life by some combination of time, place and social relationships – and rationalised – organised so that tasks are performed as efficiently as possible and with no incentive to maximise job satisfaction. Opportunities to do things for the pure pleasure, for the intrinsic satisfaction, thereby become concentrated within people's 'own' time.
- Second, the family, community and religious controls that once prescribed entire ways of life must be relaxed. The modernisation of work, which led to individuals receiving money wages, assisted this relaxation. In pre-industrial times both work and recreation were normally part and parcel of family and community life (see Malcolmson, 1973) whereas modern leisure allows – indeed requires – individuals and households to make lifestyle choices.
- Third, although governments may (and in practice always do) make some provisions for people's leisure, the leisure that we experience depends on governments not being totalitarian and trying to do everything. Rather, they must uphold laws that protect socio-cultural space in which civil society can develop. People must be free to form associations for religious, political and recreational purposes, and businesses must be able to market leisure goods and services. Such provisions will only be made when people have free time and money to spend, but this in itself is not a sufficient condition to produce modern leisure. There must be space for diverse uses of leisure to be offered. People can select and act on leisure interests, thereby making lifestyle choices, only when a wide range of provisions are 'out there' rather than interwoven in their family and neighbourhood lives.

As we have already seen, it is impossible to draw a clear line between leisure and the rest of life, and this applies to provisions as much as to people's activities and spending. Leisure goods and services are bought by or for private individuals rather than businesses. In economists' language, leisure provisions are counted among 'consumer goods and services'. The problem is to separate spending on consumer essentials like food, housing, clothing and fuel and other social necessities such as education and health care from pure leisure goods and services. The boundary is blurred, which is why estimates of leisure spending, as above, and leisure time also, often give minimum–maximum ranges. However, all leisure goods and services share two features which are important from every provider's point of view. First, because they are not as essential – or not essential in the same way – as things like food and shelter, leisure goods and services are subject to flights of fashion, and this makes catering for leisure high-risk. Second, there is the above-average rate of overall growth, which means that exceptional returns are available for those who provide successfully.

What the leisure industries offer

There are alternative ways in which the leisure industries can be classified. One is according to the kinds of goods and services that they offer. The big three in this classification are tourism, out-of-home eating and drinking (usually alcohol), and the media. Government statisticians and the industries themselves use these labels, and, of course, they are recognised by members of the public. Now there are different ways in which the relative sizes of leisure industries can be measured: in terms of the proportions of the population involved, the total amounts of time, or the amounts of money that are spent. All the big three leisure industries score highly on at least two of these measurements.

- Tourism, conventionally defined as spending at least one night away from home, is top in terms of spending (see Table 2.1, p. 19). Households save continuously for the big break, or, increasingly nowadays, for their major and minor holidays. Roughly 60 per cent of the UK population take at least one holiday (with at least four nights away from home) each year. The non-participants are mostly old and/or poor.
- Drinking is an overlapping leisure activity. Whether people are at home or 'away', drinking is what they are most likely to do when they 'go out' in the evening. Seventy-five per cent of adult men and 60 per cent of women drink alcohol at least once during a typical week. The total spend on alcohol is second only to tourism. If out-of-home eating is combined with drinking, this becomes the top leisure activity in terms of spending.
- Nowadays television is the market leader among the mass media. 'The box' alone accounts for roughly 40 per cent of all leisure time in all modern societies (Robinson and Godbey, 1999). Over 95 per cent of UK homes contain at least one television receiver, and the TV is normally switched on whenever people are in and doing nothing else. Television also ranks highly in terms of spending when purchases and rentals of hardware, the licence fee, plus subscriptions for satellite and cable channels are taken into account. To these it is now customary to add spending on videos and the internet because the boundaries between these media are increasingly blurred.

Note that, if spending on motoring was to be counted as leisure expenditure, this would easily be top of the list, well ahead of holidays. Are cars leisure goods or simply necessities? Maybe driving *as* a leisure activity is a thing of the past but the cost of driving *to* a leisure activity should really be included in leisure spending.

Mention leisure and many people's thoughts are likely to switch immediately to sport, the arts, the countryside, stately homes and heritage sites. These are actually minor components of the leisure market, however size is measured, although they may act as the magnets within, or at least be part of, larger uses of leisure. For example, people may visit theatres and heritage sites while on holiday, and these attractions may influence where their holidays are spent. Sport may be the reason why people subscribe to satellite or cable television. Simple quantitative measures may understate the importance of particular uses of leisure. Nevertheless, the facts remain that sport and the arts (even when spectating and participating are aggregated), and countryside and heritage visits, lag well behind not only the big three, but other activities which may not spring immediately to mind as uses of leisure. We spend more on telephone calls than on sport, all hobby-type activities, or visits to cinemas and other places of entertainment. With meals-out, motoring, telephone usage, clothing and housing (the home is where most leisure time is spent) it is impossible to separate out the proportions of spending that should be classified as leisure. Moreover, some leisure activities are (money) cost free: casual conversation and relaxation, and also window shopping and its armchair equivalents. Shopping itself, the act of purchasing and all the preliminaries, probably unlike motoring, can be a pleasure in its own right (see Chapter 11) as well as, sometimes, for the purchase of leisure goods. An implication of all this is that all the statistics understate the total amounts of time and money that could – and should in principle – be classified as leisure.

There are other industries which really ought to be included but are sometimes ignored, and thereby rendered invisible, in the literature on leisure. Gambling is a bigger leisure industry in Britain than either sport or the cinema, more so since the National Lottery began in 1994. Tobacco and other leisure drugs of choice are another major leisure market. The participation rates are much lower than for television and alcohol, but those who partake regularly spend considerable proportions of their leisure budgets on tobacco products, and on other (illegal) drugs in some cases. Americans spend more on illegal drugs than on cigarettes (Campbell, 2003). All these uses of time and money (like motoring and the telephone) are usually overlooked in books and courses on leisure. There is a tendency to focus on activities which are clearly leisure and to ignore 'grey' ones, and also to concentrate on the bright side rather than the dark side of leisure. Sex is a moderately large leisure industry. Nowadays the leading component in the sex industry is pornography. USA porn (with the sex video as its main product) has a larger turnover than the mainstream cinema, the theatre, and the combined worth of rock and country music (Sharkey, 1997). America produces over 200 new porn video titles every week (Campbell, 2003). The internet has become a profitable outlet. In 1997 there were around 22,000 porn websites; by 2003 this number had risen to around 300,000 (Campbell, 2003). USA strip clubs have a bigger cash turnover than Broadway, regional theatres and orchestral performances combined (Campbell, 2003). Sex tourism has become a distinct branch of the global holiday industry (see Davidson, 1994; Jeffreys, 1999). Then there are all the paid-for sex-centred services – difficult to quantify, as the tax authorities will testify.

Chris Rojek (2000) has insisted that the study of leisure should pay proper attention to the dark side. Some writers define leisure in terms of seeking or obtaining 'peak experience'. If such definitions are taken literally, then, as Rojek points out, serial murder has to be included. 'Dark leisure' is not just for a minority of deviant individuals. Rojek contends that 'edgework' and 'liminality' are features of much leisure behaviour. People gain tingle, excitement, by pressing the limits of what they themselves, and society, will tolerate, hence the pleasures of football hooliganism, joy-riding, adultery and dangerous sports. Totally safe, hygienic leisure is relatively boring. Everyone wants to take some risks, though they may also seek – even demand – to be protected from the more serious consequences.

Leisure activities change constantly. The market is notoriously unstable. Some say that people's lifestyles will be revolutionised by the internet – that in the future they will increasingly not only shop online but form cyberspace friendships, and use multimedia to supply 'virtually' any experience that they want to any place at any time. This may happen, but not necessarily (see Chapter 10, pp. 148–52). Will the internet make as great a difference as electricity, or the internal combustion engine, or television? We cannot know, but the biggest leisure revolution in Britain to date occurred in the second half of the nineteenth century, just after the country had become the world's first industrial nation. It was then that the modern holiday was invented, likewise most modern sports, and the pub became a place that would be recognised by today's patrons. It was also the period when the foundations were laid for our present-day commercial, public and voluntary systems of catering for people's leisure. This book is about these systems and the leisure opportunities that they offer.

Issues

A book on the leisure industries can be justified by their importance in the present-day economy and in people's day-to-day lives. However, this book is also intended to be timely. This is an age in which the thinking of the new right threatens to become hegemonic, having replaced an earlier social democratic consensus, but with more and more people seeking some kind of third way (see Giddens, 1998). The earlier social democratic consensus embraced a regulated (planned) and mixed (private and public sector) economy, and a progressively expanding welfare state and social services. This consensus held in most Western countries from the Second World War until the 1970s when the new right mounted a successful challenge. The new right claims that private enterprises and markets, not governments, are the best servants of the public's interests. This was the case for privatisation and deregulation, thereby allowing the expansion of commerce governed only by consumer demand. In their view the earlier dominance of the state was a tragic historical mistake or a temporary necessity while consumers were still too poor or too immature to look after themselves – conditions which, it is said, no longer apply.

The new right has proved as factious as the old left. A libertarian wing advocates a minimal state, maybe doing no more than safeguarding the external defence of the realm and internal law and order plus providing sound money. If a case for additional state services is admitted (health care and education, for example), libertarians favour the state acting as a purchaser (from independent hospitals and schools, for instance) rather than a direct provider, and replacing free-to-user services with vouchers (or an equivalent entitlement) which consumers could top up if they desired and with which they could always shop around. This libertarian right has been extraordinarily influential in leisure in many countries. Commercial sectors such as tourism have been allowed to expand. Deregulation (and expansion) have been pursued in shopping, gambling, and out-of-home drinking and dining. Commerce has been allowed to make inroads in fields such as sports, which were formerly governed by voluntary associations, and in areas such as broadcasting, which in Europe used to be basically a public service. Many parks, playing fields, indoor sport facilities and other public amenities have been contracted out to private sector management. Is this the best way of running the leisure industries?

There is an authoritarian wing of the new right which advocates minimal state provisions but favours heavy (moral) restrictions on the goods and services that other bodies are allowed to supply and consumers to purchase. Authoritarians want the public to be protected from base temptations. They favour the state acting paternally (critics say like a nanny). The authoritarian right wants restrictions on the 'exploitation' of sex and violence, and on trade in alcohol, drugs, gambling and whatever else gives offence to those who believe that they know better. This position is compatible with a low-tax, low-spending state. Intervention is basically restrictive rather than facilitating.

The old social democratic left was suspicious of, if not altogether hostile to, the market economy. It favoured similar restrictions to the authoritarian right but envisaged the market being progressively replaced as the public was converted by the appeal of superior state and voluntary sector provisions. People were to express their support for this regime as citizens through the ballot box rather than as consumers in the market place. Most people would probably not fancy a return to this system. If none of the above models are practicable, you will understand why so many are searching for another way.

This book stakes out a third way in leisure, a 'modern left' position. Here the market is unfettered, more or less as envisaged by the libertarian right. Commerce is not crowded out but complemented by state and voluntary sector provisions which are not regarded as superior but different. State provisions are based on the public sector's special capabilities which, to anticipate later arguments, include making leisure opportunities accessible to all citizens. The voluntary sector is used when cranking up its efforts through public support serves a public interest. For example, governments might give financial support to voluntary youth organisations as well as, or instead of, creating their own youth movements. Commerce is restricted only in so far as some territory is occupied by the public and voluntary sectors. Otherwise markets are liberated. Thus the voluntary and public sectors do not squeeze the market so much as widen citizens' and consumers' options.

This book makes the case for a 'third way'. Maybe readers will think of further alternatives. Some may prefer to resurrect the old left or to back one of the new right positions. This book challenges everyone with a stake or interest in the leisure industries to decide where they stand.

Analysing the leisure industries

One of the core arguments – a thread that links all the chapters in this book – is that the commercial, voluntary and public sectors have different, very distinctive, capabilities. We shall see that these sectors are not just alternative ways of providing much the same range of leisure goods and services. Each sector has its own 'engine', and the provisions that result are distinctively commercial, voluntary or public sector products. It is in terms of the 'logics' of commerce, voluntarism and state intervention that we find our most powerful explanations of what the leisure industries offer. Dividing the field into tourism, the media, sport and so on is helpful, indeed necessary, for descriptive purposes, that is, to portray the range of leisure opportunities with which individuals are confronted. However, we find that we cannot explain the kind of holidays, for example, that are made available simply by searching for facts and explanations, however deeply and assiduously, solely within the field of tourism. We need to identify the main sector and thereby the main 'engine' which drives this segment of the leisure industries, which turns out to be commerce, which is always run for profit – the very same engine which also provides most popular entertainment, and most opportunities to gamble and to spend evenings-out eating or drinking. Sport, in contrast, developed from a voluntary base, and most sport is still run by volunteers, acting as members of voluntary bodies. Commerce has claimed segments of top sport and, as explained in Chapter 7, in doing so it has not merely replaced one supply mechanism with another but has changed the character of the sports themselves. Likewise, we shall see in Chapter 10 that, as television has become increasingly commercial, the product itself has been modified.

There are two organising principles within this book. One is explicit in the chapter headings in Part II (Chapters 5–13). We systematically examine tourism, sport and so on – how each industry developed, and how it is run. We cover leisure's dark side (alcohol and gambling, for example) as well as its brighter aspects, and some marginal activities such as shopping are included. The other organising principle is that throughout all the examples in successive chapters the book seeks to identify and then illustrate the special capabilities in leisure of commerce, voluntary associations and the state. It aims to explain the strengths and limitations of each. Commerce is not subjected to blanket praise or condemnation. Likewise the voluntary sector is shown to have both special capabilities and limitations. State intervention is shown to be neither good nor bad in itself. A major aim of this book is to identify the state's special capabilities in leisure which could, and should, become the foundation for coherent and effective third-way leisure policies.

We proceed in Part I (Chapters 2–4) by examining systematically the character of the commercial, voluntary and state-based systems of leisure provision. Commerce (driven by profit) is treated briefly at this point. It provides many different kinds of leisure goods and services and therefore features in every chapter about particular kinds of leisure, but its distinctive features are simple, straightforward, and easy to explain and understand. Chapter 3 deals similarly with voluntary associations – what they are, why they exist, and what is special about what they offer. Chapter 4 treats public sector leisure in the same way, identifying how it is 'driven', and its special capabilities. These special capabilities of the public sector are considered again in Part III (Chapter 14), but the intervening chapters will illustrate repeatedly that the state has capabilities which are simply beyond the reach of both commerce and the voluntary sector.

A recurrent issue in this book, and necessarily so, is the progressive commercialisation of leisure provision which is partly an outcome of the recent strength of the new right. This is despite the fact that, as we will see in Chapter 2, commerce still tends to receive far more criticism than praise. Commerce has been accused of debasing sports, films, music, catering, broadcasting, holidays and the arts, and promoting less desirable uses of leisure such as drinking and gambling. Commercialisation occurred at different times in different areas of leisure. So critiques of Hollywood and popular music date from the 1920s whereas, in Europe, complaints about business taking over sport and broadcasting have mounted only during the last 20 years. The case against commerce differs somewhat from leisure industry to leisure industry, but there are numerous overlaps and cross-overs in the arguments, and these are highlighted in Chapter 2. Governments, especially in recent times when they have been influenced by new right thinking, have been criticised for creating or defending the conditions which enable commercial businesses to expand their operations willy-nilly, failing to do enough themselves, failing to protect the voluntary sector, and, within the latter, favouring the more commercial high-profile projects – funding performing arts companies, and subsidising the reconstruction of Wembley – while neglecting community arts and grass-roots amateur sport. Some of the more detailed critiques of commerce are introduced in the chapters about the particular leisure industries to which the arguments were originally applied. So the arguments of the Frankfurt School are presented alongside Hollywood and popular music in Chapter 9, while the McDonaldization thesis is considered alongside the hospitality industry in Chapter 11.

This book's third-way position is as follows:

■ First, commercialisation is certainly a powerful trend. It developed throughout the twentieth century and it is continuing, aided by new right policies
■ Second, commerce is not a wholly malign force in leisure. It can spread only when there are willing consumers who always have alternatives.
■ Third, commerce is just one of three main systems that cater for leisure, and it is simply incapable of dowsing either the voluntary or the public sector unless volunteers and politicians decide to stand aside.
■ Fourth, while commerce and the voluntary sector can be relied on to perform to their strengths, the public sector may not. Here everything depends on policy-makers recognising their special capabilities in leisure, and, up to now, they have failed to do so.

The selection of leisure industries, and the order in which they are introduced from Chapter 5 onwards has an underlying logic. We begin with tourism, a leisure industry in which commerce now has a long history as the principal provider. We then consider modern sports, which have voluntary sector roots that, as we shall see, are still largely intact. Commerce services sport, but Chapters 6 and 7 explain why it is unable to take over the core organisation without changing the character of the sports themselves. Chapter 8 deals with events, which are always about tourism plus the event, which may be based on sport, an art form, wine or anything else that attracts visitors. Chapters 9 and 10 are about the media. Some of these – printed media, films and recorded music – have always been basically commercial, whereas in Europe broadcasting was originally developed as a public service. During the latter part of the twentieth century, there was a commercial take-over. Recent commercial inroads in sport and broadcasting, together with the controversies about the costs and benefits for countries that host events such as the Olympics, highlight what is distinctive about each of the three main types of leisure provider. Chapters 11 and 12 discuss a group of commercial leisure industries which are often neglected in courses and texts on leisure: shopping, out-of-home eating and drinking, and gambling. Chapter 13 then switches to the arts – high culture – which is supported primarily by a combination of voluntary effort and state largesse. This chapter serves as a reminder that commerce may well have become the leader but it is still not our sole leisure provider.

The final chapter returns to the role of the state in leisure. It draws on evidence presented in the intervening chapters, and expands on the analysis, in Chapter 4, of the public sector's special capabilities; what governments alone can realistically hope to achieve by intervening in leisure. Up to now these capabilities have never been properly identified. This is bound up with the failure to develop coherent leisure policies and, despite all the carping about commerce, to offer a strong modern alternative to the new right's system. One outcome is that, although the UK's and other governments still spend quite a lot and do quite a lot in leisure, their populations fail to derive maximum benefit. They endure debacles such as the Millennium Dome. There were bound to be arguments over whether Britain should commemorate the new millennium and, if so, whether this should be with a building and, if so, what kind of building and where it should be located. There are plenty of past examples of commemorative buildings and parks, bequeathed for public benefit, which have come to be regarded as local or national assets once their birth arguments faded away. Courtesy of the funding available from the National Lottery, the Dome could have fared similarly. If it had been built, then handed to trustees, to be used indefinitely for public benefit – very likely in ways that could not be envisaged at the beginning of the millennium – people would now be enjoying the maturation of the project. In the event, the Dome was treated as if it was a business. Commercial sponsors were sought. The public was charged admission prices appropriate to a commercial attraction, but in this case one which had been built mainly with their own money. The plan was always to sell off the Dome after just one year. In the event, it was virtually given away. Success was defined in terms of getting the sums right. The all-round embarrassment, and the net cost of the Dome (over £1 billion), make this a particularly high profile example of the penalties of failure in leisure policy-making.

Governments have yet to develop sound policies to pursue in leisure, and we shall see in Chapter 14 that they have hardly begun to face up to some of the wider policy issues – sustainability, and the quality of employment offered by the leisure industries – that the growth of these industries poses. Another way, if not this book's proposed third way, is surely needed.

Part

I

PROVIDERS

2 Commercial Leisure

Introduction

This chapter pivots around one of modernity's great debates – the one between pro- and anti-marketeers. Economists have usually been in the pro camp. Their discipline is basically about how markets work. There have always been exceptions who have preferred some type of workers' or consumers' cooperative, or state ownership and control, but most economists have applauded the virtues of markets. Competitive markets are said to give people exactly what they want, when they want it, and at the lowest possible cost. While usually conceding the case for some regulation and complementary state provisions (for policing and defence, for example) most economists have concluded that markets are basically good. Sociologists, in contrast, have criticised the immense concentrations of wealth (and therefore power) which market economies produce. They have deplored the exploitation of workers and consumers whose interests are said to be sacrificed before the altar of profit. Needless to say, there have always been exceptional voices in sociology (as in economics), but the big issue in this chapter is what is right rather than who said it first or loudest. This book's third-way stance accepts and seeks to benefit from the virtues of markets while arguing that setting markets free does not diminish the value of complementary voluntary and public sector provisions.

The basic case for commercial, market-disciplined leisure provision is laid out in this chapter. There are two main planks to this case. First, there is the historical story which is summarised in the next section. This shows that in Britain, the world's first industrial nation, the expansion of commercial leisure provisions did not precede but followed the creation of strong voluntary and public sectors, and that the growth of commerce eliminated nothing; rather it added considerably to people's options. This is one reason why the left was misguided in so far as it sought to reduce the role of commerce. The second plank in the case for markets, and a second set of criticisms of the traditional left, are laid out in the subsequent section which examines the main criticisms of commercial leisure and concludes that they are unfounded.

This chapter is not a tour around everything that commerce offers. This comes later. Rather, this chapter simply identifies the 'engine' that drives commerce. This is profit, which is easily identified and explained. Note that the engine is profit, not money, which is a crucial fuel in most types of leisure provision – by the voluntary and public sectors as well as by commerce. Charging customers and paying staff (whether the staff are sport players, artists, entertainers or managers) do not of themselves make something commercial. Commerce arises only when there is a separate class of proprietor – profit-seeking owners or owner-workers – while other people are involved as hired hands, clients and customers. Having identified the engine, this chapter then reviews the distinctive features of commercial leisure provisions. It will be shown that, although the full frontal criticisms are mistaken, commerce has serious limitations. There are things which commerce simply cannot do, hence the scope and need for leisure contributions from voluntary associations (see Chapter 3) and the public sector (see Chapter 4).

A brief history of leisure provision

The nineteenth century

Leisure may be distinctively modern but recreation is timeless, and when nineteenth-century Britain was transformed from a mainly rural into a mainly urban society and became the world's first industrial nation, the migrants took with them many of their traditional village pastimes. They took their drinking, animal sports and fighting, and fairs continued to travel the country. Gradually these pastimes were either replaced or modernised. Town and city streets became places for daily shopping, so fairs lost their role as market places and henceforth specialised in entertainment, amusement and unprecedented thrills with their new mechanically-powered rides. Modern sports, suitable for play in urban areas and compatible with industrial time rhythms, were invented then popularised as participant games and spectator events. Traditional inns and ale houses were replaced by more specialised institutions – hotels, restaurants and pubs. Hobbies and other new uses of leisure were pioneered. The 'straight' theatre and music hall were separated, and the modern holiday was popularised.

These innovations were not all led by commerce. In fact commerce was not at the forefront of developments in leisure provision in nineteenth-century Britain. The new modern sports were run by voluntary bodies. The holiday 'away' was initially promoted by churches, progressive employers and other social reformers. Museums, parks and art galleries were provided by local authorities. Throughout the nineteenth century most leisure innovations were run by local authorities and the voluntary sector. City and town councils opened bath-houses, designated playing fields, and built concert halls and other cultural facilities. The nineteenth century was the age of the municipality, of civic pride and local council-led efforts to establish civilised ways of urban life (Meller, 1976). Clubs were formed by the various hobby enthusiasts, and the voluntary sector created the now traditional youth organisations. Even sports which permitted professional (paid) players (mainly football) continued to be run by voluntary bodies. As far as we can tell, the middle classes have always been the main joiners, but in nineteenth-century Britain it was not only the middle classes who formed and joined clubs. Churches and chapels, trade unions and the social clubs that they supported, became bases for organised working class pastimes which included sports, educational activities and a host of additional interests such as pigeon racing and brass bands. Some of the non-commercial developments were part of a movement for 'rational recreation' (Bailey, 1978). The aim of these social reformers was to encourage the new urban populations to use their free time and money sensibly, meaning in wholesome, edifying ways which would lead to self-improvement. Their enemy was the 'dark side of leisure' at that time – drink, gambling and prostitution (all usually illegal).

Commerce was very much a subsidiary force in the development of leisure provision throughout the nineteenth century; understandably so once we appreciate that, for leisure goods and services to be profitable, people must have money to spend on non-essentials. Commerce offered pubs, fairs and music halls, the theatre and eventually holidays, but even these provisions were heavily regulated. Holidays were regulated (governed) by working time which, in the nineteenth century, left precious little time for leisure. Fairs, the theatre and the music hall were regulated by local government bye-laws. Drinking was regulated by increasingly tough licensing laws and taxation. The rest of the dark side of leisure (gambling and prostitution) was mostly illegal.

The music halls (theatres with programmes consisting of a variety of acts) were probably the highest profile type of commercial leisure that was created in the second half of the nineteenth century, and the music hall remained extremely popular until the cinema and broadcasting began to compete just before, during and after the First World War. Music halls made fortunes for some proprietors and became renowned for the spectacular yields that investors could earn, so they became popular with speculative investors (like football clubs and dotcom companies in the 1990s). Another parallel with their recent counterparts is that, as a matter of fact, music halls were always extremely high-risk ventures (Crowhurst 2001). Leisure is usually a risky place to invest.

Nowadays commerce is the most powerful engine driving leisure provision. It is important to realise that things were not always so. When the growth of commercial provision really took off in the first half of the twentieth century it did so amidst established competition which was becoming ever stronger. Local authorities were extending their own leisure services – opening new swimming baths, and taking on responsibility for the youth service, for example. Participant and spectator sports were also growing strongly. New non-commercial uses of leisure were constantly being pioneered. As city populations overflowed into suburbs, gardening became a popular pastime, and local authorities created allotments for the use of gardenless households. The development of public transport (and the bicycle) opened up the countryside and enabled rambling and hiking to become popular recreations with their own voluntary bodies. These included the Youth Hostels Association which was formed in 1931 with, at that time, just 73 hostels and 6000 members (it now has around 300,000 members). Commerce, when it developed, did not eliminate anything that already existed. It simply added to people's leisure options. No-one had to use what commerce offered. There were alternatives. Indeed, there were, and still are, direct public or voluntary sector competitors in all the main fields of leisure where commerce operates.

Between the world wars

The growth of commercial leisure in the first half of the twentieth century was dependent on rising living standards, but it was aided considerably by scientific and technological innovations or, rather, by entrepreneurial responses to such innovations which led to businesses marketing bicycles, motor cars and aeroplanes (all of which could be, and were, used for leisure as well as for other purposes). Further technological developments made it possible to sell radios and, later on, television sets. In Britain the BBC was nationalised in 1927 (it had previously been a private company which had already been subjected to state regulation and given a broadcasting monopoly), but only when commerce had already demonstrated that the best way to make money out of radio was to sell receivers and to broadcast to households. Recorded music and the cinema were further technology-led innovations that commerce pioneered as leisure industries. The dance palais was another commercial innovation but, in this instance, not new technology-rooted.

It was during the inter-war years that mass markets were developed for a new range of 'white goods', most of which became viable when dwellings were connected to mains electricity. These goods included cookers, irons, refrigerators and washing machines as well as radios, gramophones and, later on, televisions. Thus consumption-based lifestyles began to spread (see Bowden, 1994; Cross, 1993). The 1920s and 1930s are best remembered (still in living memory as well as in history books) for the unemployment and attendant poverty, but in Britain unemployment did not significantly affect the south of England and people who remained in work experienced real increases in their earnings. It was between the wars that department stores began to cater for a mass rather than just an upmarket clientele (see Lancaster, 1996), and when multimedia advertising and consumer credit were first introduced.

Post-1945

However, commercial consumer culture has been the dominant leisure culture only since the Second World War after which Western governments adopted Keynesian methods of economic management (part of the social democratic consensus which then prevailed). An outcome was the '30 glorious years' of full employment in most regions of most Western countries, and more or less continuous economic growth and year-on-year rises in standards of living. In the 1950s the TV set became standard domestic equipment. The market for recorded music was enlarged considerably through products specifically designed to be sold to young people. Scooter and motor cycle sales rose. During the 1960s most British households acquired motor cars. Simultaneously, the markets for fashion clothing and cosmetics were expanded, and likewise the holiday industry, with a rising proportion of holidays being taken abroad. The transistor radio, the music cassette, the Walkman and its competitors, then the CD, further enlarged the music market during the remainder of the twentieth century. The video-recorder, then satellite and cable television transmissions and the DVD, led to further growth in the audio-visual and entertainment markets. Alcohol consumption per capita in Britain doubled between the 1950s and the 1980s. The meals-out market expanded dramatically, assisted by the popularity of ethnic restaurants. Night clubs offering combinations of different types of recorded and live music, and alcohol, opened in virtually all towns and cities which thereby acquired booming night-time economies and became 24-hour places. By the end of the twentieth century the strength and variety of consumption-based lifestyles was helping to inspire debate about a postmodern condition (Featherstone, 1991). Commerce has now become the main leisure provider, but it was not the first, and it is still far from being the only one.

Critiques of commerce

The tirade

Commerce is now not only the main, but also the most criticised, leisure provider. Throughout the second half of the twentieth century the expansion of the commercial leisure industries was accompanied by wave upon wave of academic critique. As explained above, most of the exceptions have been economists whose skills include the analysis of markets and most economists seem to like what they see (see Taylor, 1992). They have been the ghosts in the debates (they attend different conferences and publish in different journals) with whom other social scientists, especially sociologists, have taken issue. Betsy and Stephen Wearing (1993) contend that the commercialisation of leisure constrains rather than extends individual freedom. Jeremy Seabrook (1988) argues that leisure is deformed by market relationships and that people today sustain richness in their lives only within their families and other small social groups. Harry van Moorst (1982) claims that, in capitalist societies, leisure is nothing more than the ransom paid for industrial peace. John Clarke and Chas Critcher (1985) argue that citizens today are doubly exploited – at work where surplus value is creamed off by their employers, then in their own time when they are enlisted as consumers that capitalist businesses need if they are to be profitable. They also claim that the variety in the public's uses of leisure is less a sign of freedom of choice than crude underlying inequalities. Somnez et al. (1993) argue that the extension of market forces has corrupted earlier, more innocent, purer uses of leisure. Vittoria de Grazia (1992) argues along very similar lines in sketching how people's lives have changed in Italian villages since the 1930s when, whether communists or fascists were in power, the leisure ideal was the politically mobilised citizen engaged in uplifting activities. By the 1990s affluence and commerce had invaded the villages. So had tourists. Some traditional festivals were being preserved as tourist attractions. However, everyone's leisure, the tourists' and the locals', had been depoliticised. It had become a relatively vacuous end in itself.

The 'engine': profit

Is the tirade of criticism justified? An elementary fact is that commerce will provide anything on which people are willing to spend their time and money, provided it is profitable and (usually) legal. In practice some commercial operators are invariably willing to circumvent or break the law. Hence the buoyancy of the dark side of leisure. Leading internet operators will carry hardcore porn because it pays well. Commerce will deliver whatever makes money, but only if it makes money: commerce has no deeper commitment to sport, the arts, any other specific form of leisure, or to leisure in general. A cinema or bingo hall will be transformed into a supermarket or a car park if doing so secures a better return on capital. Profit is the engine that drives commerce. This is not to say that private sector investors, employers and workers are never personally interested in the kinds of leisure that they cater for, or that they are never elated by the enjoyment that they facilitate. The point is that intrinsic interest and enjoyment alone are never sufficient to sustain commercial provisions. The provisions must also be profitable. And if provisions can be made profitable, then, irrespective of providers' personal interests and consumers' experiences, commerce will deliver.

Mistaken criticisms

Some criticisms of commerce can be dispensed with quickly because they are so plainly wrong.

- First, commerce does not cater only, or even mainly, for the well-to-do. There is more money to be made in mass markets. However, it is true that the commercial sector is most used by the better-off (see Table 2.1). In Britain the richest 10 per cent of the population spends over 6 times as much as the poorest 10 per cent. In leisure most of the spending inequalities are wider: 8 times more on alcohol, 11 times more on meals out, 21 times more on visits to cinemas, theatres and other entertainment, 25 times more on sports and camping, and 27 times more on holidays. The relatively 'democratic' paid-for leisure activities (those that are least sensitive to income inequalities) are reading matter, audio-visual media, hobbies, tobacco, and gambling.
- Second, commerce does not target a lowest, or any other, common denominator. Quite the reverse: whether building houses, publishing newspapers or opening restaurants, commerce generates diversity. Providers target specific market segments or even smaller niches. Commerce offers thousands of holiday packages and hundreds of different alcoholic beverages. Every provider tries to offer something different and either better or cheaper. So commerce produces

Table 2.1 Household spending per week, UK 2000–01

	A Poorest 10% £	B Average £	C Richest 10% £	C as percentage of A
Housing	21.0	63.9	141.1	671
Fuel and power	8.6	11.9	16.6	193
Food and non-alcohol drinks	25.8	61.9	111.4	432
of which:				
Restaurant and café meals	2.4	10.4	27.4	1141
Alcoholic drink	4.2	15.0	33.8	804
Tobacco	3.9	6.1	6.5	167
Clothing and footwear	6.7	22.0	45.8	683
Household goods and services	19.7	54.6	125.4	637
of which:				
Telephone	0.2	8.4	15.2	7600
Personal goods and services	5.0	14.7	32.7	654
Motoring	8.6	55.1	118.3	1376
Fares etc	2.7	9.5	28.2	1044
Leisure goods and services	20.2	70.3	187.5	928
of which:				
Books, maps, diaries, newspapers, magazines etc	1.9	4.7	9.2	484
TV, video, audio equipment, rentals, licences	5.4	13.7	23.8	441
Sports, camping	0.5	4.2	12.9	2580
Toys, hobbies, photography, gardening	1.6	5.4	11.3	706
Cinema, theatre and other entertainment	0.3	2.6	6.4	2133
Education and training	3.3	6.5	27.7	839
Holidays	2.5	21.8	68.7	2748
Gambling	1.7	3.9	5.0	294
Gifts and donations	2.2	8.1	22.5	1022
Miscellaneous	0.2	0.7	1.6	800
Total	126.7	385.7	849.0	670

Source: Office for National Statistics (2002), Family Expenditure Survey, 2001, London.

more and more brands whether on supermarket shelves or in leisure goods and services. Some argue that the differences between many products are superficial and trivial, but it is the variety that makes commercial market places attractive to consumers. It is the public sector that offers standardised fare whether delivering houses, health care, education or holidays. Even though they tried, the East European communist authorities were never able to offer Western-type holidays. It was simply not the same when all the state-owned souvenir shops carried exactly the same range of goods.

■ Third, commercial leisure markets are not dominated by monopolies. Once again, exactly the reverse applies. The big multinationals never have the field to themselves. All leisure markets are distinguished by the large number of small businesses, many run by enthusiasts about tropical fish, dance music, fitness or whatever. With leisure, the economists have been basically correct: in commercial leisure markets consumers are offered choices, and their choices really are sovereign.

Limitations of commerce

So why not let commerce run everything? One of this book's central arguments is that the original left was wrong to condemn what commerce actually offered. The left lost these arguments because the public obviously enjoyed commercial leisure. A modern left or third-way stance does not dwell on weaknesses of the market system so much as the complementary strengths of the voluntary and public sectors. Complementary provisions are needed because there are limits – two important limits – to what commerce can do. First, commerce will only cater for demands which can be met profitably. Commerce always seeks maximum profit. It always endeavours to expand or deepen its markets by increasing the number of customers, or persuading existing customers to purchase more often, or to spend more on each occasion. All businesses do their best to attract customers and to keep them loyal. The effect of all the advertising and other forms of marketing is to generate a consumer culture – the images and beliefs that come to be associated with particular goods, places and experiences. Commerce is rather good at stimulating desire. But all this happens only when the process of providing can be made profitable. The second important limitation of commerce is that it requires a clear division between the provider and the customer. There can be consumer benefits here: people seem to like being served, to some extent and for some of the time, at any rate. The limitation is that commerce often, but not always, removes much of the potentially interesting work. It makes things easy and therefore they may be tempting but undemanding. Yet peak experience appears to arise only when things are challenging – hard work in fact (see Harper, 1997). Commerce simply cannot afford to allow people to do it all whether the 'all' is preparing food for their own consumption or producing a play.

Commerce cannot do everything, but free market economists claim that the things that commerce offers are what people manifestly want, and that competition keeps prices low and quality up. In claiming this, the economists have always been correct. Therefore, it might appear, the more commerce can do, so much the better. Why do we need a third way? The case for complementary provisions is signalled by the current disquiet about how commerce is changing areas of leisure where it is expanding. As top-level soccer has become more commercial, fans have complained about the rescheduling of fixtures, the escalation of prices, and the emergence of super-teams. In television the industry appears to have decided that we should purchase widescreen sets. With UK government backing, the industry has decided that we should all go digital. If in 1989 (prior to UK satellite broadcasting) members of the public had been asked whether they would prefer to have just five channels for the price of the licence fee, or 500 channels (and have to pay separately for most of them while accepting premium charges for the latest films and the most popular sports events) at a total cost roughly quadruple the licence fee (which they would still have to pay), it is quite possible – most likely in fact – that the majority would have voted for the status quo. Change always has critics, and the critics are especially vocal when the changes involve matters as important to so many people as television and football. However, we shall see in later chapters that in the above instances there are countervailing benefits. It will serve no-one's interests to sacrifice these benefits and haul back commerce. New commercial innovations should be welcomed, but we should always bear in mind that commerce has limitations and these do not change. The expansion of commerce has not weakened the case for state (public service) contributions in broadcasting. Likewise the commercialisation of certain segments of certain sports does not, in itself, reduce the scope for the voluntary involvement that is still responsible for most participant and spectator sport events.

CONCLUSIONS

This book could well have been subtitled 'the commercialisation of leisure' because over the last 100 years commerce has become far and away our main leisure provider. All of the big three leisure activities – holidays, out-of-home eating and drinking, and the media – are basically commercial enterprises nowadays. Every chapter of this book has to deal, in some way or another and to some extent or another, with the effects of commercialisation.

This chapter has examined the basic criticisms that the commercialisation of leisure has provoked. These criticisms have been rejected on two grounds. First, there is the historical story which shows that commerce has always added to people's options without eliminating any of the voluntary or public sector alternatives. Second, some of the harsher and most sweeping criticisms – those that accuse commerce of seeking out the rich and neglecting the masses, homogenising provisions and reducing choice, and leading to leisure markets being dominated by monopolies – are simply mistaken.

Commerce is not basically malign, but this chapter has also explained that it has limitations. This means that commerce needs to be complemented. The next chapter will explain what is special about the voluntary sector, and Chapter 4 will identify the public sector's special capabilities. The strengths of commerce need to be recognised and indeed can be applauded, but not to the point of drowning the case for the maintenance of alternative and complementary provisions.

3 Voluntary Associations

Introduction

A question that is always in the background – when it is not up front in discussions about voluntary associations – is whether the sector is in decline. This indeed is the overarching issue in the present chapter. The issue has been made topical, first by Robert Putnam (2000), an American political scientist who alleges an all-round loss of 'social capital' in North America, and secondly by governments in North America and Europe adopting a version of this thesis to explain low turn-out at elections (and other imperfections in present-day democratic politics) and the creation of excluded groups, then envisaging a revival of the voluntary sector as a source of democratic renewal and a way of fostering inclusion. The Putnam thesis has proved attractive to some powerful groups. No blame for maladies sticks to politicians or the economy: 'society' is apparently to blame!

This chapter will show that, in fact, there has been no all-round decline in either the voluntary sector or social capital, but first of all we consider what is meant by the term 'voluntary'. We will explain how these associations fill the social, economic and political space between the state and the market on the one side and individuals amid their families and other primary (informal, face-to-face) social relationships on the other. We then consider the wider role (beyond leisure) of voluntary associations. We shall see that they are indeed an important source of social capital, and that social capital is very important: the voluntary sector is a crucial building block on which civil society and democracy rest. The various types of voluntary associations are then distinguished. These are not all leisure-based, but helping to run them, whatever the associations' objectives, is always a leisure time activity for the activists.

We then consider who joins, who runs and who benefits from the voluntary sector. There are variations, but we shall see that the voluntary sector plays an important role in the lives of people in all sections of the population. This leads to a discussion about the kinds of leisure provision in which the voluntary sector excels: sport, the arts and crafts, and hobbies. These leisure activities could not exist, at least in their present forms, without voluntary organisation and effort.

We then ask what drives the voluntary sector. It is members' and users' enthusiasm that is the associations' lifeblood and their principal defence mechanism, and it is not on the wane. The impetus to self-organise has not been quelled by the expansion of commerce. The chapter explains how and why the voluntary sector is able to resist challenges from commerce and state provisions. The voluntary sector can sometimes provide things more cheaply, and it can sometimes do a better job than any other type of leisure provider, but it always does things differently. It provides a kind of leisure experience which is simply beyond the capabilities of both the state and the market. This is why the voluntary sector is not a 'thing of the past', a vestige from the time when most people could not afford commercial provisions, and before the state accepted responsibility for the economic and social welfare of the people.

What is a voluntary association?

Let us be clear about the meaning of 'voluntary'. These organisations are very likely to enlist unpaid volunteers but they may also employ paid staff. The organisations remain voluntary because the people in charge, the trustees or the committee, are not there for the money. There may be state subsidies, but the organisations are not statutory, meaning that they are not brought into existence at the behest of government. Associations which are formed, or kept alive, mainly by government grants, or specifically so that government activities can be hived off, are best described as quasi-voluntary or quasi non-governmental organisations (quangos). We also need to recognise, and sideline here, a category of commercial clubs (such as gambling clubs and health and fitness clubs) that are created by the host businesses. Sometimes the club is a legal requirement, as for certain types of gambling, in order to prevent impulse participation. Sometimes the club membership fee is a form of upfront payment, or a means of excluding the 'wrong types'. These are not genuine voluntary members' associations. However, voluntary associations may have business sponsors, and they may well be business-like in their operating methods. Most clubs are perpetually fund-raising. They are indeed interested in money, but they are non-commercial in that no-one is syphoning off profit: everything is ploughed back in.

Voluntary bodies have a long history and in leisure they are still thriving. In Britain the number of voluntary societies multiplied during the nineteenth century (Tomlinson, 1979). They then created, and proceeded to run, most of our modern sports. The Football Association was created in 1863; the All-England Croquet Club in 1868 (tennis was added in 1877); the Rugby Football Union in 1871; and the Amateur Athletics Association in 1880. Voluntary effort also created the original modern youth organisations – the Boys' Brigade (founded in 1883), the Boy Scouts (1908) and the Girl Guides (1910), for example. Thousands of other clubs were based on hobbies such as coin and stamp collecting, gardening, photography. The list is endless. Because Britain was the first industrial nation it was among the first to acquire an impressive array of non-governmental organisations (NGOs).

Subsequently, forming a committee, which then founds an association or club, has sometimes been seen as a distinctively British way of addressing any problem. However, other European countries, and North America, have equally strong voluntary sectors.

Voluntary sector leisure is neither derivative, residual nor on the wane. The sector is not a poor relation of commerce. Nor does it exist only with permission and funding from public bodies. In catering for modern leisure, the voluntary sector was a first mover. Public sector and commercial provisions typically followed, and, in the cases of the arts and sport, have always rested on a broader voluntary base. The voluntary sector nurtures artistic and sporting talent from which professionals are recruited. It creates the interest which generates the spectators and audiences for professional performances. Likewise, the voluntary sector fosters interest in hobbies which commercial enterprises can then service. Voluntary action fills local authority arts and sports centres with users. The centres exist because of the interest, not vice-versa. Voluntary provision is more than a fallback: it is more often a base or at least an equal partner with other sectors. Most crucially, we shall see that voluntary clubs and societies provide kinds of leisure experience that are simply beyond the capabilities of commerce and the public sector.

Civil society

Voluntary associations are important within and far beyond leisure. They are the 'stuff' of civil society on which liberal democracy rests. These associations fill the socio-cultural space between the state and market on the one side, and individuals and their primary groups on the other. Civil society is created when citizens voluntarily form themselves into associations. Sometimes the label used is 'third sector', or 'non-profit', or 'non-governmental organisation'. These terms are used interchangeably here. Some voluntary associations are run democratically by their members. In other cases control is vested in trustees who are required to respect the constitution and purposes for which the organisation was founded, maybe by a donor. People may form voluntary associations for recreational purposes, but the same socio-cultural space is available for, and is also populated by, churches, trade unions and political parties. The sector includes charities. In the USA some of these are sufficiently strong to take on responsibilities performed by state welfare in European Union countries (see Wright, 2000).

Some socialists are enthusiastic about the voluntary sector. In their ideal society, rather than everything being run by state bureaucracies, they envisage the voluntary principle being extended, certainly in leisure, to encompass the mass media, for instance. Thus newspapers and television channels would be run by their workforces on a non-profit basis, or by their readers or audiences (see Tomlinson, 1990).

Social capital

Describing voluntary organisations as a sector is convenient for this book's, and other, purposes, because all the organisations do share a great deal in common.

However, it must be said that the activists do not necessarily regard themselves as contributing to a sector. People are more likely to become involved through an interest in sport, more likely a particular sport, and sometimes just one particular club, rather than to contribute to any wider effort. Most of the organisations are aggressively independent and, therefore, impossible to organise. Voluntary associations are not a co-ordinated movement. Nevertheless, each association creates social capital – social bonds and trust – on which other organisations can draw. There are different kinds of social capital. Robert Putnam (1995, 1996, 2000) distinguishes 'bonding capital' (which strengthens relationships within a group – within a neighbourhood, for instance), from 'bridging capital' (relationships which straddle different groups and which may therefore facilitate social mobility), and 'linking capital' (which links different sections of a population and helps to bind them together). 'Bridging' and 'linking' capital are considered especially valuable. Social capital is an asset. Where it is high, people tend to be wealthier and healthier, children have higher educational attainments, crime rates are lower, and levels of civic participation are higher than elsewhere (Harper, 2001); hence social policy-makers' interest in how to boost social capital. Throughout the world, sports organisations, which have the capacity to involve so many people from all kinds of backgrounds, have been regarded as important generators of the socio-cultural capital on which democratic grassroots politics depends. Hence Putnam's (2000) claim (but see below, pp. 32–3) that the trend in recent years for Americans to go 'bowling alone' is weakening the country's political fabric. The existence of a vigorous voluntary sector is widely regarded as a hallmark of any genuinely democratic society. So the development of 'third sectors' has been used by the European Union as one of its indicators in assessing candidate countries' progress towards fulfilling the conditions for full membership.

Types of associations

There are many ways in which voluntary associations can be classified, but some bodies always straddle the boundary lines. This sector is notoriously untidy. There is certainly no clear division between associations that exist for leisure and those that serve other purposes. Organisations can be grouped into those which exist to meet a common interest of the members, which may or may not be a leisure interest; those seeking to promote the welfare of another target group – the disabled or senior citizens for instance – which, again, may or may not embrace recreational programmes; and those promoting a cause or interest which, those involved are likely to claim, is for everyone's benefit. Such causes may be leisure-based, in the arts or sport for example, or leisure-related, such as the conservation of nature, or only indirectly if at all leisure-linked, such as opposition to genetically modified foods. However, most voluntary bodies are involved in leisure to some extent in some way or another. Whatever its original purpose, running the association is most likely to be a major leisure interest of the office holders. Volunteering is a major leisure activity for some of those who are involved. Only the voluntary sector is able to mobilise voluntary effort. Associations which are based squarely on leisure interests may develop on their own or as offshoots from any other organisation – a school, firm, trade union, church or any other place which initially draws people together.

Who joins, who benefits?

No-one knows exactly how many voluntary associations exist in Britain or any other democratic country. One of the hallmarks of these political regimes is that citizens do not need official permission in order to bond together and can do so without registering with any authority. Handbooks which list arts, sports and other types of associations are always incomplete, and likewise local directories of voluntary societies. Researchers who try to survey the sector thoroughly invariably rely heavily on 'snowball' methods – being informed about additional associations from any starting point. This method always seems to find that every district within every town and city, and every rural village, is dense with clubs and societies. Any church, further education college or university will have dozens of clubs. This is what Bishop and Hoggett (1986) discovered when they began to research the voluntary sectors in Bristol and Leicester. They were so overwhelmed by cases that it was necessary to restrict the study to just a section of each city. In her study of Toxteth, an inner-Liverpool district, Ruby Dixon (1991) contacted 54 different arts organisations. The district appeared to be an artistic hotbed but there is no reason to believe that Toxteth is outstanding in this respect. On the basis of her fieldwork in Milton Keynes, Ruth Finnegan (1989) estimated that between 5 per cent and 6 per cent of the local population was involved in making music of some type or another. Most of those involved in Milton Keynes were in contact with other musicians through a dense network of bands, orchestras, choirs and clubs of various types. Perhaps less surprisingly, Sara Cohen (1991) located scores of rock bands on Merseyside, but these groups are best understood as a periphery of the commercial pop music industry. Unlike other music-makers, amateur rock musicians depend on private resourcefulness and networks, which are linked to the professional tiers of the business, rather than a base of voluntary clubs.

It is difficult to estimate the proportion of the population that is involved in the voluntary sector. Unless a long prompt list is used, individuals may not recall all the groups to which they belong, especially when one can 'belong' simply by being an occasional attender. People will not necessarily think of their participation as being in a voluntary sector. They will not necessarily be aware that a sports centre that they use, or a museum or wildlife reserve they visit, is under voluntary management. The figures in Table 3.1 should therefore be regarded as under-estimates. Even so, the figures show that in 1999 over a half of all adults belonged to at least one voluntary body. The associations with leisure as the main purpose will mostly be within the 'sports', 'social' and 'other' categories, but, as explained above, any kind of voluntary participation can be regarded as a leisure activity. The point is that the voluntary sector in leisure is certainly not the preserve of a minority or, indeed, any distinct section of the population. Virtually everyone would notice and their leisure would be seriously affected if the voluntary sector disappeared

Table 3.1   Voluntary association membership, Great Britain 1999

	Men (%)	Women (%)
Sports club	23	12
Trade union	18	12
Social club	17	6
Tenants'/residents' group	8	9
Political party	4	3
Environmental group	3	3
Voluntary services group	3	5
Parents'/school association	2	4
Religious group	9	14
Other organisation	20	22
At least one membership	58	50

Source: British Household Panel Survey, Institute for Social and Economic Research, University of Essex.

completely. The labour market would be seriously depressed if the voluntary sector disappeared: it is responsible for 7.9 per cent of all civilian employment in European Union countries (European Commission, 2003).

Members and particularly office-holders in voluntary associations tend to be male and middle class (Hutson, 1979; Tomlinson, 1979) but this is only a tendency (see Table 3.1). There are plenty of women's organisations, not necessarily linked to second-wave feminism. The working class's capacity for self-organisation has produced the trade unions and political parties which, in many countries, have been the governing or main opposition parties for a century and more. Unsurprisingly, members of different social classes tend to join different clubs (see Chapter 6, pp. 84–5, and see also Hill, 2002, pp. 130–45). The voluntary sector has often played an important political role in forming social bonds between members of particular classes with an economic base. The social capital generated by the voluntary sector can harden divisions and may therefore contribute to the formation of included and excluded groups. Contrary to Putnam's (2000) inferences, social capital is not always beneficial, or equally beneficial, for the members of all social strata. That said, it remains the case that all sections of the population have stakes of some description in the voluntary sector.

Contributions in leisure

The voluntary sector caters for all kinds of leisure interests and activities, but its contributions are much greater in some fields than in others. Churches and trade unions still operate some holiday centres, and some holidays are arranged by voluntary groups – for children and adults with special needs, for example – but the tourist industry is primarily commercial. So is the evenings-out (eating and drinking) industry despite the contributions of working-people's clubs, student unions and so on. Most voluntary associations run raffles as part of their fund-raising, but the major forms of gambling – the National Lottery, football pools, casinos and betting shops – are commercial businesses. Most voluntary associations also publish, at least to the extent of producing newsletters. Some operate local radio and even local television networks. Nowadays many have internet sites. Even so, the main players in broadcasting and publishing are state organisations and commercial enterprises. The types of leisure where the voluntary sector is pivotal are sport, artistic production and performances, and hobbies.

In Chapter 6 we shall see that most popular modern sports were invented, provided and, for the most part, are still managed by voluntary bodies. All sport, except the very top levels of the most popular spectator sports, still happens only because volunteers organise it. The extent and manner in which commerce has taken over sections of top sport in recent years, and the implications for the wider sports-interested public are considered in Chapter 7. Suffice it to record here that the voluntary sector is still far and away the main provider in both the participant and spectator branches of sport.

The voluntary sector is also the mainstay of the arts and crafts. Most painting, pottery, drama and musical production is organised by amateurs. No-one is paid. People do it for enjoyment. Professional productions (where people are paid) are different and are usually structurally separate. There is a difference here between sport and the arts. Whereas even professional sport (where the players are paid) may remain under voluntary management, the professional theatre, musical productions and so forth (where the artists and other producers are paid) are nearly always run either on a commercial basis or with state funding. Which arts benefit from state support, and why, is considered in Chapter 13. Here we can simply note that both commercial considerations and state largesse are wholly irrelevant to most artistic production. All the work is done voluntarily, and the professional tiers of the arts industries could not exist without the voluntary sector acting as a seedbed, nurturing the talent and interest that produce professional performers and their audiences.

Hobbies are the third type of leisure in which the voluntary sector is the main provider. Hundreds of interests – in coins, cars, stamps, animals, fish, plants, railways and so on – are expressed and nurtured in voluntary societies (see Boxes 3.1 (p. 30) and 4.2 (p. 44), for examples). Individuals who do not belong to any club may do gardening, coin or antique collecting as hobbies, but they are most likely to read voluntary associations' publications and visit their events. Most hobbies are served by commercial profit-seeking businesses, many run by enthusiasts who are trying, with varying degrees of success, to base paid occupations on their hobbies. The relevant businesses and voluntary societies feed off each other, but it is hobbies that are served by commerce: businesses may invent games but they do not develop these into hobbies. Likewise, hobby groups may use public sector facilities, especially meeting rooms, but local authority leisure services departments do not create hobbies. These are always the work of like-minded individuals who get together, maybe informally to begin with, but before long it is most likely that a club with officers will have been brought into existence.

Tourism, broadcasting, publishing, gambling, and evenings-out eating and drinking could all manage without any voluntary sector input. Hobbies, the arts and sport are different. They could not exist, or, at any rate, they would take quite different forms, if the voluntary sector's contributions were stripped away. This sector has unique capabilities.

The engine: enthusiasm

> We believe that involvement in such groups [voluntary associations] offers people something probably unique in our society: the chance to come together with others to create or participate for collective benefit or enjoyment rather than for sale to an anonymous audience or purchaser (Bishop and Hoggett, 1986, p. 3).

Spectator crowds and audiences generate special types of atmosphere and elation. The voluntary experience is not better or worse, more or less intense, but simply different. Shared enthusiasms bring people together and are then sustained and strengthened by their interaction. There is no intermediary. There is no division between the provider and the consumer. These roles are fused. Within such contexts there are special satisfactions to be gained from developing skills and expertise. The intrinsic enjoyment, plus the recognition and esteem of fellow members, become sufficient reward. Members' enthusiasm can migrate to the associations themselves. So people are prepared to offer the same commitment, and sometimes as many hours per week, as in their paid occupations. Some club officials devote more time to their voluntary work than others (and sometimes they themselves) devote to their paid jobs. The voluntary sector is proof that money is not the only effective motivator. People will push themselves to peaks of sporting and artistic achievement for personal satisfaction, and for the respect and esteem earned among others who share their passions. Enthusiasm drives voluntary associations. It is their life-blood. They thrive on it. While enthusiasm is sustained, the associations cannot be threatened, or even seriously challenged, by either commercial or public provisions (see below). Once enthusiasm dries up, the associations are extinguished.

It is within voluntary associations that people are most likely to experience what Robert Stebbins (1992) calls 'serious leisure'. People can have careers in serious (as opposed to casual) leisure, gradually accumulating experience and skills. Enthusiasts inspire each other. So amateur musicians, actors, astronomers, archaeologists, comedians and sports-players sometimes become as skilled and knowledgeable as professionals. Why do they do it? Why do they work so hard at their leisure interests? This does not happen to audiences at the cinema or crowds at spectator sports unless some of them form themselves into clubs. The dog enthusiasts studied by Dair Gillespie et al. (2002) were devoting huge amounts of

BOX 3.1 HOBBIES

Pigeon racing

The specially bred homing pigeons that had been used for centuries to carry messages became redundant with the invention of the telegraph. However, the simultaneous development of railways, and the broader modernisation of leisure that was then in progress made it possible to organise pigeon racing as a hobby.

The 'sport' began in Belgium, spread to Holland, France and Great Britain, then to North America. Nowadays the two main US pigeon racing organisations have 11,000 and 3000 members respectively. The main Canadian association has 2500 members. In Europe the big annual event is the Blackpool Show which is attended each year by around 30,000 pigeon fanciers, and upwards of 2000 pigeons are on display competing for the prizes that are on offer.

Races of up to 1000 miles (but usually no more than 500 miles) are normally between birds that 'home' in the same region so as to standardise distances travelled and weather conditions although the sport has procedures for taking account of these variables. Nowadays birds are normally transported to a race's start point in specially constructed air-conditioned trucks. The sport has developed its own complicated technologies and organisations to verify race results. Pigeons have been traded for prices up to $250,000.

Pigeon racing is now a veteran hobby/sport, but research is still continuing into exactly how the pigeons find their way home.

Sources: www.rpra.org, www.pigeon-racing.co.uk

Tiddlywinking

This game is not 'just about flicking counters into a cup. It is a complex game of tactics and strategy which involves a fascinating mixture of manual dexterity and intellectual activity.' Who says so? You guessed!

The game was invented by Joseph Assheton Fincher of London and patented in 1888. There was a tiddlywinking craze in England during the 1890s. Many variations on the basic game were invented and over 70 patents were issued for tiddlywink games.

However, the development of tiddlywinks into an organised hobby did not occur until the 1950s. The first known tournament was held at Cambridge University in 1955. Oxford University followed before long, and in 1962 its team returned undefeated from a tour of the USA.

A North American association was formed in 1966, and Americans then dominated world play until the 1990s. The American association has held over 150 tournaments typically with over 500 competitors.

There are sister national associations in England and Scotland. The first world singles championship was held in 1972, since when there have been 40 champion challenge matches. The winner of the English, Scottish or US national championships is allowed to challenge the reigning world champion over 7 games. In 2001 Patrick Barrie of Cambridge became the new world singles champion.

Sources: www.tiddlywinks.org, www.etwa.org

→

$\longrightarrow$

Subbuteo Table Soccer

This is a relatively new hobby The game was launched in 1947 and became an instant success for its manufacturer. The first sets comprised two cardboard teams, one celluloid ball and metal-framed goals with paper nets. Players were instructed to mark a pitch (chalk provided) on an ex-army blanket.

The game was at the peak of its popularity in the late-1970s and early-1980s. At that time the manufacturer produced teams in over 300 club and national strips. Since then Subbuteo has been failing to recruit younger players through competition from computerised games. However, there are sufficient enthusiasts to keep the game alive worldwide.

There are national associations, and an international federation. These amateur associations have drawn up their own rules of play. There are affiliated associations in over 30 countries. World championships are held annually. There are more frequent grand prix tournaments, and video-recordings are available of some major events.

Sources: www.americansubbuteo.com, www.subbuteoforum.org.uk, www.peter-upton.co.uk

time, and large amounts of money, to their hobby. In some cases the dogs appeared to be taking precedence over everything else. Some of the enthusiasts were sleeping with their dogs instead of their human partners! The rewards obtained from serious leisure careers are similar to those that some people obtain from paid employment: enrichment, improved self-image, feelings of accomplishment and belonging. The rewards can become deeper the longer a leisure career extends: as one-time players or performers become officials in their sports or arts, and then become organisers of local, regional, national and even international events. Stebbins claims – although up to now this remains unproven – that serious leisure can perform the social and psychological functions usually associated with paid jobs and can thereby avert the socio-psychological loss and damage that are otherwise likely during spells of unemployment or following retirement.

Undermined?

There is always talk of crisis in the voluntary sector. Up to now all obituaries have proved to be, not premature, but plain wrong. There is always movement: births and fatalities, growing and contracting segments. In a mixed leisure economy there are constant boundary adjustments between voluntary, public sector and commercial providers. There are always some voluntary societies that are experiencing limitations and pressing the bounds of their capabilities. Most of the problems are symptoms of health rather than terminal sickness.

That said, the associations face some common and seemingly perpetual problems. To begin with, most of the organisations are always short of money.

Fund-raising is usually perpetual. Every meeting may feature a fund-raising raffle. The associations are constantly trying to hold onto existing premises, or are seeking new places to meet or play – maybe looking to larger voluntary bodies, such as churches, or to use local government premises. Second, the organisations invariably want more members, and especially more volunteers. This latter problem may well have become more acute in recent years. Most women, as well as men, have paid jobs nowadays. Men are doing more in their homes. Full-time employees of both sexes are working longer (see Roberts, 1999a). However, there are more old people, many of whom expect to have decades of active life after they have retired from their main occupations and relinquished their main family responsibilities. The 'young old' have become a major source of volunteers. The over-45s, especially women and those who are not in employment, are more likely than other age groups to be volunteers and to help others in less formal ways (Rushton, 2003). Even so, voluntary organisations complain about the difficulty of recruiting new blood. Recruiting members, and especially volunteers, may or may not have become even more difficult than it was in the past, but it has always been a problem for societies. Few associations have ever had 'enough' volunteers.

The crucial point is that the sector is definitely not fizzling out. Over a half of all adults in Britain belong to at least one voluntary society. There are roughly 1.5 million people in Britain who do voluntary work for sports teams and clubs on a more or less continuous basis – acting as referees, club secretaries or whatever. As many as 7.5 million people do a sports-related voluntary activity at some time during any year. The number of volunteers vastly exceeds the number of sports-related paid jobs of roughly half a million (Gratton and Taylor, 2000). The latter figure is rising – evidence of the growing economic importance of leisure – but professionalisation is just a trend. As yet it is far from an absolute state. The 2002 Commonwealth Games in Manchester created 6100 (temporary) full-time equivalent jobs but as many as 20,000 members of the public applied to become volunteers. Just 10,500 were accepted. It was the largest volunteer force ever assembled for a single event in the UK in peacetime (Ralston et al., 2003).

There are instances – whole areas of leisure in some countries – where clubs are in decline. For example, in recent years some European countries' sports clubs have experienced a loss of members (see Deckers and Gratton, 1995). The reason is not that people are quitting physically active recreation. It is more a case of them engaging in recreational swimming, surfing, skiing, sailing and so on without joining clubs and teams, and participating in competitions. This does not mean that competitive sport is threatened with extinction. It is more a shift in the constantly moving boundary between club sport and self-organised recreation (see Chapter 6).

As explained above, Robert Putnam (2000) has written a gloomy treatise on the decline of social capital in America. *Bowling Alone* is a catchy book title but bowling is just one of the more trivial examples that Putnam presents. He finds that more Americans are living singly; that families are dining together less frequently; that there is less activity in politics, and a decline in other forms of civic activity and church attendance; that fewer people are playing team sports and more are taking individual exercise. Putnam claims that although the USA has more voluntary associations than ever before, collectively they have fewer members than in the past. Moreover, he claims that members are becoming increasingly passive, paying donations instead of doing.

However, it is not clear that there really has been an overall decline in voluntary organisation membership across America (see Paxton, 1999), and there is no evidence of an all-round decline in Britain or in other European countries (Harper, 2001). In Britain there has been a decline among males in membership of trade unions and working men's clubs. This has increased the social-class skew towards voluntary association membership being most common among the middle classes (Li et al., 2002). Middle-class adults appear to transmit their superior propensity to join to their teenage children (Egerton, 2002). All that said, there does not appear to have been any decline in most types of leisure-related voluntary associations. As in America, there does seem to have been a general decline in trust among citizens, most of all towards politicians, and in (broadly defined) political activity, but the reasons for this are more likely to be politics-specific rather than an all-round decline in civil society. In Britain more people are taking individual exercise but as many as ever are playing team sports such as football (see Table 3.2). Since the 1980s there has actually been a decline in jogging (often a solitary activity), though more people are 'walking', doing keep fit and yoga, cycling, golf, and weight-lifting and training. Cue sports and darts have been in decline but football remains buoyant.

What about the internet? Is it going to keep people online instead of going out and joining clubs? At present the evidence is not clear-cut. In America there is evidence of heavy internet use leading to less face-to-face social interaction (Kraut et al., 1998). Virtual cyberspace relationships may replace the traditional variety. However, a study in Switzerland has found that internet users in that country have

Table 3.2 Participation in sports and other physical activities (percentages aged 16 and over taking part in the 4 weeks before interview)

	1987	1990	1993	1996
Walking	39.9	40.7	40.8	44.5
Swimming	13.1	14.8	15.4	14.8
Keep fit/yoga	8.6	11.6	12.1	11.3
Cycling	8.4	9.3	10.2	12.3
Cue sports	15.1	13.6	12.2	11.3
Darts	8.8	7.1	5.6	1.3
Weight lifting/training	4.5	4.8	5.5	5.6
Golf	3.9	5.0	5.3	4.7
Jogging	5.2	5.0	4.6	4.5
Football	4.8	4.5	4.5	4.8
Any activity other than walking	44.7	47.8	47.3	45.6

Source: Office for National Statistics (www.statistics.gov.uk).

larger social networks, and experience more face-to-face interaction, than non-users (Franzen, 2000). The impact of the internet may vary from place to place, although convergence is likely as people in all countries become more familiar with the technology (see Chapter 10, pp. 148–52). Every innovation in home-based leisure has been accompanied by forecasts of mass withdrawal from wider social networks. In the past, the more active forms of out-of-home leisure have been unaffected. Television did not kill the voluntary sector. In the 1980s it was computer games that were going to keep young and old 'kids' locked to the screen. These forecasts were confounded, and the internet is unlikely to replace actual with virtual associations because, at present at any rate, the new technology cannot deliver the same satisfactions.

It is true that some pundits in Europe, as in America, believe that the individualisation of biographies and trends towards privatism in daily life will drain voluntary organisations of their lifeblood, namely, members and volunteers. Home-centred, family-based lifestyles and a general decline of community are frequently identified as threats to the voluntary sector. Note, however, that the 'decline of community' thesis is as old as industrialism. The character of home-centred lifestyles is sometimes misunderstood. Being home-centred does not mean never going out. Extreme privatism is usually due to exceptional constraints – lack of money, and child-rearing couples juggling their domestic and paid work schedules, for example – rather than choice (see Devine, 1992). In the absence of such constraints, the home usually acts as a base from which individuals and couples can venture out into wider social networks (see Allan and Crow, 1991). Traditional neighbourhood communities (as we now describe them) are in decline, and have been declining for many years. People have become more mobile. Most neighbourhoods no longer provide communal roots in which voluntary associations can grow. When people go out they are most likely to do so privately, by car. If they go out for a drink this is not necessarily to 'the local'. Much the same has happened to occupational communities, and for much the same reasons. Labour is more mobile than in the past. People are no longer constrained to live within walking or cycling distance from their workplaces. But people still go out and associate with one another. They participate in interlocking rather than 'traditional' superimposed social networks in which kin, neighbours, work colleagues and friends are all largely the same people and all the participants have much the same circle of acquaintances. Interlocking networks have no definite bases either in neighbourhoods, churches or workplaces. The people who join a particular club will not necessarily have any other social bonds with one another. The older communal formations (which could be experienced as warm and friendly, or stifling) are in decline, but they are being replaced with other forms of sociability.

Coping with success

Fund-raising and recruitment are problems with which voluntary organisations have proved able to cope. They do not threaten the entire sector. Some clubs fizzle out and are replaced by others. In this respect voluntary societies are like small businesses. More serious threats to the sector may appear to arise from its successes. Voluntary organisations include local camera clubs and pub quiz leagues, and also bodies with national, sometimes international, profiles – the International Olympics Committee, the Scouts and the YMCA are all basically voluntary and, nowadays, global in scale. There are many internationally renowned orchestras, opera and ballet companies, and art collections, that are under voluntary management. If the work of an NGO is considered to be of sufficient national importance – that it would be too great a loss to the nation if everything foundered – then state support is likely to be forthcoming. This process may be repeated at regional and local levels. A possible, but sometimes exaggerated, problem is that eventually an NGO may come to depend on state support. It may begin to gear its operations to retaining state largesse. Other fund-raising may be wound down. If it becomes necessary to appoint paid staff, as is likely, the affairs of the association may be left in their hands. So an organisation may become, in effect, a loosely coupled branch of state administration. All this may happen but, as explained below, it is less likely to occur in leisure than in other, more 'serious', fields such as education and health care.

The next chapter explains that governments become involved in leisure provision in numerous ways and for a variety of reasons, but, to anticipate arguments developed fully later on, the sole ground that is likely to sustain state involvement in the long term is a general public interest in the maintenance of a particular leisure activity or facility. Now it is certainly possible that, once the state has shown that it will intervene if and when voluntary effort fails, the volunteers may simply withdraw. This happened during the expansion, to the point of universal provision, of state-provided schooling and health care. In some instances voluntary associations may become hollow shells which enable responsibility for the delivery of public services to be privatised, but there are invariably calls, eventually, for such quangos to be placed under proper public management if only to prevent the misuse of public funds. There have been well-publicised fraud scams and scares in recent years in Britain's quasi-privatised further education and training industries. This is far less likely to happen in leisure-based voluntary associations because in genuine NGOs members supervise and police each other. Fraud is rare. State support does not usually drive out voluntarism. This is because voluntary associations have capabilities – specifically their capacity to harness and fuel enthusiasm – that government agencies simply cannot replicate. Enthusiasts are usually willing to take on the form filling and accountability that state support requires. Youth, sports and arts organisations are thereby enabled to crank up their operations to the levels justified by a public interest. Government intervention is not a threat to the voluntary sector provided politicians and civil servants do not attempt to run things, and they usually have no inclination to take on hobbies, the arts or sports management. It is usually possible for these different providers to agree a mutually acceptable division of labour, which often takes the form of the state providing land and buildings, and the voluntary sector filling them with activists.

A similar 'threat' may appear when voluntary associations are so successful in promoting their activities that they become commercially viable. Players or artists may then demand that the associations be run professionally, presumably in order to maximise their own incomes. Alternatively, the stars may go independent as has happened in professional golf, tennis and snooker. Or the people who officiate in NGOs may decide that their organisations should be converted into PLCs, or an association may be, in effect, taken over by an existing commercial enterprise, such as a media business, for example. Very few voluntary bodies face this particular threat. That said, hobbyists played an important part in the early development of radio technology and its uses. In more recent times hobbyists have developed computing and internet technology and related skills (see Hesmondhalgh, 2002). The Apple company was formed by a group of hobbyists, but its transformation into a PLC has not eliminated computing as a hobby. Some associations may be lost to the voluntary sector, but the entire sector is not at risk.

Commerce does not threaten the entire voluntary sector for the same basic reason that state intervention is not a threat; namely, that these different providers have quite different capabilities. When the public wants variety, choice and a consumer experience, commerce offers suitable products. When involvement is needed – as in amateur sport, the arts and hobbies – commerce will provide relevant goods and services but it will not, because it cannot, actually run the show. Neither state agencies nor commerce can arouse or sustain comparable enthusiasm, dedication, and the corresponding satisfactions, to those that are found in the voluntary sector.

Professionalism is sometimes regarded as the threat from within. It arises when growth allows or requires voluntary bodies to appoint paid staff. Hanson (1982) gives examples from the railway clubs which were formed in Britain when steam engines were retired from the rail transport industry, and when, with the spread of the private motor car, many loss-making branch lines were closed. Before long voluntary associations were taking over and restoring some of these lines, plus the old steam locomotives and their original carriages. By the 1970s the more vigorous and successful railway clubs had developed money-raising activities. They were using their trains to convey paying passengers (mostly day-trippers and tourists) as a way of covering the clubs' costs. This, more likely than not, required the appointment of paid staff to sell tickets and to maintain the tracks and rolling stock to the required safety standards, and to drive the trains. Hanson describes some of the tensions that can arise within clubs between paid employees and fun volunteers. The former are likely to want the associations to be run 'professionally' – their own livelihoods are at risk – and they do not expect to be asked to volunteer their own time.

Such conflicts may be resolved by the separation of the amateur and commercial branches of a leisure industry, which is what happens in most of the performing arts where, for example, there are distinct amateur and professional theatres. The exception is rock music, which is also exceptional in being a commercial invention (see Chapter 9, p. 126). There is no clear division in this business between players who are basically amateurs with other paid jobs who may do occasional paid gigs, or, if they are becoming successful, regular gigs, and the 'big time' stars (who may be in this position for only a year or two, or even just for a few weeks).

A fact of this matter is that there are non-artistic forms of leisure where, in some voluntary associations, neither the professionals nor the volunteers can manage without the other. It would be impossible to stage the Olympic Games (or the Commonwealth Games – see p. 32) without any paid staff, and these events would also be impossible without the worldwide interest and participation that depend on voluntary action. There may always be tensions, but the major sports and youth organisations now have long histories of achievement in which they have combined voluntary management and volunteer help on the one hand with the employment of paid administrators and professional players and leaders on the other.

CONCLUSIONS

One message from this chapter is that the voluntary sector is alive and well. Its vibrancy is evident in the health of sports, hobbies, and the non-commercial arts organisations. Overall leisure has been commercialised but the expansion of commerce has been in addition to, rather than at the expense of, what the voluntary sector offers. Neither the expansion of commerce nor the growth of state provisions have undermined voluntarism. This is why a third way is possible: the different providers have complementary, non-substitutable capabilities. There are constant boundary adjustments, but there can be no wholesale take-over because of voluntary associations' distinctive capabilities and the satisfactions that they can offer. In recent years in Britain commerce has developed new markets for the individualised pursuit of health and fitness through exercise, but this has not been at the expense of the competitive sports that remain under voluntary management (see Chapter 7, pp. 106–7). Likewise, holidays are still self-organised by members of churches, schools, by employees at specific workplaces, wine lovers and Elvis worshippers. After 70 years, the Youth Hostels Association is still active. Commercial holidays have surrounded rather than taken over or extinguished the voluntary sector's contributions, and as it usually does wherever it expands, commerce has widened holiday-making citizens' options (see Chapter 5). Commercial and voluntary provisions are not head-on competitors. It is unnecessary to oppose one in order to support the other.

4 The Public Sector

Introduction

What are the special capabilities of public leisure services? This is the question that takes us to the heart of this book's central argument. If there were no special public sector capabilities – if everything could alternatively be done by the voluntary or commercial sector – the big policy issue would be whether the public sector performed better or worse than one of the alternatives. On this basis support would flow to the right or the left. The case for a third way in leisure is that the public sector is basically different with special, very distinctive, capabilities. Thus public provisions should not be conceived as alternatives to voluntary sector and commercial fare. The state can, if it wishes, restrict both voluntary and commercial enterprise simply by occupying space with its own free-to-use or heavily subsidised provisions, or by taxing and legislating in order to limit the permissible. Equally, governments can support voluntary associations and commercial businesses. And, most important of all, we shall see that governments can achieve things that are simply beyond the capabilities of any other leisure providers.

Seeking the public sector's special capabilities matches the questions addressed in Chapters 2 and 3 about the roles of the commercial and voluntary sectors but we should immediately note two crucial differences. First, neither commerce nor voluntary associations are likely to be swayed by intellectual arguments, and this applies whatever the quality of the argument. Commercial businesses have to be profitable or else they sink. They cannot be persuaded to stay in unprofitable markets. Conversely, if a good or service can be supplied profitably, then some enterprise is going to fill the market niche however harshly the product is condemned. Voluntary associations are driven by a different engine – their members' enthusiasm – and, just like commerce, not by outsiders' rational arguments. The public sector is different. Once accepted by politicians, arguments can be acted upon. A second crucial difference is that commerce and the voluntary sector each has a dominant engine – the profit motive and enthusiasm – whereas governments can authorise leisure interventions for all manner of reasons. It follows that, whereas commerce and voluntary associations can be relied on to act on the same motives, if not in exactly the same ways independently of time and place, the public sector is less reliable and far more complicated.

This chapter begins by noting the universally recognised importance of public sector leisure. All modern governments make leisure provisions. Wholesale withdrawal would provoke public outrage and this would never be contemplated, even by the most right-wing and market-oriented governments. All modern societies have histories of state leisure provision that extend throughout modernity, if not longer. Yet there are paradoxes. One is that, while most local, regional and national governments now have departments and ministers with responsibilities covering leisure, most of these departments have been created quite recently, whereas the leisure provisions are much longer standing. In other words, many provisions preceded the creation of dedicated branches of government. Another paradox is that the work of these departments is still not governed by clear and explicit leisure policies.

This chapter proceeds by asking how these paradoxes have come about. Britain is used as a case study. It is not a typical country in all respects but many of its experiences in pubic sector leisure are representative. We shall see that Britain's public leisure services developed haphazardly. They were not known as leisure services originally because they were introduced at various times when different problems – health and crime, for example – became matters of public concern. During the second half of the twentieth century the provisions came to be regarded as leisure services and their administration was rationalised within dedicated government departments, but this happened without leisure becoming a party political issue and therefore without clear leisure policies being developed and adopted. This policy vacuum has been widely recognised. Public providers have looked for assistance from academics who produce theories about leisure but nothing yet offered has proved both convincing and acceptable. However, there is no reason why the policy hole should remain unfilled. One way to proceed is the course taken in this chapter: to consider arguments for public leisure provisions which have been taken seriously and, indeed, have proved efficacious in loosening government purse strings. We then examine the evidence and the inherent plausibility of the arguments and decide which are beyond, and which are within, the real capabilities of state leisure provisions. It will be argued that redressing economic disadvantages (reaching out to the poor), spreading virtue, and enabling people to fulfil their own leisure ambitions, fall into the former (unrealisable) group. The genuine capabilities which are special to public provisions are investing in loss leaders in order to trigger an economic multiplier, extending citizenship, enhancing national (or local or regional) prestige and identities, and setting standards. We all have much to gain from public leisure services and much to lose if resources are frittered away in pursuit of the impossible or if potential benefits from public provisions are ignored.

The paradox

The importance of public sector leisure can be demonstrated quickly by listing some things that would be lost if the state withdrew entirely and left everything to the commercial market and voluntary effort.

■ There would be no recreational land in urban areas. All parks, playgrounds and playing fields would become more profitable as supermarkets, car parks, office blocks or residential developments. Local authorities are sometimes tempted to sell off open space, but this is akin to liquidating the family treasure. The land is initially free. All that is necessary to retain land for leisure is to designate it for recreational use. Once sold it is gone for good.
■ Physical recreation would be offered mainly indoors in towns and cities, in fitness suites and multi-purpose space for 5-a-side football, badminton, tennis and such like, on a members-only or pay-per-session basis. Oblong swimming tanks would be closed. Commercially viable swimming would usually be in the kind of fun pools associated with holiday destinations, and in small splash-arounds as found in up-market hotels. Many full-scale golf courses would be replaced by putting and driving ranges.
■ Access to the coast and countryside would be restricted, and usually by payment.
■ Large art galleries and museums would be replaced by commercial shops with paintings, antiquities and other works on display for sale, small exhibitions by groups of local artists, and private collections to which public access would depend on the wishes and charging policies of the owners.
■ Full-scale high culture – opera, ballet and symphony – could not be sustained by a combination of admission charges and commercial sponsorship. There could still be Wembley- and Hyde Park-type concerts featuring international stars with mass appeal performing popular acts.

There is no danger of a total government pull-out. The British state (like all other governments in modern societies) has a long record of intervention in leisure. The state was another early starter, alongside the voluntary sector. By the end of the nineteenth century Britain's local authorities were administering parks and playing fields, libraries, swimming baths, art galleries and museums. Chapter 2 explained that the main spurt in commercial provision came later. Before the twentieth century, commerce had little to offer except the pub and the music hall, plus the fast-developing holiday industry. At that time, public authorities and voluntary societies had little competition.

Despite the long history of state intervention in leisure, the UK's central government 'ministry for free time' was created only in 1992. It was then called the Department of National Heritage, and retitled the Department for Culture, Media and Sport (DCMS) by New Labour in 1997. Nowadays virtually all countries have a branch of government with broad responsibility for leisure, although the word 'leisure' is rarely in their titles. Culture, tourism and sport are more likely to feature. The departments are often quite recent creations (as in the UK) and/or have experienced numerous reshuffles of their responsibilities. All this reflects a worldwide uncertainty as to exactly what governments are trying to achieve in leisure.

In the UK, DCMS is a small central government department in terms of staff (roughly 600) and in terms of the size of its budget from the exchequer (roughly £1 billion excluding television licence fees which amount to around £2.5 billion), to which should probably be added the £1.5 billion or thereabouts that is raised for good causes through the National Lottery (see Chapter 12). This money is distributed by boards that make decisions independently, but within a framework of government policy directions. It all adds up to around £5 billion a year. The UK central government is not a big leisure spender. If lottery money and the TV licence fee are excluded from the calculation, we find that local authorities spend much more in total on leisure services (just over £2 billion). The total public sector spend on leisure is just over £7 billion. Meanwhile, private consumers spend over £10 billion on sports goods and services alone (a minor leisure industry in cash terms). The gambling industry has a turnover of £42 billion (but stakes less winnings amount to just £7.5 billion). Sport employs roughly 500,000 and gambling around 170,000 compared with the DCMS's 600. The DCMS is a relatively modest player. However, it does not use most of its budget on its own leisure services. Rather, via the financial support that it offers (over 90 per cent of its budget is distributed to other service providers) and the regulations that it issues (which can be enforced by legislation if necessary), it exerts considerable influence throughout the commercial and voluntary sectors, and on the rest of public sector (mainly local authority) leisure provisions. So how does the DCMS try to use its influence?

The obvious question to pose is, 'Why do governments support, or at least permit, some leisure activities but not others?'. This question has often been addressed, but no-one has found a brief and convincing answer. There turns out to be no master explanation (see Coalter et al., 1988). Some interventions have been inspired by concern for the health and fitness of children, workers and soldiers. Sometimes the concern has been the welfare of disadvantaged groups. Sometimes one aim has been to reduce delinquency. National or local prestige has been another motive. Government largesse has sometimes followed a belief that particular leisure activities are especially worthwhile. Governments may be swayed by pressure groups that lobby for particular activities. Sometimes, and increasingly in recent years, governments have invested in leisure hoping to trigger an economic multiplier.

The crucial fact of this matter is that, in leisure, governments can do anything that they wish, subject to the normal political checks and balances, that is, they must have the support of members in parliament or council chambers who are likely to be swayed by judgments as to whether votes will be won or lost depending on whether a facility is opened or a request for support turned down. Politics is the 'engine' that drives the public sector. It is a different kind of engine from those that drive the commercial and voluntary sectors. The political engine has many more 'cylinders' and 'spark plugs'.

Leisure is rather unusual in that it has never become a party political issue. This is despite the high profile of leisure in local government where nowadays, in the UK, it is among the high-spending departments, and one of the few areas in which local councils still have significant discretion. In recent years, leisure's profile in national politics has risen. The Millennium Dome was rarely out of the news in the UK around 2000. The government's subsequent role in the reconstruction of Wembley Stadium and its support for London's bid for the 2012 Olympics then kept the UK's 'ministry of leisure' in the news. Yet none of Britain's main political parties has ever campaigned on a distinctive leisure policy. Suffice it to say here that policy-making has usually been left to 'policy communities' (see Houlihan, 1990) composed of interested politicians, representatives of leisure interests, plus, sometimes, interested academics. These communities usually operate out of the public gaze, which can be a haven for woolly thinking.

The development of public leisure services: The case of the UK

Incremental growth

Britain's public leisure services (as they are now described) developed incrementally and haphazardly. From their nineteenth century beginnings, the long-term growth of leisure time and spending played a part, but only as a hidden hand. In the nineteenth century neither central nor local government had any intention – or even an aspiration – to cater comprehensively for the people's leisure. Proposals for state intervention in education, health care and housing were controversial. The case for public leisure services was way outside all political agendas. Public sector leisure provision developed in an ad hoc way, not in response to leisure demands so much as to address a variety of other problems that arose during the transformation of Britain into an urban industrial society. There was no landmark legislation comparable to the 1870 Education Act (which made elementary schooling universal). The legislation under which public leisure provision began includes the Baths and Wash-houses Act of 1846 (see Box 4.1), the Public Health Acts of 1875 and 1890, the Local Government Act of 1894, and the Open Spaces Act of 1906.

One problem to which nineteenth-century governments responded was the (lack of) cleanliness and the general unhealthiness of the urban masses. They were also concerned with encouraging respectable, edifying ways of life; hence the public libraries, museums and art galleries. Sometimes the problem was a specific section of the population. The youth service has its origins in nineteenth century efforts to keep young people, especially young males, out of trouble. Sport was supported for all the above reasons: health, shaping character, and keeping young males out of mischief. Over time provisions were introduced for other needy groups such as the retired and the disabled. Local authorities sometimes became leisure providers by force of circumstance. When they became responsible for children's schooling they were obliged to make provisions for the pupils' leisure. Later, when they began to construct council houses, they could not but give consideration to the recreation facilities that were needed on the often sprawling estates. Holiday resorts, of course, had particular reasons to enhance their public amenities.

BOX 4.1 BATHS AND WASH-HOUSES

These were the precursors of present-day swimming pools. They were opened in all major towns and cities in Britain in the decades following the 1846 Baths and Wash-houses Act. There were facilities for washing clothes. Typical charges in the nineteenth century were one penny per hour, or threepence for two hours, including drying. There were also 'slipper bath' facilities. These were so-named because of the appearance of the baths when, in the interest of modesty, users draped large towels over the tubs while they bathed.

By the 1870s local authorities were adding swimming pools to the basic facilities. Ashton Swimming Pool in Lancashire was among the first. It was built in 1870 at a cost of £16,000, most of which was donated by a local mill owner. The main pool (100 feet by 40 feet) was used exclusively by men except for a three-hour slot each Thursday when it was allocated to ladies. The latter normally had to use a smaller (27 feet by 15 feet) pool.

The first association of swimming clubs, which evolved into the Amateur Swimming Association, was formed in 1869 in London. Its main initial responsibility was the management of games of football played in water (which became known as water polo). However, in 1869 there was also a one-mile race. Before long other distances were added. The first recorded diving championship was held in Scotland in 1889.

Sources: www.britishswimming.org, www.northflow.fsnet.co.uk, www.ashton-under-lyne.com/baths.htm

There are three noteworthy features of the historical beginnings of Britain's public leisure services. First, local rather than central government was the main provider. Second, most of the provision was under permissive rather than mandatory legislation, meaning that local authorities were allowed, but not required, to provide. Third, wherever possible the provision was made via the voluntary sector or with major philanthropic contributions (see Boxes 4.1 and 4.2). This also applied during the development of state education and health care. In the second half of the nineteenth century Britain's municipal authorities set about encouraging rational recreation and creating civilised ways of urban life by harnessing and co-ordinating voluntary effort and filled any gaps with their own facilities only as a last resort (see Meller, 1976). The Philharmonic Hall (see Box 4.2) is just one of many grand buildings in Liverpool which were erected in the nineteenth century with most of the initiative and initial funding coming from the voluntary sector.

The outcome was an untidy hotchpotch. Local authority leisure services varied considerably in quantity and quality from place to place. There were no nationally approved benchmarks or yardsticks. At the time the provisions were not known as leisure services. Local authorities added new committees and departments for each service that was introduced – parks, libraries, baths, allotments, youth clubs and so on. Each service had its own aspirant profession. So by the 1930s there was extensive public sector leisure provision, but no overall leisure services departments, no single leisure profession, and, most crucially, no leisure policies.

Public leisure services (as they are described today) somehow missed out during the overhaul and strengthening of Britain's welfare state that followed the Second

---

BOX 4.2 LIVERPOOL'S PHILHARMONIC HALL

This building is still owned and managed by the Royal Liverpool Philharmonic Society, which is one of the oldest concert-giving organisations in the world. The Society gave its first performance in 1840. It is the only orchestral society in Britain which owns and operates its own hall.

The original hall opened in 1849 but was destroyed by fire in 1933. An art deco replacement was opened in 1939. It was re-opened in 1995 following a complete refurbishment. The Hall is now the home of the Royal Liverpool Philharmonic Orchestra, the Royal Liverpool Philharmonic Choir, and the Merseyside Youth Orchestra.

Choral music predominated in the Society's programme up to the First World War, and a full-time professional orchestra was established only after the Second World War. The orchestra's annual programme now includes the Summer Pops which are regularly attended by over 30,000 people.

The 200-strong choir remains entirely amateur. It travels the length and breadth of Britain, and overseas as well, and has sung regularly at the BBC Proms in London's Royal Albert Hall.

Sources: www.rlpc.freeserve.co.uk/backgnd/hall.htm, www.liverpoolphil.com

---

World War. Secondary education for all was introduced. The National Health Service was created. Council house building accelerated to replace the remaining slums and war-damaged properties. Local authority leisure services continued much as before. By the end of the 1950s they offered some of the starkest examples of public squalor – Victorian swimming pools, water-logged playing fields, and changing rooms with no water supply – amid private affluence. The affluent consumer society was then coming into existence, and the Albemarle Committee (1960) concluded that youth clubs in draughty church halls could not compete with glitzy dance palais and café bars.

However, by the 1960s central government was playing a larger role in leisure provision, often – as had happened in local government previously – by sheer force of circumstance. Problems were arising which required a national response or, at any rate, national co-ordination. Central government already had more than a toehold in leisure. Much of the country's heritage was owned by the government or by the crown, and was being visited by increasing numbers of tourists and day-trippers. Since 1927 the BBC had been the monopoly state broadcaster (see Chapter 10). Roads and railways (and canals) were always, in part, leisure resources, and were increasingly being used for leisure travel. The government was already regulating gambling and alcohol sales, and had legislation prescribing the limits of decency that were permissible on stage, in print and on film (albeit, in the latter case, via the industry's own board of censors).

An Arts Council was created in 1946 in recognition of the fact that the production of high culture was becoming unsustainable without state support. In 1949 legislation was passed enabling National Parks to be designated, and creating a National Parks Commission (which was renamed the Countryside Commission in

1968, and is now the Countryside Agency). This was a response to the fact that more and more people were visiting the countryside. They needed facilities, and potential conflicts between the various demands on the countryside had to be addressed. The Sports Council (now split into UK Sport, Sport England, Sportscotland and so on) was created in 1965 as an advisory body, and became an executive body with a royal charter in 1972. The case for central government support for sport was basically the same as for the traditional arts. Most (still genuinely voluntary and amateur) sports associations needed state support if they were to maintain the organisation and facilities required to produce internationally competitive players. A push from central government was needed if grass-roots facilities were to be improved so as to make sport attractive to young people and other sections of the population. Purpose-built local authority sport and leisure centres began to be constructed in the 1960s, under the auspices of, and with part-funding by, the Sports Council, and by the end of the century the UK had around 2000 of these facilities. VisitBritain (its present title) dates from 1969 when it was created in recognition of the growing importance of international tourism in the country's trade balance, and to co-ordinate planning so as to accommodate the anticipated growing stream of visitors.

The end result of these developments was a public leisure services organisation that was even more fragmented than before. As well as the local authorities, each with separate departments catering for different kinds of leisure, there were several central government ministries with substantial leisure responsibilities – those responsible for local government, the environment, transport, education, trade and industry, plus the Home Office. Outside commentators who surveyed this scene were appalled by the untidiness (Travis, 1979).

Rationalisation

The administrative rationalisation of Britain's public leisure services began in the 1970s as part of a broader re-organisation of local government. This reduced the number of separate local authorities and thinned out the committee systems within them all. It was the start of ongoing attempts to create more streamlined, joined-up, local government. Most local authorities emerged from the 1970s' overhaul with combined departments under leisure, recreation services, or some similar title. The staffs of the former baths, parks departments and so on were also merged, and they created an umbrella professional organisation, the Institute of Leisure and Amenity Managers (ILAM). ILAM has subsequently set up its own training provisions, accredited other (higher and further education) institutions' courses and qualifications, and established procedures for professional certification (see Bacon, 1990). Thus, since the 1970s, there has been an aspirant, emergent association of (mainly) public sector leisure professionals (although membership is also open to persons who work in the voluntary and commercial sectors).

From the outset the local authority leisure services departments realised that they needed leisure policies. They became interested in what economists, psychologists and sociologists were writing about leisure: a possible source of theory on which they might base professional practice. The new local authority departments began to commission leisure research, initially to discover who was using their facilities, to identify under-represented groups and unmet needs. This research was encouraged by the Sports Council (and to a lesser extent by the Arts Council and the Countryside Commission). The Sports Council had adopted 'sport for all' as its main policy, and was working in partnership with local authorities to raise overall levels of participation, especially within sections of the population that were known (or believed) to be under-represented, namely, women, ethnic minorities (though there is evidence that they are not all under-represented), the working class, and particularly the unemployed. A theory that some of the new leisure professionals embraced, envisaged leisure services as a branch of the mainstream social services – an integral part of the welfare state – ensuring that all citizens had access to a full range of approved leisure opportunities. Academics based in the university and polytechnic leisure studies and related departments which were being created in response to the new profession's need for qualified staff, and to undertake the research which 'the industry' required, sometimes endorsed this thinking (Coalter, 1990; Coalter *et al.*, 1988) which, in the event, turned out to have arrived too late. In the 1950s and 1960s social democrats (the old left) had envisaged the welfare state expanding indefinitely, transforming what had formerly been privileges of the few into rights of all. By the time that a public sector-based leisure profession began to develop, 'the party' was already over. State spending was being capped. New right thinking was ascendant. Governments were seeking cost savings. This was not to be the temporary pause which, in the 1970s and 1980s, social democrats may have hoped, and leisure policy-making has still to catch up with the 'new times'.

During the 1990s there was an administrative rationalisation of the UK central government's leisure responsibilities, mirroring what had happened in local government 20 years earlier. As explained above, in 1992 most of central government's leisure responsibilities were drawn together in a new Department of National Heritage, which in 1997 was retitled the Department for Culture, Media and Sport (DCMS). Since 1994 this department has had oversight of a greatly enlarged budget, provided by the National Lottery (see Chapter 12). Twenty-eight per cent of the National Lottery's stake money is channelled to 'good causes' which have included the arts, sport, the heritage and, up to the turn of the millennium, a millennium fund.

Actually the DCMS does not have a monopoly of state leisure policy-making and implementation. It never will. The exchequer will always retain a say in spending plans. The health ministry will always be involved, in some way or another, in promoting healthy lifestyles. The education ministry will always have some responsibility for the recreation of pupils and students. The government department responsible for trade and industry will always need to be involved in the development of what is now a major economic sector. The Home Office is unlikely to relinquish control over 'public order' matters related to alcohol, drugs, the conduct of spectators at sports events, or whatever is causing concern and offence at a given time. Nevertheless, since 1992 UK central government has possessed a lead ministry in leisure.

Provision without policy

Like UK local government 20 years earlier, the central government's lead leisure department has needed leisure policies, and, as explained above, such policies have not been delivered through the normal party political channels. The UK's main political parties have never developed and campaigned for election on distinctive leisure policies. Leisure provision has always been non-party political. Although it is possible to construct ideal-types of conservative, neo-liberal and socialist leisure policies (see Henry, 2001; Henry and Bramham, 1986), none of Britain's main parties has ever taken this step. The Labour Party, even when it was 'old' Labour, never sought to nationalise the commercial leisure industries. Nor have the parties of the right ever sought to privatise most of the public leisure services that have developed incrementally over the last 100 years or so. In leisure, all the parties have always accepted a mixed economy.

Why the political reticence? Maybe it has been an outcome of an Anglo-Saxon reluctance to allow the government to tell people how they should use their own time and money. A minister for leisure would sound presumptuous. French governments, for example, have been less hesitant, whether promoting France's cultural achievements and seeking to democratise their culture, producing world sports champions, or prescribing the proper length of a working week. UK politicians have always been more cautious. However, leisure has never been party political in France, or anywhere else except the ideological cauldron that was the Soviet Union in the years immediately following 1917. Leisure is not normally 'political' in the everyday sense because the main capabilities of state intervention (see the section on capabilities) are unlikely to be divisive unless political parties are based on national, ethnic or religious schisms. A consequence has been the delegation of leisure policy-making to 'policy communities' composed of interested politicians, civil servants, representatives of interest groups and other experts. They have sought consensus, thereby keeping a steady hand on decision-making. Now policy communities exist in all policy areas, but in leisure the policy communities have been only weakly attached to party political processes and thereby to public opinion.

> As with sport policy generally, sports development lacks the systemic embeddedness that exists in other service areas such as health and education where the organisation and professional roots are multiple and go deep into the infrastructure of political parties, the government and the state.
>
> (Houlihan and White, 2002, p. 231)

Another problem with the leisure policy communities is that they have formed not around leisure in general but around sport, the arts, the countryside and so on. This reflects the fragmentation of the leisure industries. There are many leisure policy communities. Even individually they usually find consensus difficult to achieve and sustain. The interest groups based on particular sports and arts are often aggressively independent. So although there is now a lead leisure department in central government, its work is guided by a series of discrete sports, arts, heritage, and media policies and so on, which are not orchestrated by an overarching leisure policy

When politics leaves a policy vacuum, the space is likely to be filled by other forces. At local and national levels, leisure policy has always been exceptionally open to influence by the enthusiasms of individual ministers and councillors, plus the lobbying of interest groups.

> Incoming ministers for sport, of which there have been far too many in recent years, have a capacity to translate their particular enthusiasms into policy priorities in a way that is inconceivable in other government departments.
>
> (Houlihan and White, 2002, p. ix)

The creation of the UK Sports Institute (see Chapter 6, p. 93) owed much to the fact that prime minister, John Major, was a sports enthusiast. Alternatively or in addition, ministers may decide to make their mark through seeking administrative efficiency, becoming business-like, meaning, in practice, cutting costs, setting measurable targets and demanding results from the departments, and other organisations which receive support. They may, thereby, seek better value for money – which is never a bad thing in itself, but can be dangerous in the absence of any clear sense of what counts as value (see Box 4.3).

There is always a danger of scoring own goals. Many leisure services are labour-intensive. Opera and sports coaching are cases in point. It is impossible to replace labour with technology. Leisure services differ in this respect from most manufacturing industries and many business services. In leisure it is often impossible to save on labour costs without degrading the service. Over time the services inevitably become more expensive as labour costs increase. So, for example, in the Arts Council-supported national performing arts companies (see Chapter 13), pressure to enlarge their non-government streams of income (which the companies have generated themselves) has been accompanied by a decline rather than an increase in the total number of productions that they stage and the total audiences reached. Government subsidies, ticket prices and box office revenue have all increased. The audiences have spent more and, therefore, may have become even more socially and economically exclusive than formerly (Evans, 1999). There is no possibility of achieving economies of scale. Over time the arts become more expensive. To maintain quality they need to do less for more, not more for less. If they are to do more while retaining their present shape and sources of funds, they will need a lot more (government) money. This is not due to archaic forces of conservatism; rather, the quest for efficiency gains is flawed.

Business language is often completely inappropriate in state leisure departments. In recent years government ministers have been keen on targets. They have spoken of 'deliverables' and expect targets to be achieved in exchange for state funding. But do we really want politicians to decide what arts organisations should deliver? In sport there must be losers as well as winners. Ministers who believe that they can

BOX 4.3 COMPULSORY COMPETITIVE TENDERING (CCT) AND BEST VALUE

In 1989 the Audit Commission (an accountancy-led central government body) issued a scathing report on the management of the UK's local authority sport and other leisure services. It criticised the lack of clear objectives, customer research, and cost-benefit comparisons. The government's response was to insist that from 1992 onwards the management of the services should be put out to competitive tender and that the task should be handed to either the voluntary or the commercial sector if they could do a better job.

There were instant howls of anguish and anger. Critics forecast full privatisation as the next step, balance sheets taking precedence over social objectives (Ravenscroft, 1993; Stabler and Ravenscroft, 1994), and two-tier provisions with plush facilities for 'good citizens' who could pay and utility standards for the rest (Ravenscroft, 1993, 1998).

In the late-1990s the New Labour government removed the compulsion and incorporated competitive tendering within a broader 'best value' regime (see Henry, 2001). By then most of the earlier controversy had subsided. Many local authority staff had decided that there were advantages in the new system, such as making services more efficient and responsive to customers (Coalter, 2000; Edwards, 2000). Equally important, the impact had been far less dramatic than expected.

■ Most contracts have been awarded to in-house bidders (Taylor, 1992; Coalter, 1995). Commerce has displayed little interest. In 2001 local authority facilities were being operated by 10 commercial organisations and 15 voluntary bodies whereas over 300 local authorities were still managing their own facilities (Audit Commission, 2002).

■ There has been virtually no change in levels of participation in sport or in the social profile of participants (see Table 3.2, p. 33). However, CCT and its successor may have restrained the public sector and thereby created scope for the development of commercial health and fitness clubs (see Chapter 7, pp. 106–7).

■ Social objectives have become less prominent. For example, there are now fewer staff with responsibility for promoting women's sports participation (Aitchison, 1997; Yule, 1997), though there has been no decline in participation by women.

■ Lower grade staff have been losers. Their terms and conditions of work have been degraded (Aitchison, 1997) as has happened more widely with the introduction of market forces into the UK's public services (Nichols and Davisdon, 1993).

control the flow of Olympic gold are deluded. They need proper leisure policies which square with the public sector's genuine capabilities.

Leisure policy is constantly exposed to broader political tides. During the last 30 years a priority of successive UK governments has been to modernise the economy and to make businesses more competitive in European and wider markets, all amid an assumption (evidence of the success of the new right) that private enterprise and market forces are preferable to state intervention and direct government provision. So there has been a tendency to treat state leisure spending as an 'investment' which should lead to jobs and overseas sales, and a willingness to allow the commercial sector to deliver everything that it is able to take on. The danger here is the sidelining of softer, more difficult to measure, social and cultural benefits that can accrue from state interventions in leisure. The big failure in public sector leisure provision is not operational but political. The political process has never yielded satisfactory leisure policies. Business-like management and practices, such as cutting unit costs, are not just insufficient but often misconceived. Politicians need to say what the public leisure services are to achieve, and why. Up to now they have been either myopic, muddled or silent.

Where should the search for leisure policies begin? Driver *et al.* (1991) are helpful: they argue that public services always need to be benefits-driven because the test of their effectiveness and value is never how much they do but the results. Then, as John Crompton (2000) has added, the benefits need to be public benefits, shared by all or most of the population, not just the participants. Public subsidies for purely private benefits such as enjoyment are unlikely to be politically sustainable in the long term however efficiently such benefits are delivered and however appreciative the individual recipients may be. In addition, the benefits sought need to be consistent with the public sector's leisure capabilities.

Incapacities

One way to proceed, therefore, is to identify the kinds of public benefits that state interventions are able to deliver. To begin with, and in order to clear the ground of garbage, we can identify some important functional incapacities of state leisure provisions: aims that are frankly unrealisable, however important they may often be as intentions and/or rationalisations, and however efficacious they may be in loosening government purse strings.

Reaching the poor

First, public provisions are unable to redistribute leisure opportunities in favour of the socio-economically disadvantaged. Some state measures – support for high culture and tourism, for example – are clearly not aiming to achieve this. It might be argued that free-to-use or subsidised provisions will be accessible, and therefore of particular value, to the disadvantaged. In practice, however, we find that it is nearly always the better-off who make the most use of free-to-use and subsidised facilities – national parks and sports centres, for instance. The social-class skew varies in strength according to the type of leisure, but the evidence in Tables 4.1 and 4.2 shows that the higher socio-economic strata usually participate more irrespective of whether the activity is state supported.

The reasons for the skew are straightforward: the better-off are the most likely to possess the transport, equipment, interest, skills and social networks that allow them to take advantage. Time and again sport facilities have been opened with the declared intention of servicing the financially weak and have then been used by the strong. The main UK public leisure provisions that are used as much by the poor as by the rich are BBC television which is funded by what, in effect, is a regressive poll tax (the licence fee), and (if it counts in this context) the National Lottery. It is true that most local authorities have programmes targeted specifically at disadvantaged groups such as the unemployed and the retired, and that subsidies are sometimes

Table 4.1 Sport participation by socio-economic group in the four weeks prior to interview, adults aged 16 and over, UK, 1996–97 (in percentages)

	Professional	Employers and managers	Other non-manual	Skilled manual and own account workers	Semi-skilled and personal service	Unskilled	All
Walking	56	48	46	44	39	33	44
Swimming	23	19	17	11	11	6	15
Keep fit/yoga	14	12	17	7	9	5	12
Cue sports	10	10	8	15	9	7	11
Cycling	19	12	9	11	10	7	11
Weights	10	5	6	5	3	2	5
Football	5	4	3	6	3	3	5
Golf	11	9	4	5	3	1	5
Running	9	6	4	4	2	2	5
10-pin bowls/skittles	4	3	4	3	2	1	3
At least one activity (including those not listed separately)	63	52	48	45	37	24	46

Sources: General Household Survey, Office for National Statistics, London; Continuous Household Survey, Northern Ireland Statistics and Research Agency, Belfast (www.statistics.gov.uk).

Table 4.2 Participation in home-based leisure activities by gender and socio-economic group in the four weeks prior to interview, UK, 1996–97, adults aged 16 and over (in percentages)

	Professional	Managers and employers	Other non-manual	Skilled manual	Semi-skilled	Unskilled	All
Males							
Watching TV	99	99	99	99	98	99	99
Visiting/entertaining relatives or friends	95	96	96	95	94	88	95
Listening to radio	93	92	93	87	85	83	89
Listening to records, tapes or CDs	83	80	85	74	73	67	78
Reading books	81	69	68	48	49	39	58
DIY	66	65	59	60	48	40	57
Gardening	62	63	50	52	46	42	52
Dressmaking, needlework, knitting	4	4	3	3	3	2	3
Females							
Watching TV	98	99	99	100	99	98	99
Visiting/entertaining relatives or friends	96	98	97	95	97	96	97
Listening to radio	96	89	90	85	82	78	87
Listening to records, tapes or CDs	93	83	80	72	70	64	76
Reading books	91	80	77	63	61	54	71
DIY	41	36	32	30	27	22	29
Gardening	49	55	51	42	41	39	45
Dressmaking, needlework, knitting	30	36	39	40	36	36	36

Sources: General Household Survey, Office for National Statistics, London; Continuous Household Survey, Northern Ireland Statistics and Research Agency, Belfast (www.statistics.gov.uk).

targeted (free admission on proof of being in receipt of unemployment or some other state benefit, for example). However, all the evaluative studies have shown that most members of the target populations are missed (Glyptis, 1989; Kay, 1987; King *et al.*, 1985; Town, 1983). Some of the target population do not like being treated differently from other people. A rather different problem is that selective subsidies are expensive to administer. Above all, a blunt fact of this matter is that, in a market economy, leisure opportunities are among the rewards of success. Leisure providers – whether commercial, voluntary sector or public – have no option but to flow with this tide. Redistribution is a job for economic and social policies, not the public leisure services. Note that these arguments apply only to socio-economic disadvantages, not disadvantages which may be associated with age, gender, sexual orientation, ethnicity or place of residence.

Spreading virtue

A second incapacity is that state leisure provisions are unable to make people use their leisure in ways that the authorities would prefer.

> The latent energy in bars, waste ground and street corners, poised perhaps for violence, can be released effectively and enjoyably into sport and recreation.
> (Sports Council, 1985)

Wrong! The authorities have been backing this theory for over a century. It has been tested to destruction. If people were susceptible to leisure education and state-promoted opportunities we would now be a nation of church-goers and Shakespeare readers. 'Social control' arguments still appear to be an excellent way of unlocking public funds (see Centre for Leisure and Sport Research, 2002). The willingness of the authorities to act on a manifestly false premise suggests that the official rationale of the relevant measures may perform latent functions. It enables governments to be seen to be 'doing something' about conditions in 'problem areas' whether the problem is the sectarian conflict in Northern Ireland or the more widespread inner-city and council-estate syndromes. The wider public may thereby be persuaded that the target population's ill-health and misdemeanours are outcomes of their own lifestyle choices rather than the surrounding economic and housing conditions and inequalities (Ingham, 1985). The crucial fact of this matter is that when people have a choice of commercial, voluntary and public sector leisure provisions, they will use the latter only if the provisions coincide with their own inclinations. The authorities can try and try again to persuade the public to use their leisure in what, to the authorities, appear to be rational ways. Public sector leisure professionals are still expected to act as 'soft cops', countervailing against harmful temptations. The nineteenth century ideology of rational recreation lives on (see Heeley, 1986) but its measures are destined to fail at one or another of what are now well-known hurdles. The target populations either decline to take part (in sport, arts programmes or whatever), or they drop-out after initial visits, or they stay and overwhelm the provisions with their own culture (see Skogen and Wichstrom, 1996).

Fulfilling dreams

The third incapacity is assisting the various sections of the public to fulfil their own leisure dreams, whatever these might be. This implausible rationale was surprisingly popular among some public sector leisure professionals during the second half of the twentieth century. Some were inspired by France's state-funded animateurs who do 'missionary work' among the people, attempting to unlock their latent artistic creativity (see Kingsbury, 1976). Many public sector professionals like to appear non-judgemental, non-authoritarian, willing to listen and respond to the public's wishes. They have envisaged leisure professionals bringing together politicians and members of the public to identify leisure needs which can then be met (Coalter, 1990; Rapoport, 1977). The crucial fact here is that the agenda is hopelessly unrealistic. John Crompton's (2000) 'rule' applies: public subsidies are likely to be politically sustainable only if there is a public benefit, or at least a perceived public benefit, in what is being provided. Public sector leisure professionals are not going to be licensed to cater for the leisure interests of all the various sections of the population, be these philosophy, ocean cruises or sexual fetishes. The public sector is always going to be judgemental. There is a sense in which it is inherently paternal, deciding to facilitate some but not other leisure demands (see McNamee et al., 2000, 2001).

Capabilities

The economic multiplier

So what are the public sector's special capabilities? These are fourfold. First, public investment in leisure facilities can trigger an economic multiplier. Holiday resorts realised this ages ago. By laying out parks and generally taking care of the environment, the attractiveness of a holiday destination is enhanced, and (hopefully) the visitors' spending more than repays the investment. In more recent times, rural districts, declining industrial towns and major cities have become equally keen to attract tourists, day trippers and people on nights out. City councils vie with each other in their progress towards becoming 24-hour hotspots with booming night-time economies (including gay quarters in some places). Leisure spenders may be enticed by clean environments and open spaces, the conservation of any natural beauty and historic buildings, pop concert venues, or museums and art galleries. Cities need tempting facilities and, equally important (but slightly different), nowadays they need attractive images (see Hughes and Boyle, 1992; Street, 1993). These measures can work. Private investment is just as able as public investment to attract visitors and spending but only public bodies are able to invest in loss-leaders. The local tax-payers pick up the bill and (they hope) recover their investment from visitors' spending on provisions that operate at a profit.

The problem is not that the economic rationale is fundamentally flawed. Rather, the problem for most places is that leisure is a highly competitive market. Different coastal and inland resorts and cities compete against each other for market shares. It is a case of 'beggar my neighbour'. There are winners and losers. There are cases where investment in culture has triggered urban regeneration but there are also examples of failure (see Bianchini and Parkinson, 1993). The leisure policies and provisions of different countries, regions and cities affect the distribution of leisure spending but not the global level which is dependent on macro-economic conditions, levels of employment and unemployment, overall levels of government spending, interest rates, and whether the public accounts are in deficit or surplus. Moreover, a leisure-based local or national economy can be a mixed blessing (lots of jobs, but mostly seasonal or part-time), and pre-occupation with economic goals may sideline other special capabilities of public leisure provisions.

Citizenship

Another special public sector capability in leisure is extending citizenship – rights that we all enjoy simply by virtue of our citizenship. Public leisure provisions can be intended for, and accessible to, everyone. This is most easily accomplished with land. The state can simply designate coastline, rural tracts and urban parks for public enjoyment. All citizens can be given access. No-one need be charged. The same principle can be applied to buildings: stately homes, art galleries, libraries and museums (see Box 4.4). Even people who do not visit can still enjoy the feeling that the facilities are theirs and that they themselves, their children, grandchildren,

---

BOX 4.4 PUBLIC LIBRARIES

Britain's first 'circulating' (lending) libraries were opened in the first half of the eighteenth century.

The 1850 Public Libraries Act enabled local authorities to open libraries. However, at that time there were severe restrictions on how much the authorities were allowed to spend. At first they could rarely afford to actually purchase books. So even public libraries needed wealthy patrons. Andrew Carnegie (1835–1919) helped to finance over 380 libraries in Britain. By the time of his death over half the library authorities in Britain had Carnegie libraries and he had set up more than 2800 libraries across the English-speaking world.

A further 18 Library Acts were passed between 1850 and 1900 which expanded provisions towards the service that we know today. During the twentieth century new services were added. The first mobile public library service was introduced in Perthshire in 1920. In 1935 Middlesex County Library became the first to loan gramophone records. In 1972 Cardiganshire became the first to loan cassettes. In 1995 Marylebone became the first public library to offer public access to the internet.

Today the UK has over 4000 libraries which are open to the general public plus over 650 mobile libraries. Fifty-eight per cent of the UK population hold library cards. There are around 350 million visits to public libraries every year – more than six times the number of attendances at professional football matches. It is in a public library that most children receive their first civic recognition through their right to a library card.

Sources: www.spartacus.schoolnet.co.uk/library.htm, www.la-hq.org.uk/hot_news/mediapk.pdf

neighbours and indeed all their fellow citizens, can use them if they so desire. A society can decide to conserve and open some facilities to all humankind thus helping to create a global citizenship. Until recently in Britain public service broadcasting enlarged citizenship. The main channels and programmes were available to all (see Chapter 10). Commercial provisions cannot create citizenship in the same way – the benefits are restricted to people who are able and willing to pay. Voluntary associations cater for their members or a target group. They are normally unable to reach out to the entire population unless enabled to do so by public subsidies.

The manner in which public facilities are managed sometimes fails to exploit their citizenship potential. For example, Parker and Ravenscroft (1999) argue that Britain's national parks (where most of the land remains in private ownership) have always been administered in a paternal way: that the public has been made to feel that access is a privilege rather than a right, and conditional upon their good (as defined by the authorities) behaviour. Public leisure provisions do not automatically enlarge and strengthen a population's sense of citizenship. They cannot achieve this if they are managed as if they were businesses. The situation is rather that they have a unique citizenship-enlarging capacity.

Prestige and identity

A third unique public sector capability is enhancing national prestige and identity. These two usually go hand-in-glove. People experience pride if their country's (or a region's or a city's) historic buildings, art collections, sites of natural beauty, performing arts or sporting achievements win wider admiration.

> Sporting success for Britain makes people proud to be British. To some degree which is difficult to quantify, this justifies public investment.
>
> (Sports Council, 1985)

True! Governments may seek to strengthen national identity and prestige by supporting traditional games (Irish, Scottish, Asian or whatever) but nowadays, like the Chinese authorities, they are likely to be more concerned with success in the major world sports, especially Olympic sports (see Tan Ying and Roberts, 1995). The City of Manchester Stadium is a recent, somewhat controversial, prestige project (see Box 4.5). Governments are better-placed than either commercial businesses or voluntary associations to use leisure provisions for nation-building. The success of a business is due to, and benefits most of all, its own investors, managers and workers. A voluntary association's achievements bring credit to its members – their skills and enthusiasm. Governments alone can act for their countries.

Standards

A fourth special capability is that state leisure policies and provisions can articulate a clear moral and aesthetic order. Public provisions may be unable to change the

---

BOX 4.5 CITY OF MANCHESTER STADIUM

This stadium was originally owned by Manchester City Council, but the costs of its construction (£110 million) were covered mainly by a £77 million grant from Sport England (with money from the National Lottery). It was built for the 2002 Commonwealth Games with seating for 38,000. In addition to its contribution to the cost of the main stadium, the government spent another £40 million on the Games (in security, protocol and general organisation).

The stadium is located on a 146-acre former industrial site, which also contains another athletics track (the warm-up track at the Commonwealth Games), an indoor tennis centre, England's national squash centre, and indoor athletics facilities.

Controversially, after the Commonwealth Games the stadium was long-leased to Manchester City AFC (in exchange for the club's older, 1923 vintage, Maine Road ground). Manchester City have converted their new facility into a 48,000 seater football stadium. Has the public investment been justified by public benefits?

Manchester City Council believes that the benefits have justified the outlay. The council welcomes the fact that the Commonwealth Games attracted a million visitors to Manchester and that staging the games helped Manchester to secure an additional £600 million of public and private investment. The council also claims that, as a result of the publicity generated by the games, Manchester will attract an additional 30,000 visitors a year, spending an extra £12 million in the region, that these benefits will continue indefinitely, and that nearly 30 million extra people worldwide now consider Manchester as a possible visitor or business destination (Manchester City Council, 2003).

Manchester can afford to smile. Most of the investment that made the Commonwealth Games possible was found by the wider UK public.

---

public's tastes and behaviour, but they can send out clear messages about what is approved of and what is deplored. State support places leisure activities on the 'bright side'. High culture and sport clearly benefit from these rays. Types of leisure that are outlawed, restricted or taxed heavily (alcohol, tobacco, cannabis and other recreational drugs, commercial sex and, until recently, most gambling) are thereby placed on the 'dark side'. People may still participate but they know that they are venturing into the shade by so doing. Governments must inevitably make moral choices over what to support and what to prohibit. The state is always the arbiter of last resort. It must intervene when there are conflicts over the use of water space or urban precincts (between those who want lively night-time economies and those who prefer peace and quiet, for example), or on moral grounds (such as that between those opposed to and those who wish to practise so-called country sports).

> Leisure is part of the struggle for the control of space and time in which social groups are continuously engaged.   (Wilson, 1988, p. 12)

Governments are inevitably drawn into these conflicts and are thereby required to define which uses of leisure are to be admired and applauded, and which should be deplored.

CONCLUSIONS

Needless to say, leisure policies may fail to transmit any clear moral and aesthetic messages, just as they may fail to enhance national identity and prestige, and to extend citizenship. Failure in any of these areas is likely – highly probable in fact – when governments fail to recognise all the unique capabilities of public leisure provisions. In the rest of this book we shall encounter examples of the penalties that everyone is paying for this failure. Governments do not spend huge sums of money on leisure (compared with their spending on health, education, pensions and defence, for example) but they make a disproportionately large impact on what is provided via their ability to influence the commercial and voluntary sectors.

This chapter has reviewed how public sector leisure provisions developed within a leisure policy vacuum. It then proceeded to separate incapacities from the public sector's true capabilities in leisure. The public sector's special capabilities are not necessarily either explanations or actual consequences of what governments do in leisure. In politics there is no benign hidden hand. Nevertheless, the public sector's genuine capabilities, as outlined above, can serve as a template for appraising actual interventions in the various leisure industries that are examined in the following chapters. The third way in leisure requires the public sector's special capabilities to become cornerstones of state leisure policies. This is the pre-condition for the public sector to deliver genuine best value.

Part

II

PROVISIONS

5 Tourism

Introduction

Tourism is not just the largest among all the leisure industries. Globally it is now larger than every other industry. It accounts for 12 per cent of the global economy, 8 per cent of all exports and 8 per cent of all employment (Urry, 2001). During the second half of the twentieth century tourism was among the world's top growth sectors. In 1950 there were just 25 million international passenger arrivals whereas by 2000 there were 698 million. The latest wave of information technology will change many leisure industries but tourism is unlikely to diminish. The experience of actually being there cannot be bettered or closely simulated by guide books, TV holiday programmes or the internet (see Urry, 2001, 2002). The events of 11 September 2001 led to a global dip in international travel of 7.4 per cent. This was a crisis for some airlines, and for tourism-dependent economies, but the industry was always confident that it would bounce back as it had following all earlier crises – wars, oil price hikes and so on. The world's thirst for travel seems unlikely to diminish.

The growth rate has been spectacular and 698 million international arrivals is a huge figure. However, each international trip involves at least two arrivals (outward and returning). Some people take several trips per year so there will be some double and triple counting, and so on. The world's population is over 6 billion. The figures show that tourism is certainly a massive industry, yet no more than 5 per cent of the world's people can be international travellers during any year. Most of the 5 per cent are from the most highly developed countries (in economic terms), and we have already seen (Table 2.1, p. 19) that in countries such as Britain consumer spending on holidays is more strongly related to income than spending on most leisure activities, and that across leisure spending overall the income gradient is steeper than for all consumer spending.

Everything that applies to leisure in general seems to apply to tourism on an even grander scale. Tourism is the biggest and the fastest growing leisure industry. It is arguably the most extremely modern in so far as 'differentiation' is a hallmark of modernity (Meethan, 2001). In modern societies work and leisure are differentiated, and in the case of tourism the separation is extreme. The tourist is separated not just from work but from the whole of normal everyday life, and by place as well as time. Tourism is extreme in the amounts of money that the world's richer people spend, and in the huge imbalance in flows between richer and poorer countries. It is also extreme in being one of the most thoroughly commercial leisure industries.

Tourism is not 100 per cent commercial. The public sector has always played a role, but usually just a supportive part. Perhaps not surprisingly in view of all its extremities, tourism is among the more heavily criticised leisure industries. Commercial tourism is accused of packaging experiences which become necessarily inauthentic. It is accused of degrading natural and cultural environments. Everything and everybody – visitors, visited and habitats – are said to be subjugated and debased by the industry's commercial rationality. We shall see that the criticisms contain at least a kernel of truth. Why is all this allowed to happen? The answer is simple; in all commercial businesses profits take precedence. So why has commerce been allowed to take over and expand this industry so successfully (against its own criteria)? That is this chapter's top question. We shall see that the only plausible answer is that commerce delivers what people genuinely want and that, if people are given the choice, voluntary sector and state provisions simply cannot compete.

Another big question arises from the extent to which tourism today receives worldwide public sector support. National, but more usually local, governments have always provided tourist infrastructure – parks, drains, gardens, electricity supply, open spaces and other attractions. Public authorities have recouped their outlay through charges which tax-payers have contributed – willingly, it appears (even amid never-ending complaints) until recent times, because the tax-payers, in turn, have recouped the costs from the spending of tourists. The political process has (presumably) ensured that governments have spent roughly the 'right' amounts. Too much or too little has led to protests and maybe a loss of votes rather than run-of-the-mill carping. However, matters have become more complicated in recent years as the tourist industry has expanded, the trade has become more and more competitive, and more regions, towns, cities and countries – not just a limited number of holiday destinations – have joined the business. There are many places where any infrastructure created mainly for tourists benefits only the sectors of the local economy, and the sections of the population, that are involved in tourism-related businesses. So why should everyone pay towards the infrastructure? These questions are examined fully in Chapter 8 because they arise in a particularly acute form when public money is needed to host one-off events, especially expensive mega-events. These can give a spectacular, if short-lived, boost to inward tourism, but huge megas are likely to require huge public outlays on appropriate infrastructure – sport stadiums for instance. Governments face a dilemma. They either cough up or the entire business goes elsewhere.

The next section charts the development of the modern holiday industry from its nineteenth-century beginnings in Britain and other European countries. Twentieth-century developments – holiday camps, overseas package holidays, and a subsequent trend towards do-it-yourself holidays – are then examined. The chapter proceeds to explain how, as the tourist industry has grown, it has become increasingly competitive. Hence the heightened importance of 'attractions', the incorporation of 'the heritage' into the tourist industry, and the enhanced importance of the cultural dimension in the competition for business. The chapter concludes by answering its overarching question, 'Why commerce?'.

Creating the modern holiday

Beginnings

The modern holiday is possible only under three conditions.

- Working time must be compartmentalised and standardised with at least one major break of sufficient length to enable workers to 'go away'.
- There must be transport, mechanical transport, to convey the holiday-makers.
- Workers must be able to afford a holiday.

All three conditions were met in Britain during the second half of the nineteenth century, and they have been fulfilled in more and more countries as their economies have been modernised. Britain led in holiday-making and in many other types of modern leisure simply because Britain was the very first industrial nation. Employers in Britain, pressured by the trade unions that were formed in the second half of the nineteenth century, gradually reinstated the holiday weeks that had been abolished when the population moved from the countryside into the expanding industrial towns and cities. At the same time, the construction of railways made the journey 'away' possible. Railways were faster than the canal boats, and the river and coastal steamers, which had carried some of the earlier holiday pioneers. The steamers were the original reason for constructing piers at Britain's seaside resorts. By the end of the nineteenth century most piers had lost their original function but new piers were still being built as promenades and sites for entertainment. Later on (but still before the era of mass private motoring) the motor coach became the railways' main rival as a means of holiday travel. The third condition for mass holiday-making was met when manual workers' real earnings and living standards rose during and after the 1870s. This brought holidays within the means of the working masses. So by the end of the nineteenth century Britain's seaside resorts were booming (during the summer months) and all the basic elements of the present-day holiday were in place.

By then the holiday had become a primarily commercial type of leisure, but commerce was not at the forefront of pioneering holidays away from Britain's industrial towns and cities in the first half of the nineteenth century. Thomas Cook

---

BOX 5.1 THE CO-OPERATIVE HOLIDAY ASSOCIATION

This association was formed in the late nineteenth century by a Congregationalist minister, T A Leonard of Colne (Lancashire), who wanted to promote rational countryside holidays for working class people. In 1891 Rev Leonard organised a walking holiday in the Lake District for his local walking club, and this venture was subsequently expanded on a national scale as the Co-operative Holiday Association (CHA). This was to provide 'a holiday of another kind . . . a happy brotherhood spending its days on tramp and its evenings in social intercourse with music and chatty lecturettes'. Initially the CHA used empty cottages for accommodation and school halls for evening activities but it soon acquired its own centres in Keswick, Whitby and elsewhere. By the early twentieth century the CHA had expanded: to 8400 members in 1904, and 30,000 in 1914, by which time it had centres in Germany, France and Switzerland. Accommodation was primitive. Meals were taken at trestle tables. Sleeping quarters were divided into curtained cubicles. Alcohol was forbidden. Lights-out was at 10.30 pm. Rambles were accompanied by lecturers who would provide wayside talks on the natural history and artistic connections of a region. The association was based on ideals of utopian socialism, Wordsworthian high thinking, and plain living. Its motto was 'simple and strenuous'. To extend the social relationships formed on holidays, CHA members established local branches with winter programmes of walking and indoor cultural pastimes.

Although intended mainly for working class people, the CHA was meant to be a classless organisation. Social distinctions were to be neutralised. Holiday parties included school-teachers, shop assistants, warehousemen, clerks, carpenters, dressmakers and university lecturers. In practice, however, the CHA always drew the majority of its members from the middle class. It proved particularly suited to the needs of professional young adults, and especially single young women to whom it offered a safe and respectable environment.

Source: Snape (2002).

---

organised the first holiday 'tour' by rail from Leicester to Loughborough in 1841, and this is sometimes taken to be the start of the modern holiday industry. Before long Thomas Cook was organising more adventurous excursions, including trips abroad, but this type of holiday package was really a full century ahead of its time. Up until the 1850s in Britain, churches and progressive employers arranged most holidays, which were then very much the exception for the industrial working class. The holiday was conceived as a rational form of recreation (see Box 5.1). It was considered desirable for workers to escape from city grime and, in particular, from urban temptations, especially drink. Holiday-making was associated with saving, sobriety and the family (see Walvin, 1978). The early idealistic holiday pioneers did not plan the Blackpools that were to come.

Antecedents

The modern holiday has pre-industrial antecedents. During the eighteenth century sons of the gentry (and much more rarely the daughters) had begun undertaking the 'grand tour' which took in all the main European centres of culture. They would set forth, often accompanied by servants and with letters of introduction to distant relatives and other family acquaintances. This tour, intended to be educative, could last for well over a year. During this same period well-to-do English families had started visiting London, or the fast-developing spa towns (Buxton, Harrogate, Bath) for the summer season, or for at least a month. These were social occasions when the well-to-do also became well-connected, and, of course, the spa waters were supposed to be medicinal. Towards the end of the eighteenth century the seaside began to rival the inland spas. Brighton's popularity was boosted by the Prince of Wales' regular visits. Sea air and water were believed to confer health benefits, but not the sun: sunbathing did not become fashionable until the end of the nineteenth century.

Going to the seaside

It was seaside towns that were adopted as holiday destinations by Britain's working class during the nineteenth century. There is still debate as to whether the decline of Britain's spas was due to the overwhelming natural attractions of the coast, or whether failure to invest in the spas led to their decline. Inland resorts have remained popular in many European countries, but in these countries people are likely to live further from the coast than in Britain. This argument rumbles on (see Bacon, 1997). Whatever the reason, by the end of the nineteenth century it was Britain's seaside resorts that were most popular. Commerce was providing all the main ingredients. Private railway companies offered travel. Landladies provided board and lodging. Showmen and other entrepreneurs opened fairgrounds, piers, amusement arcades, stalls selling holiday paraphernalia, theatres and pubs. At that time holiday-makers usually remained within their home regions. Towns would close for the holiday week. People who worked and lived together would travel together, or, at any rate, meet each other while on holiday. Families sometimes visited the same resort, and may have stayed at the same boarding house, year upon year.

Blackpool was by far the most popular holiday resort in north-west England, catering for families from the Lancashire textile towns. Blackpool Tower (inspired by the Eiffel Tower, see Box 5.2, p. 71) was opened in 1894 and the town's pleasure beach also opened during the 1890s. Skegness was the east coast equivalent. Skegness was an insignificant coastal village before it was connected to the railway system at the end of the nineteenth century. Then things took off, and Skegness became a favoured holiday destination for east-Midlands families. At one time it was not unusual for 60 trains to arrive in a single day. This was during 'the season' which lasted for just 6 to 10 weeks. Skegness's popularity peaked in the 1930s. By then it had 4 cinemas, 4 theatres and 5 dance halls. Most of these have now been converted into amusement arcades, night clubs, shops, car parks and bingo halls.

As the working class 'invaded' resorts close to the industrial cities, Britain's well-to-do families went further afield – overseas to the Mediterranean or to the 'English Riviera' in the south-west. They also adopted mountains, lakes and snow as alternative holiday destinations to the spas and seaside (Hill, 2002). Most resorts were keen to attract the masses (and their money) but some places, including

Bognor Regis, preferred to remain exclusive and took care to stay off the (railway) track. Torquay was among the south-west resorts that deliberately sought to establish a superior, distinctly up-market, appeal (Morgan and Pritchard, 1999).

Local authorities played their part in attracting the expanding tourist trade. They laid out parks and promenades and kept the streets spick-and-span. Attracting tourists has now become a science. Researchers try to identify features that make holiday destinations attractive, and to calculate exactly how much people will be prepared to pay to get there and still visit all the facilities. It appears that cities are most attractive to tourists when they have historic buildings, plenty of shops and places to eat and drink, and attractive countryside nearby (Martin and Mason, 1988). Destinations now try to present an image of themselves that appeals to tourists (see McCrone *et al.*, 1995; Morgan and Pritchard, 1998). Nowadays marketing a tourist place is a far more sophisticated business than just issuing a brochure containing information and photographs. The destination itself may need a radical face-lift. If they are not already present, beaches or traditional mountain chalets may be constructed, and an appealing history can always be discovered, if required. The image may sometimes become the reality in the minds of tourists and even locals, although some claim that this is the age of the sceptical tourist who sees behind the images. In the nineteenth century resorts had to rely on what was already there plus whatever commerce added. Initially, the crucial assets were simply sea, sand, and a railway station.

Holiday-making habits have certainly changed over the last 100 years, but when we see photographs of Blackpool at the end of the nineteenth century we have no difficulty in recognising it as a holiday resort. The basic ingredients of the holiday remain unchanged: going away for a week or two, probably to the seaside, sitting on the beach, venturing into the sea, being catered for in hotels, boarding houses and restaurants, and having a wide choice of entertainment. Blackpool at the end of the nineteenth century bore less resemblance to either a stage on the grand tour or the pre-industrial spas than to its twenty-first century self.

Twentieth-century developments

There have been many developments in the holiday business since the nineteenth century. Some have become established while others turned out to be mere ripples, but none have overhauled the basic shape and features of the modern holiday.

Holiday camps

The holiday camp was an inter-war innovation. The idea was to provide everything – accommodation, food, recreation and entertainment – on site and for an all-in price. The first purpose-built holiday camp – Butlin's at Skegness – opened in 1937. It was soon followed by other Butlin's camps and competitors (see Bandyopadhyay, 1973). The camp then enjoyed what proved to be a brief period of popularity which was ending by the 1960s. By then more and more British holiday-makers were venturing abroad. Those who were still taking their holidays in Britain were seeking something less regimented. In any case, the facilities in the existing camps were too basic for post-war tastes. However, there are still Butlin's 'resorts' at Minehead, Bognor Regis and Skegness, and there are even more Pontin's holiday villages. The scaled-down UK industry specialises in family holidays.

The true present-day counterparts of the original holiday camps are probably the hotels which have their own swimming pools, a choice of restaurants, child care, and organised recreation and entertainment for those so inclined, and the holiday 'villages' (operated by Center Parcs, among other companies) where the core attraction (in non-tropical countries) is most likely to be an enclosed tropical facility. Club Med has villages all around the Mediterranean and in other parts of the world which offer different holiday 'menus' at different sites and at different times – family holidays, adults-only, singles, couples, and activity holidays. Sandals is more specialised. It caters exclusively for 'couples in love' at ten idyllic beachfront resorts on the Caribbean's most exotic islands (the adjectives are taken from publicity materials). Absolutely everything is part of the package including a choice of gourmet dining at prices (in 2002) ranging upwards from USA $355 per person per night.

The overseas package

As already mentioned, from the 1950s onwards the British masses began deserting domestic resorts in favour of guaranteed sun. They followed the trail that the well-to-do had pioneered when domestic resorts began to cater for the working class. The first true overseas package holiday from the UK was to Corsica in 1950, organised by Horizon. By the 1960s the jet engine and charter flights had made the Mediterranean as accessible, and usually as cheap, as Bournemouth. Wide-bodied jets, flying since the 1960s, have brought down the costs of long-haul flights, and more and more holiday-makers have been travelling further afield. Of course, the long-term rise in people's incomes has helped. In 2001 UK residents took a total of 59 million foreign holidays, roughly one per head of population. Ever since the 1950s Britain's domestic resorts such as Blackpool and Skegness have been trying, unsuccessfully, to regain their popularity. Holiday-making visitors to Britain, whose numbers have increased, are rarely seeking seaside sun. Blackpool recorded its all-time peak number of visits (17 million) in the early 1970s, when it was the largest resort in Europe. By 2001 the number of visits had declined to 10.9 million, which is still an impressive figure. Surprisingly, the number of people visiting Blackpool has not declined but they are visiting less frequently, staying for shorter periods, and spending less. The economic effects in Blackpool have been devastating even though the town is still the UK's number one resort (Cavill, 2002).

Since people began going abroad, 'the package' has become the staple holiday product. Thomas Cook's time finally arrived with the jet airplane. The basic package is simple: air travel, transfers and accommodation. There are numerous variations. The travel may be by air, ship, train or motor coach. The accommodation may be hotel or self-catering. Excursions may be included. A package may be to just one place or a tour with one or two nights at a series of destinations. Customers can select from an endless mixture of places and grades of accommodation. There are specialist packages for families with young children, senior citizens, young singles, wine lovers, mountains, white-water, city culture, desert treks, *ad infinitum*. For most overseas holiday-makers during the last 40 years, whatever their home countries, going away has meant buying a package, put together by a tour company, advertised in its brochure, and probably sold by a high street travel agent.

D-I-Y holidays

There is now a countervailing trend to the package holiday. More and more holiday-makers have been deciding to do more for themselves. In Britain this trend began in domestic tourism. By 1973 80 per cent of all holiday-makers in Devon and Cornwall were car-borne, and 49 per cent of all holidays in the region were self-catering (South-West Economic Planning Council, 1976). Families have taken to towing their own accommodation – tents and caravans. More accommodation is now room-only rather than full-board or half-board. Rooms can be rented by the night rather than only by the week. People are opting to pick-and-mix, creating their holidays as they travel: they can decide en route where to stop and where to eat.

Britons abroad are increasingly doing likewise. They take their own car, or hire one, which enables them to travel independently away from the congested hotspots. Visitors to Britain are reciprocating. Nowadays over 70 per cent of incoming tourists have visited Britain previously (Henley Centre, 1993). Their first visit may have been a package tour to London, Stratford-upon-Avon and Edinburgh. Next time the visitors are likely to want something a bit different, perhaps customised to their particular interests. They are becoming more confident, and may be prepared to hire a car and plan their own routes. The holiday has not been decommercialised but it has been partly decommodified.

Competing for business

Information technology may not diminish the desire to go away – the virtual experience is not really a satisfactory substitute – but it is changing the ways in which holidays are arranged. The internet has made it easier for people to fix their own packages. They can book air travel, hotels and car hire separately online. Hotels and airlines can by-pass both high street travel agents and the tour companies. The implications for the industry are profound. However, we shall see in Chapter 10 (pp. 148–52) that, just because technology makes something possible, this does not necessarily mean that people will do it. They may prefer the convenience of buying an all-in package, and they may prefer leafing through traditional printed brochures to surfing the web.

Whatever the long-term outcomes, the ability and willingness of some holiday-makers to do more for themselves has intensified competition in the travel industry. The present-day industry is incredibly competitive. As tourists have become more mobile, regional resorts have lost their captive markets. Competition is now international, and as the economic importance of leisure has grown, more and more places have tried to attract tourists. The trade is no longer confined to traditional inland and coastal resorts. Cities want cultural tourists. Farms want agricultural tourists. Declining industrial towns want heritage tourists. Everywhere wants tourists! Businesses which offer travel and accommodation are competing more energetically than ever for the tourist's money, and the same applies to regions and countries. As already noted, public authorities have always played a crucial, albeit supportive, role in promoting tourism, and this role has become more complicated than arranging for a railway company to open a line (or to have an airport built), to lay out parks and gardens and keep a place tidy, then issue a brochure.

All countries now have government agencies which are responsible for promoting inward tourism. The British Tourist Authority (BTA), now called VisitBritain, was created in 1969. It has a government budget of £37 million, supplemented for some campaigns by contributions from airlines, hotel chains and local authorities. VisitBritain calculates that every £1 it spends yields an increase of £27 in spending by incoming tourists, and aims to improve this ratio. It now targets specific segments of the tourist market. The USA is a crucial source of tourists for Britain, partly because there are more of them than from any other single country, and partly because they spend more per head than visitors from mainland Europe. The problem with Americans is that they are difficult to persuade to travel; only 22 per cent have passports. All countries are now targeting specific market segments. Spain has decided that it is no longer seeking 'more'. Indeed, Spain has decided that mistakes were made during the rapid expansion of tourism which led to over-congested beaches and coastlines blighted by high-rise hotels. Spain is now seeking tourists who spend more per head per night, and hopes to leave the bottom end of the market to poorer countries such as Greece and Turkey.

Promoting tourism has also become more difficult because there is local opposition to it everywhere. People complain about religious and cultural traditions being debased and environments degraded, about the congestion that tourists create, and also, in some cases, about residents' rights being subordinated to tourists' interests. So everywhere the search is now on for ecologically sound, sustainable tourism. This is partly a matter of not blemishing the features of a place that attract tourists, but equally of harmonising tourism with the economic, social and cultural interests of all sections of a host population. It is never easy. Roughly 50 per cent of visitors attempt to climb Ayers Rock (see Box 5.2, p. 71). Aboriginals consider this behaviour inappropriate for reasons of cultural respect. Whereas Western culture seeks to control and subjugate nature thereby achieving progress and improved living standards, Aboriginal culture respects the sacredness of all life, connectedness with nature, and has a strong sense of place (Brown, 2002).

Attractions

How does a location tempt tourists? One tactic is to create an attraction. In some places the natural environment or the historic buildings may be sufficient. If not, attractions can always be created. This has happened throughout the history of modern holiday-making. Blackpool Tower was inspired by the Eiffel Tower over one hundred years ago (see Box 5.2). Blackpool's authorities had noted that the Eiffel Tower was attracting a never-ending stream of visitors and hoped to replicate this.

Pleasure beaches – basically fairgrounds – were another early, much replicated, and enduring type of attraction. However, the attractions that have brought far and away the most attention from academics are the Disney parks. There is now a Disney literature (see for example Bryman, 1995; Rojek, 1993). Disneyland opened in southern California in 1955. It was followed in 1971 by Florida's Disney World, Tokyo Disneyland in 1983 and Euro-Disneyland (20 miles east of Paris) in 1992. These are all commercially successful. They are among the very few built attractions that are holiday destinations. Other theme parks, zoos, stately homes and castles attract day visitors and tourists during their holidays. They may add to the appeal of a holiday destination, but it is really only the Disney parks that have become holiday destinations in their own right. Sociologists have noted that the Disney parks celebrate a particular moral and political order. They exalt the American way of life, present a depoliticised view of the world, applaud the triumph of the individual, especially the little man (Mickey Mouse), and provide an escape into an asexual world of fantasy. Academic interest has been heightened by the fact that the Disney organisation itself takes its social mission seriously, and the company is extremely protective towards the public image that it presents. George Ritzer uses Disney as an example of rationalisation (see Chapter 11, pp. 154–60), but does Disney really exemplify anything except Disney? The attractions are unique. They have no peers. They rank alongside the world's most spectacular waterfalls and deepest canyons in drawing tourists from all over the globe.

Some places have historical buildings that attract tourists from all over the world. India has the Taj Mahal. Egypt has the pyramids. London has its Tower, the Houses of Parliament, Westminster Abbey and so on. Other cities have built new interesting structures. Bilbao's Guggenheim Museum (see Box 5.2) is an example.

Las Vegas also has a special attraction, but in recent years other cities have discovered that gambling attracts visitors and persuades them to part with large sums of money. As an economic engine, gambling is far more successful than museums. In 2001 Blackpool Council received (with interest) a proposal to build a set of Vegas-type casino hotels. If Britain's gambling laws are relaxed so as to make this possible, and if this plan goes ahead in Blackpool and nowhere else in Britain, the resort will almost certainly recover its earlier glory (see Chapter 12, pp. 177–8). However, gambling will cease to be a special attraction for destinations like Las Vegas and Monte Carlo as more and more places emulate them.

Another way of boosting visitors is to host a temporary attraction, like a sports or cultural mega-event. These are always intended to benefit the local economy (see Chapter 8). There is always a net cost to public funds, but far more money usually flows to the local economy. Is this always good business? Gratton and Taylor (2000) estimate that Euro 96 (the European soccer tournament) added 0.1 per cent to Britain's GDP during April–June 1996. A host city or country can hope to derive

BOX 5.2 POPULAR ATTRACTIONS

The Eiffel Tower

The Eiffel Tower was built for the 1889 World Exposition (World Fair), which celebrated the centennial of the French Revolution. It is 302.6 metres high and was the winning entry from 700 proposals. Gustave Eiffel always referred to it as the 300-metre tower. His critics, who were opposed to its construction, called it the Eiffel Tower and this name has stuck.

Nowadays the Eiffel Tower receives around 5 million visitors each year. There have been around 200 million visitors since the tower opened.

Source: www.tour-eiffel.fr

Bilbao's Guggenheim Museum

This spectacular building was opened in 1997. The Basque authorities provided political and cultural backing, and the funds for the museum to be built and operated. The Guggenheim Foundation contributes collections of modern and contemporary art, its programme of special exhibitions, and its experience in international-level museum administration and management.

The Guggenheim is one of the central ingredients in a plan to redevelop the city of Bilbao and to revitalise the entire region's economy. Within a year of opening the museum had already received over 1.3 million visitors.

Source: www.guggenheim-bilbao.es

Ayers Rock

This is a red sandstone monolith, the world's largest single rock. It is 9.4 kilometres around with steep slopes rising to 340 metres. The Rock is situated in Central Australia, 335 kilometres south-east of Alice Springs.

For many thousands of years the Rock has been the focus for religious, cultural, territorial and economic inter-relationships among the Aboriginal peoples of Australia's Western Desert. Caves around the base of the Rock were once used for shelter and are decorated with paintings. In 1993 the area in which the Rock is located was renamed the Uluru-Kata Tjuta National Park, reflecting the Aboriginal heritage of the site.

However, the Rock has featured prominently in recent years in Australia's efforts to promote international tourism. Visitor numbers to the Rock have been rising steadily, to over 300,000 per year. Above all else, the Rock is now a tourist attraction

Source: www.justclickaustralia.com/guide_ayersrock.htm, www.auinfo.com/aboutayresrock.html

long-term benefits from the facilities that are built and the publicity received, but these benefits are difficult to measure. There are always too many intervening variables. Rather than a one-off mega, a recurrent mini-event, like an annual arts festival, could be a better investment. Calculating the cost-benefits of different sports and arts events is now a subsidiary branch of the tourist industry (see Gratton *et al.*, 2001; Shibli and Gratton, 2001).

However, the natural environment can also be an exceptionally good attraction. Nothing man-made can truly match the Swiss Alps or the Grand Canyon. Australia has discovered that Ayers Rock (see Box 5.2), situated in a desolate, inhospitable region, is probably its best single asset (superior even to Sydney's Opera House, see Box 13.1, p. 184) for attracting additional international visitors.

The heritage business

Nowadays the heritage business is regarded as an export industry. The heritage is anything man-made from the past: landscapes, gardens and battlefields; objects which are stored in museums and art galleries; buildings such as castles, palaces and stately homes, and industrial mills also. Wigan Pier, which was built to load coal onto canal boats and long-known only from the title of George Orwell's book, *The Road to Wigan Pier*, is now part of England's heritage industry.

At one time it was mainly local people and historians who were interested in relics from a locality's past. Children were taken to local museums as part of their education (and they still are). Nowadays, however, all the world's main heritage sites draw most of their visitors from further afield. They have discovered that some tourists are keen to learn about the history of the places that they visit. Site owners have welcomed the revenue. Tourist authorities have recognised that heritage sites can be powerful tourist magnets. Presentation has improved: tourism is a competitive business. Working models, animated displays and multilingual descriptions have become standard in museums. The heritage industry has enabled visitors to do more than just imagine, but to actually experience something akin to life as it used to be. In York visitors wander (on a miniature railway) around a Viking village. In Scotland they can experience life in a highland croft. In North West England they can walk down a traditional terrace street and gaze into the local shops, either in Salford's museum or down the road in Manchester on the television set of *Coronation Street*. Tourism has made it possible for us to experience an evening in a gypsy camp, a rail journey across rickety wooden viaducts or travel in the luxury of the Orient Express. We can experience desert life, or stay in a stately home and sleep in a four-poster bed.

Some places are heritage rich. The lands of ancient Greece are superbly endowed. Likewise all the European capitals except those, like Warsaw, where little was left standing after the Second World War. The UK has approximately 500,000 listed heritage buildings, 17,700 scheduled monuments, and 850 designated conservation areas. Central government sponsors 17 national art galleries and museums, including the British Museum which is one of the country's top tourist attractions. Australia and America do not have comparable histories. They need to rely more on their natural assets (Ayers Rock and the Grand Canyon), recently built attractions such as the Disney parks, and gambling (see Chapter 12).

Tales of places inventing appetising histories for the benefit of tourists are usually much exaggerated, but sometimes true (see, for example, Grunewald, 2002). All countries must have sections of history that they would prefer to airbrush out – slave-trading for example. It may seem embarrassing, and bad mannered, to celebrate military victories in the presence of visitors from the defeated country, especially when the battles occurred within living memory. However, local historians and interest groups are forever vigilant and will not permit blatant distortions, and today's tourists (and hosts) can be objective in viewing the facts. Some Second World War concentration camps have become tourist attractions.

It may seem strange at first that we conserve and maintain objects and memories from our pasts, restore them to life, for the benefit of others but, given the economic importance of present-day tourism, it is really anything but. It is often people from afar who are most interested. New Zealand's Maori cultural sites attract far more overseas visitors than domestic tourists, who display relatively little interest (Ryan, 2002). In a similar way, natural habitats and wildlife in Africa are preserved and protected because of their value as tourist attractions.

The cultural dimension

In recent years researchers have been highlighting tourism's cultural dimension (see, for example, Aitchison et al., 2000; Crouch, 1999). This is not confined to so-called cultural tourism: everything has a cultural aspect. Appadurai (1986, 1996) argues that all 'things' – including things from the past – are always given their meanings in their present contexts. So 'traditions' are always modern inventions. The sociological gaze has been redirected by the so-called cultural and post-modern 'turns' in academia, and also by the huge efforts and sums of money that destinations and holiday companies now spend on constructing appealing images. The actual built and natural environments may or may not be modified. Locals (certainly those who are paid to work in tourism-related businesses) are trained to enact scripts that tourists are led to expect. The visitors' gaze is pre-focused by all the publicity, so they know what to look for and the hosts know what to lay on. Sociologists have drawn attention to how the present-day tourist industry creates identities for places and peoples – their national characteristics and sexual inclinations, for example.

> More and more, local identities become associated with the significance places have for people from elsewhere. (Lengkeek, 2000, p. 11)

All the parties may internalise the identities that have been constructed for them (see Morgan and Pritchard, 1998; Urry, 1990). Some astounding claims have been made for the cultural impact of international tourism. It is not only (some) sociologists who claim that cross-national understanding and friendship are strengthened, but few people could realistically imagine that 'pilgrimages' to each other's places, where 'sacred' objects are 'worshipped', might unify all humankind (MacCannell, 1976).

The 'cultural turn' has led to some valid observations, but three points should be borne in mind. First, the voices of tourists themselves are strangely absent from much of this literature. More attention is paid to holiday brochures and adverts, which are then subjected to cultural analysis. Surveys of people are relatively expensive. In any case, the statements made by tourists (see the TV holiday programmes) are typically bland. Speculating about the meanings of travel brochures can be much more exciting.

Second, who believes the brochures? People who do may return home gravely disappointed. The host population may not have enacted the expected scripts. A place may not have lived up to expectations. Visitors may feel cheated by misleading publicity, or at not having been shown what they had believed – and continue to believe – is the 'real thing'. This is not yet the era of the post-tourist who decides that the best information and sights are obtained from television and printed matter, and that actual travel has become redundant. The so-called post-fan, who considers televised football superior to actually being there, is probably another myth. However, the public surely realises that adverts can lie. Some tourists do their own in-depth pre-travel research by visiting libraries, talking to people who have already been, and 'triangulating' different bundles of information. During their holidays, some D-I-Y tourists make every effort to seek authenticity behind the scenes. Some are surely every bit as sophisticated as sociologists. Writers on tourism sometimes contrast the earlier 'traveller' with the modern tourist. For the latter, everything is said to be pre-packaged, laid on especially. Maybe, but surely all concerned realise this. Locals in particular surely know the difference between what their places are really like and the images and displays that are presented to tourists. Current knowledge of other places and people may be heavily media-filtered. Daily newspapers and TV reports undoubtedly influence our knowledge (see Chapter 10, p. 139). Tourist paraphernalia alone surely makes far less impression.

Third, cultural analysis may over-estimate the cultural sensitivity of the tourists who stick in their own groups, enjoy their usual food and drink, and TV programmes, and return home without much exposure to the regions and countries that they have visited. Various typologies of tourists have been proposed (see Murphy, 1985; Smith, 1995). The Cohen (1979) typology is among those more frequently cited. Cohen distinguishes five kinds of tourist:

- Recreational tourists who are seeking entertainment.
- Diversionary tourists who are hoping to 'recharge their batteries'.
- Experiential tourists who are in search of an authentic and rich experience.
- Experimental tourists who are trying to discover their own true selves.
- Existential tourists who are looking for a better world.

Maybe tourists do not divide neatly into these five particular groups, but the typology alerts us to the fact that tourists differ in their cultural sensitivity.

Sociologists are unwise to ignore the 'basics' of holiday-making, or to leave the obvious to economists. First and foremost, tourists are going away. 'Where to' can be less important than just going away – from work and home, probably to somewhere warm and sunny. There are scores of acceptable, largely interchangeable, destinations for many tourists. From the brochures these people seek packages that offer value for money. The tourist trade is price sensitive. Cultural analysis risks obscuring what is often a blander reality. The most powerful cultural meanings of tourism are surely within the tourists' normal home-based social networks. The holidays that people take do indeed signify who they are. By virtue of the frequency with which people go away, and how far they go (the further the better), they tell others something about themselves. The 40 per cent of the population that does not go away, and those who 'only' go somewhere within their own country, are still among those affected (culturally) by international tourism.

Why commerce?

This is the crunch question. Why is commerce the lead actor in holiday provision? It does not have to be this way. Alternatives have been offered. People have had a choice. They can still reject commerce if they wish.

The role of governments

As we have seen, the public sector has always played a crucial, if strictly supportive, role in attracting holiday-makers in what are basically market economies. Local authorities have always taken care of the environment and have often contributed free-to-user attractions such as parks, gardens and museums. In recent years most public authorities have become even more pro-active, and they are now anxious to promote sustainable, ecologically sound tourism. They want to ensure that visitor numbers do not devalue or degrade whatever attracts them. The public sector, via the tourism departments and agencies that now operate in virtually all parts of every country, tries to ensure that host territories retain a decent share of the tourist spend. Public authorities are aware of the dangers of profits being syphoned off by hotel chains and airlines with bases elsewhere, leaving local firms with just a minor share of the proceeds. They are equally aware that local residents and businesses must bear the costs of the infrastructure required to accommodate influxes of visitors – the drains and water supplies, and so on. Public authorities are also aware nowadays of the dangers of tourist regions becoming locked in subordinate positions in economic dependency relationships (Davis, 1978; Turner and Ash, 1975). Most local authorities, therefore, aim for balanced economic development in which tourism does not become the sole base of the local economy. They know that over-dependence on tourism creates many low-level, seasonal jobs, and high unemployment out of season.

If it already does so much, why cannot the pubic sector do it all? This is what happened in Eastern Europe under communism. The holiday away was defined as a need and a right, and the system delivered. The state, usually via employers and trade unions, created holiday centres in coastal and mountain regions. These centres were for relaxation, and some had sanatorium facilities. The official purpose of vacations under communism was to restore workers' bodies and souls. The Communist Party youth organisations provided opportunities for young people to stay at holiday centres, to visit young people in other communist countries (which was supposed to be good for international socialist solidarity), and to join work brigades thereby contributing to the construction of communism (always, according to the party line, an ideal future state). The drawback was the drab uniformity. Western tourists were never impressed when they were tempted by low-cost packages to the Black Sea. Throughout the communist era, the private dacha where families could self-organise their own holidays was a perk of the privileged and an aspiration of the many. During the first wave of the post-communist reforms entire state holiday systems were allowed to disappear in most of the countries, but families have retained their dachas. The Western-type holiday, preferably at a Western destination, is still a privilege of those who are succeeding in the new market economies, but it has become a realistic medium-term aspiration for virtually everyone. The lesson is that a successful holiday industry may depend on state assistance but, if the state ever tries to do everything, the entire industry is devalued.

The voluntary sector

Some of the earliest holidays away from Britain's industrial towns were run on a non-profit basis, but before long commerce had become the principal provider. Even so, voluntary initiatives have never disappeared. Churches and Sunday Schools still organise annual trips for local children, though nowadays these events are usually overshadowed by the children's family holidays. The Youth Hostels Association is still alive and well (see Chapter 2, p. 16). The scouts run camps, and other youth organisations have similar social highlights. Schools organise excursions to concerts and theatres, plus holidays away which may be cultural (city) or adventure breaks – whatever the schools care to arrange and parents will pay for. These expeditions may have educational value. They are often highlights in children's lives when they go away with their own friends rather than with their parents: foretastes of what it will be like when they can fix their own holidays without any adult supervision. Many members of older age groups in ex-communist countries have fond memories of holidays with the Komsomol (the Communist Party youth organisation) and feel that their own children are being denied a valuable experience. In Western Europe, and to a lesser extent in ex-communist Eastern Europe, charities organise holidays for senior citizens, children with disabilities and other disadvantaged groups. Early in the history of the modern holiday, some trade unions created their own holiday centres which, like their social clubs, were relatively cheap to use because they were not-for-profit. Few of these facilities are still open. Trade union members have deserted their 'own' provisions in favour of commercial facilities.

Voluntary organisations' holidays have one big disadvantage: people holiday with their own club year after year, and the holiday may always be in the same place. It is a communal experience, where the people whom participants go with or meet on arrival are already known: an intensification of the communality in early commercial holidays when a town's population would go away to the same regional resorts during the same holiday week. Commerce offers more choice and more variety, which is consistent with the apparent desire of present-day families, couples and individuals to do their own things rather than act communally. So the voluntary sector fills niches in tourism, as illustrated above. It also arranges specialist holidays for special interest groups ranging from Elvis fans to wine lovers.

The strengths and limitations of commerce

Commerce wins most of its business only because it offers a distinctive product which no other providers can truly replicate, and, given the choice, all over the world the vast majority of holiday-makers make it clear that this is what they prefer. That said, commerce has limitations. One is that services are provided only if they are profitable. So roughly 40 per cent of the present-day UK population, and a much higher proportion of the global population, remain holiday-less. The holiday-less proportion of the UK population has not declined since the 1960s. Meanwhile, the holiday-goers have been going away more frequently: an excellent example of leisure polarisation. This must be regarded as an example of serious social deprivation and exclusion in the world's richer countries where holidays are obviously important to those who take them: the very top in terms of leisure spending. Why are holidays so important? There are senses in which the holiday is the purest form of leisure that people can experience; it is 'the ultimate change' (Hill, 2002). People may enjoy the Friday afternoon feeling at the end of the working week. This feeling is intensified when people go away entirely, for a full week or longer, and get away not just from work but also from their homes and all familiar faces (except their travel companions). The holiday is a total break. It can be hard work in its own way. People may return shattered rather than with batteries recharged. They may actually look forward to returning home at the end of the break. But the holiday is an exceptional opportunity to get away from everything. People can leave their everyday selves behind and, among strangers, adopt holiday persona – jocular, flirtatious, adventurous – irrespective of their reputations back home. Whether it is the first lager in the airport departure lounge, or the first Gallic coffee on the cross-channel ferry, it symbolises liberation. Being excluded from what has become a normal and major leisure activity must be considered as more than a minor privation.

It is interesting and revealing, therefore, that although there are constant initiatives, neither the public nor the voluntary sector makes a significant impression on the holiday-less proportion of the population. We shall find repeated confirmation, as successive leisure industries are examined, that redressing socio-economic inequalities is not among the public sector's special capabilities. The voluntary sector helps its well-off members as well as the poor. The public sector provides infrastructure for everyone's holidays. Neither sector succeeds, if it genuinely tries, in bucking the market. It is not too difficult to understand why. The holiday is one of the rewards for success in a market economy. It is among the outer-markers whereby people can assess each other's success in life – how often they go away, and how far they travel. 'Access for all' is one of the standard justifications for voluntary sector and public leisure provision, but there would not be sufficient support for depriving people of one of the main rewards of success –

or, conversely, a main penalty for failure – in the market economies. Leisure activities can be extremely important to those who partake, yet regarded as non-essential for others. This situation is ideal for commercial provision. Holidays fit into the category, as do certain other, overwhelmingly commercial, types of leisure: out-of-home eating and drinking (see Chapter 11), and many forms of popular entertainment (see Chapter 9).

CONCLUSIONS

This chapter has traced the development of modern tourism from its nineteenth-century beginnings to the present day. We have seen that the industry has expanded impressively; so impressively that is now the world's largest, and during this expansion the business has become increasingly commercial and increasingly competitive. Every country, every region, virtually every city, town and village is now keen to attract tourists. Hence the creation of so many special attractions, the incorporation of heritage into the industry, and all the place imaging.

The main criticisms of the kind of commercial tourism that now extends across the globe are all factually valid. The tourist experience is inauthentic in the sense that visitors to Greek islands, for example, do not see how things really were before the age of mass tourism. Visitors' and hosts' behaviour, and all the sights, are scripted by the industry. The sheer scale of tourism inevitably threatens heritage sites, natural and socio-cultural habitats.

It is tempting to deplore and to blame all this on the brute power of commerce. However, people have always had the option of eco-friendly non-commercial holiday-making and most have chosen the commercial product. In addition, as we shall see in the next chapter, this does not apply to all leisure industries; modern sports have largely retained their original voluntary sector roots. Commerce is not irresistible. So why has commerce triumphed in tourism? The only plausible explanation is that commerce delivers something that people genuinely value. The package may be inauthentic in one sense, but it seems to be the 'real thing' to most holiday-makers. It is understandable that people may enjoy their lives being scripted during their holidays. In what sense, if any, do most tourists care if heritage sites, local cultures and natural environments are congested, de-authenticated and packaged so as to cater for the sheer number of visitors such as themselves? Do they care enough to stay at home? Do most locals really mind provided the tourists bring sufficient money and create jobs? The presumption in this book's third-way leisure posture is that commerce should be allowed to deliver what people manifestly want.

What about the state? This matter becomes straightforward once the state's true capabilities in leisure are recognised. Tourism is basically a commercial business. Governments have to decide whether they want the business and how much they are prepared to pay for it. If they want tourists then they need to invest in infrastructure and promotion. Governments rarely have any sound non-business reasons to promote tourism. Are holidays to be offered as rights of citizenship? Probably not. Do tourist attractions and tourists' behaviour express standards that merit an official seal of approval? Maybe, occasionally. Do the packaged sites and sights that attract tourists enhance a place's prestige? Do they strengthen locals' identities and pride in their roots? There are rarely any sound reasons, business apart, for governments to invest in tourism. Whether to invest and, if so, how much, are best treated as straightforward business matters. Thereafter, central and local governments should realise that tourism is revenue-boosting rather than budget-draining. Promoting tourism need not, and should not, be done at the expense of public leisure provisions with social and cultural goals. Rather, the ability of governments to cater for locals' leisure will normally be enhanced by a successful tourist industry. In other words, everyone can win!

6 Sport: Origins and Development

Introduction

Sport is no match for tourism: it is not a gigantic leisure industry in terms of the numbers who play and who pay at 'the gate' to watch, or in the total amounts of time and money devoted to these activities. In these terms, sport lags far behind tourism, television and even gambling. Yet sport probably has a larger presence in our lives on account of its wide and deep cultural resonance. Non-participants endorse the value of sport, especially for children and young people, and expect governments to ensure that there are opportunities to play. Few feel this way about television, gambling or holidays. Sport is rated 'worthwhile'. People who never play are still likely to follow a favourite team or athlete, to feel elated when they win and down when they lose. Its cultural penetration creates secondary sports-related markets: sport helps to sell newspapers and attracts television audiences; sports clothing and footwear are not sold only to players; gambling is another leisure industry that uses sport to extend its appeal. The widespread following, and the goodwill extended to sport, owe much to the voluntary roots of modern sports. People may idolise film and pop stars, but they do not feel that the stars belong to them, and are representing them in quite the same way as top sport players. Most people have played sports, if only when they were children, and they know how difficult it is to excel. Local communities may be disappointed but usually acquiesce when a cinema or a theatre closes. The same people will rarely countenance the dissolution of a local football club. Somehow or another these clubs nearly always continue to attract sufficient players, officials and supporters to keep going.

In recent years academic interest in sport has increased, partly on account of the extent to which certain sections of sport have become big business. The cash value of some of Europe's top football clubs has soared, as have the top players' earnings. These players are now widely recognised like other media personalities and they earn huge secondary incomes through product endorsements. Meanwhile, other football clubs have faced crises due to their inability to pay the salaries needed to attract the top players on whom success and spectator appeal depend. Some clubs have faced crises through becoming over-dependent on TV-income which proved less reliable than they expected. The boom in certain sections of sport is a product of widespread partial, or attempted, commercialisation. The crises in other quarters testify to the uneasy relationship between commerce and modern sports.

In this book sport is a test case. It tests the proposition in Chapter 3 that, provided volunteers retain their enthusiasm, neither a (non-totalitarian) state nor commerce can take charge of a leisure industry. We shall indeed see in this and the following chapter that our main sports were developed by voluntary associations and, in the forms in which they have become popular, most of the sports are simply not commerce-friendly. This is not to say that it is impossible to make money out of sport. Similarly, governments can, and always have, used sport for political purposes, but all this is possible without destroying sports' voluntary foundations.

This chapter proceeds by defining sport, then describes how modernised sports were created in the nineteenth century, and how the sports were popularised as participant and spectator events by people who were motivated purely by enthusiasm. The chapter then identifies certain values which are linked to sports' voluntary roots (the amateur ethic, for example) which became entrenched in the main sports very early in their history. The chapter continues by considering the relationship between sports and governments: how sports have looked to governments to provide facilities such as playing fields, to promote sports in education, and sometimes more; and how governments have endeavoured to use sport for their own political purposes, be they social inclusion or nation-building and boosting national prestige. This raises the question of whether a full political take-over is possible and likely. Possible, yes; likely, no (except under totalitarian regimes) because we shall see that the political costs outweigh the benefits. The possibility of a commercial take-over is considered in the following chapter. We shall see that a commercial take-over would require radical changes in the character of sports themselves – so radical that, in places where sports' voluntary roots are strong, the attachments of many players and followers would be at risk. In other words, the commercial embrace would 'kill the goose'.

What is sport?

It is rather difficult to define sport to everyone's satisfaction. This is because the definition matters, and not only in demonstrating that sport is different from other leisure activities and provisions. There is a sociological cop-out. One can say that something is a sport if people (the ordinary members of society) regard it as such. This allows for a 'grey area' where there may be disagreement on whether an activity is 'in' or 'out'. However, it is unsatisfactory to sidestep the definitional problem in this way. Those who study and claim expertise in a subject should be able to say why some things are included. There will probably be agreement among the sports intelligentsia (that is, the people who write about it) and in the wider society that an activity can definitely be regarded as a sport if it passes four tests.

■ First, sports are games which are separated from the rest of life, or at any rate from the more serious parts of life, by some combination of time, place and rules. Since it is 'only a game' the result does not really matter; not afterwards, anyway. Sports are interesting or exciting only if the participants really want to win. Contestants are expected to do everything of which they are capable, within the rules, in order to secure victory. This expectation exists although there are no wider ramifications. Winning or losing at sport should not affect your job or family life. Losers can be 'smashed' without ending up in hospital.

There are some problems with this test. 'Battles' occasionally continue off the field. Some people are paid to play. For them, sport is a job and their occupational careers depend on the outcomes of games. Perhaps we can say that sports are basically just games which may sometimes be the players' occupations, and spectacles which may rouse audiences' passions before and after, as well as during, the actual contests.

■ Second, sports require skill. One can improve one's performance by training and practice. Games of chance such as roulette are therefore excluded.

■ Third, sports are energetic. Roulette fails this test also. Playing well at sport requires stamina and exertion, and performances improve with fitness training. At the end of play competitors are likely to be physically exhausted. Non-sporting pastimes make different demands. This test excludes not just gambling but also greyhound racing and also, probably, darts and snooker.

■ Fourth, sports are competitive. Players compete against each other or against the clock or some other criterion. The aim is to win: to beat the opposition or to achieve a target (par at golf, for example). This test separates recreational walking, skiing and swimming, for example, from the sports that are based on these activities.

There is unlikely to be disagreement about the activities that qualify as sports by passing all four of the above tests, but some people would include activities which fail on one or more counts – greyhound racing, darts, snooker, so-called country sports, and all recreational swimming, skiing and so on. Sport is a contested concept. Its definition is 'political'. As already mentioned, in modern society sports are placed among the more worthy leisure activities; somehow superior to mere pastimes, so participants in, and representatives of, 'marginal' activities will often argue for their inclusion. Recognition as a sport by government agencies may make it possible to qualify for financial support, especially if the activity also gains recognition as an Olympic sport. Activities gain more and better publicity if, instead of being treated as mere pastimes, they are covered as sports by broadcasters and newspapers. Public bodies and voluntary associations that represent groups of activities may have their own reasons for favouring broad definitions of sport. This widens the sections of the population for whom they can claim to speak, and who benefit from the agencies' spending and programmes. For example, the UK sports councils can claim that nearly half of all adults are participants provided long walks and swimming are included, and if 'participation' need be no more than once a month. In this instance we can assert confidently that a definition is of more than academic interest: prestige and money are at stake.

The modernisation of sports

Even on a narrow definition of the four tests listed above, all societies appear to have had sports. They have created sports out of the ability to run, jump, throw, climb and swim. Sports may or may not involve apparatus – balls, or wooden or metal objects of various shapes and weights. They may or may not involve animals. There have been thousands of different sports, and new ones are constantly being invented. The sports that were invented during the twentieth century include stock car racing, ten-pin bowling, five-a-side soccer, water-skiing, surfing, wind-surfing, skateboarding, snowboarding, snowmobiling, synchronised swimming and tractor racing. Scientific and technological developments which led to the bicycle, the motor car and the aeroplane made it possible to introduce new sports. In more recent times the voracious appetite of multi-channel television, with 24-hour 365-days-a-year sports coverage, has led to a new raft of sports inventions. However, the key period when the major modern sports were all invented – athletics, and the various games of football, for example – was the second half of the nineteenth century.

The early inventors

Most of the early inventions were developed in Britain, the first industrial nation, within the independent (non-state) secondary schools and universities. Existing sports were modernised, that is, made compatible with urban conditions and industrial time schedules, and, in some cases, 'civilised' by outlawing dangerous practices such as hacking in football, and by the Queensbury rules in boxing. Modernisation also involved confining play to pitches of limited size and limiting the length of contests. So instead of football games rampaging through entire towns and lasting all day, the new rules confined games to compact pitches and allowed matches to be completed in less than two hours. Some traditional sports survived without being fully modernised – county cricket and golf, for example. There are exceptions to all social science generalisations.

At the educational institutions where they were invented (and soon adopted as part of the curriculum in the independent schools) the new modernised sports were regarded as more than just enjoyable forms of recreation. They were valued for developing fitness and health, and, equally if not more importantly, character. Team sports were considered especially valuable – ideal training for the country's future 'officer class' not just in the armed forces but also in industry, commerce and the empire. Boys were taught the need for discipline, to subordinate their own contributions to a group, to observe rules, to respect the authority of a referee and, eventually, to exercise leadership. They learnt to win magnanimously and to accept defeat gracefully while vowing to improve and eventually to succeed.

Popularisation

Modern sports spread rapidly from the sites of their invention. They were taken to the working class by school-teachers, church people and the youth organisations. If the 'officers' could enjoy and benefit from sport, then, it was believed, so could 'the ranks'. Sports were promoted as a form of rational recreation – a way of keeping young men out of mischief. The ranks were not difficult to convert. They adopted sports enthusiastically, especially association football which was to become 'the people's game' the world over (Walvin, 1975). The Football Association (FA) was formed in 1863. By 1871–72 it was able to organise a national competition, the FA Cup. In 1872 the first international match was played between England and Scotland. In 1885 professional football (with paid players) was 'legalised' (it was already happening unofficially – the first reported professional footballers played for Darwen, a Lancashire club, in 1879). The national Football League competition commenced in 1888. All this occurred within a single generation.

Modern sports became popular not just throughout Britain. They are among the country's most successful exports: association football, rugby league, rugby union, cricket, tennis, boxing, hockey, netball, golf, polo, bowls, athletics, skiing. By the end of the nineteenth century the new sports were being played throughout the British Empire and, indeed, in virtually every other country with which Britain had contact. There were many such countries because, even before the industrial revolution, Britain had been a great trading nation. The one world region which did not import the new modern sports was North America. The USA invented its own modern sports – baseball and its own version of football. Later, ice hockey and basketball were to become major sports in North America. Much thought, and thousands of pages, have been devoted to this instance of American exceptionalism (see Markovits and Hellerman, 2001), especially why the sport called football throughout the rest of the world has never really taken off in North America. It has been argued that America's own sports appeal to its people largely because the sports are distinctly American (Gardner, 1974). It may also be relevant that, by having their own sports, it is likely that Americans will be world champions in their preferred games. It must also be said that, from the very beginning, spectator sports in North America were more commercial than in Europe. America's sport culture has been different from the outset. This is a point to which we shall return in the next chapter.

The success of modern sports, meaning here the speed and extent to which they were taken up, has created some problems for the original participants. One problem, partly avoided in North America (which has its own major sports), has been the danger of the 'teachers' being beaten by their 'pupils'. In modern sports all competitors occupy the same playing fields. The rules of the games and conditions of play are the same for everyone. This standardisation is among modern sports' distinctive features. It enables all classes, nationalities, religions and races to compete on equal terms. A virtue of sport is often said to be its ability to transcend, and maybe to heal, other divisions between peoples. However, it must also be said that in Britain, and elsewhere, the upper and middle classes have sometimes gone to extraordinary lengths to avoid the risk of being humbled by the lower orders. At any rate, this has been a consequence of some of their tactics. In some sports, rowing for example, the nineteenth-century governing bodies decided that members of the working class should not be allowed to enter the main competitions. The reason given was the unfair advantage that workers would enjoy due to the physical demands of their occupations. This regulation was rescinded long ago and governing bodies have rarely been so crude. It has been more common for competition to be informally restricted to social equals. So independent schools have played against other independent schools, grammar schools against grammar schools, and universities against universities. One division that helped to keep the classes apart for the first century of modern sports was between amateurs and professionals. The upper and middle classes joined amateur clubs which had their own competitions, and left professional competitions, and some entire sports which admitted professional players (association football and rugby league, for example), to the working class. Rugby's great schism – the split between the Rugby League and the entirely amateur Rugby Union in 1895 – was an unusually clear break. Cricket had 'players' and 'gentlemen' until 1962. Even if amateur gentlemen played in the same sides as professionals and the former did not excel on the field of play, the status of the gentlemen was preserved. The well-to-do have often avoided sports which have been taken up by the working class and have adopted less popular sports, sometimes expensive ones such as horse-riding where the riders, as well as the animals, are generally well-bred. Alternatively, the better-off have formed their own clubs where the location or the fees have kept the places exclusive. It seems that little has changed during the last 100 years in this respect. In Belgium (and very likely elsewhere) the higher socio-economic strata are the most likely to play sports that involve the use of 'sticks' (golf, tennis, squash, skiing and so on) plus large and ostentatious outlays of money (as in horse riding and yachting, for example). The lower strata dominate in some solitary sports (angling and cycling, for instance) and in sports which require body contact such as boxing and karate (see Scheerder et al., 2002).

Many class divisive practices have lapsed only since commerce entered sport. Commerce has proved far more effective than amateur governing bodies in opening up sports and levelling the playing fields. The upper and middle classes have abandoned reticence about competing on level terms with their social inferiors, and have decided to risk defeat, when the potential cash rewards have been sufficiently attractive. During the 1990s, given the prospect of huge sums of TV-linked cash, the Rugby Union rapidly abandoned its long-standing principled objections to professionalism. After football's maximum wage was abolished in Britain in 1961, university graduates (the cohort that included Steve Heighway, Paul Power, Alan Gowling and Steve Coppell) began to enter the professional game. In the 1990s, when the cash rewards in top-level football again rose steeply, young men from middle-class families became willing to quit the academic route towards university and take their chances in the top clubs' football academies. This story is incomplete. Sport will continue to interact with wider patterns of social stratification. Sport never completely over-rides wider social inequalities: these are a constant source of complications.

Similar problems, for the original inventors of modern sports, have followed their successful export. Specifically, the inventors' countries and competitors stand the risk of being defeated in the world's most popular sports. The British, or maybe just the English, are still not reconciled to losing their place among the very top football countries. How will the British (and other European nations) react if and when the world's top football contests are dominated by sides from Africa and Asia? Will we retain our love of the game? It can be a problem for the sports. Television rights are devalued when interest wanes in the richer countries. Up until now the richer countries have generally retained an edge in sports which require high levels of skill and specialist coaching but this edge is not going to last indefinitely. Of course, the problem (for the rich countries) can be solved by co-opting skilled migrant labour into their sides. Zola Budd, an outstanding South African athlete, was granted a UK passport in 1983 which enabled her to compete in the British team in the 1984 Olympic Games and subsequent international competitions. At that time, its apartheid regime had led to South Africa being banned from most world sport competitions. In the 3000 metres at the Los Angeles Olympics Zola Budd collided with the home favourite, Mary Decker, and was subsequently known as Decker's wrecker (Carroll, 2003). Zola never won Olympic gold for Britain but she won world cross country titles in 1985 and 1986, and set a new world record time at 5000 metres before retiring from international athletics and returning to South Africa in 1988. Zola Budd's recruitment by Britain was always controversial and she faced anti-apartheid demonstrators wherever she raced, but despite this high profile cautionary example, international traffic in sports players is very likely to increase. Migrant professionals have long been welcome at football clubs. They are now acceptable as coaches of national squads. Why not strengthen the squads themselves in this way? Such arguments are likely to receive huge support from commercial interests. Commerce wants its products to appeal to the richest potential customers.

Enduring assumptions

Despite the ever-present tensions between the rules of modern sports and the wider modern world, many assumptions – ideas that were linked to modern sports from the outset – have proved remarkably resilient. To begin with, there is the belief that playing sport makes people healthier, improves their characters, and turns them into good citizens. Most people still seem willing to believe this. As noted in Chapter 4 (p. 53), governments still promote sport with this aim in mind. In reality, even the health benefits are doubtful (see Roberts and Brodie, 1992). People who play often enough, and vigorously enough, to improve their physiological functioning, risk paying a price in sport-related injuries. Top-level athletes appear to require far more medical attention than the rest of the population. So much for the notion that getting people to play more sport will relieve pressure on the National Health Service. As regards the social benefits, there is still a lack not only of convincing evidence (see Witt and Crompton, 1996) but even of satisfactory evaluative studies (see Shaw, 1999). Some sports-based projects aimed at crime prevention have been able to present promising results (Robins, 1990; Sports Council, 1989), but after more than a century of such initiatives crime is at record levels.

Maybe the social engineers have been blind to the real potential of our sports. One UK project which can boast astounding results has created out-of-school study centres at professional football clubs. These centres have attracted the target group, namely, low achievers in education. The centres have been popular with all concerned – the pupils, their parents and teachers. Remarkably, the primary school pupils' reading scores have improved by an average of 6 months and secondary age pupils' scores by an average of 8 months, all within the space of a year (Sharp *et al.*, 1999, 2001). Conventional educational initiatives rarely match these figures. Maybe sport's social engineers have been slow to learn how to make the best use of their asset.

Another long-standing conviction is that playing sport is especially beneficial for children and young people. In practice, all the benefits – physical, social and psychological – appear to be age-independent (see Roberts and Brodie, 1992). If anything, sport is probably most beneficial to health in late adulthood. Yet the school-age group and those a little older continue to be the principal targets. Sport is a compulsory part of the national school curriculum in Britain and in many other countries. When in education, young (and older) students are well-provided with opportunities to play. Then there is a steep drop-out during the years after people leave full-time education.

Another entrenched assumption is that sport is masculine: that boys (and men) ought to enjoy sports but that these activities are less appropriate, or wholly inappropriate, for girls and women. Nineteenth-century elementary schools had

---

BOX 6.1 WOMEN'S FOOTBALL

The (English) Football Association did not recognise women's football until 1993 but by then thousands of women in Britain, and millions worldwide, were playing the game.

By 2001 England had 700 recognised women's teams with the top 34 playing in a nationwide premier league, plus 1800 girls' teams, a total of 61,000 affiliated players, and football was overtaking netball as the top UK women's sport. In 2000 Fulham Ladies became the UK's first women's professional team; the players were paid around £20,000 a year.

FIFA (football's world governing body) predicts that, globally, by 2010 there could be as many women as men playing football. In 1999 the Women's World Cup (played in America) attracted a total of 650,000 spectators including 90,000 at the final (which the USA won). The global (television) audience for this match was estimated at one billion in 70 different countries. This is impressive, but the 2002 FIFA World Cup had an estimated cumulative television audience of 50 billion.

Predictions should be made with caution. Fulham Ladies' experiment as a full-time professional side ended in 2003. There have been earlier booms in women's football. One occurred during and after the First World War. A football team formed by women munitions workers in Preston played before crowds of 25,000 at Deepdale (Preston) and 50,000 at Goodison Park (Liverpool). This team returned undefeated from tours of the USA, Canada, France and Belgium. By 1921 women's football was becoming so popular that the FA decided to ban it (on health grounds) (Moore, 2002).

boys doing drill while girls were in domestic science classes. Physical exertion, sweating and muscularity have been considered unfeminine. Apart from the social aspect, it was once believed that strenuous exercise could damage women's reproductive capability. There have always been some women, and some girls' schools, that have battled against these assumptions, but it is only since the 1990s that the Football Association has recognised the women's game (see Box 6.1), and until the 1960s there were no endurance events (races longer than 400 metres) for women in the Olympics. Many people still feel that women and boxing are unsuited to each other. But nothing is static. Assumptions change. Flo-Jo (the athlete, Florence Joyner) and the Gladiators (a UK TV programme) have shattered the idea that athletic women are unfeminine. Commerce is playing a lead role in these changes. State socialism produced somewhat different athletic heroines. Women's sport still receives far less media attention than men's games, but this will not necessarily be so for ever. There are many sports in which, arguably, the women's events are the better spectacles: in tennis, for example, and maybe even in top-level soccer, where male play (compared with women's) has become power rather than skill dominated.

The voluntary base

Many of the features sketched above are evidence of modern sports' non-commercial roots. Commerce's expansionist tendencies will always seek to overcome age, gender and social class divisions, by designing slightly different products, if necessary. However, unlike the modern holiday, the evening-out and popular music, modern sports were not created by the market. Sport as it is known today (in Europe) is a product of voluntary organisation and public sector support. Modern sports are among, if not the greatest, achievements of voluntary effort. It was voluntary bodies that originally codified the rules and organised competitions. In some sports these same bodies have remained in charge while participation has reached massive proportions all over the world, and the sports have become global industries with huge turnovers, providing the livelihoods of thousands of professional players, agents, managers and a variety of ancillary workers.

Amateurism

It is because sports were originally created and run by non-profit organisations that many people came to believe that it was impossible to run sport on a commercial basis: that by its nature the activity needed to be supported by unpaid voluntary effort and, possibly, government subsidies. The reality is that sport can be commercial, but not the sports scene that has existed in Europe for the last one-and-a-half centuries. Another belief that became entrenched early in the history of modern sports was that, even if it was possible, it was wrong to make money out of sport; that all concerned should act for the love of the games. This ideal was built into the modern Olympic movement. Baron de Coubertin, a Frenchman, was impressed by the ideals of the original Greek Olympics (see Box 6.2) on the one hand, and, on the other, by the sporting ethos that he observed in England's nineteenth-century independent schools (see Tomlinson, 1999). Maybe the baron misunderstood both, but the modern Olympics aimed to draw them together and to unite humanity through its common ability to enjoy sport, to play for its own sake, and to both lose and triumph gracefully. Outside Europe few people have ever been able to understand why it should be wrong to make money out of sport. Americans do not find this offensive, and the rest of the world tends to think like America in this respect.

In Britain, the original birthplace of modern sport, it is only during the last 50 years that, with very few earlier exceptions, any players have made good money out of sport. Even today it is only the very top players in the most popular sports who are well-rewarded financially. Olympic gold does not lead to riches for swimmers, rowers or archers, to name just three sports. Until quite recently, athletes who could fill stadiums and whose performances commanded worldwide attention did it without expectation of significant financial reward. Roger Bannister was not paid in 1954 for becoming the first human to run a recorded mile in under four minutes. At the start of their athletics careers in the 1970s, Steve Ovett and Sebastian Coe were competing in a sport that was still amateur in Britain even at the highest level. Top UK rugby union remained basically amateur until the 1990s. Maybe the players did receive generous expenses but they all had, and needed, other

---

BOX 6.2 THE ANCIENT OLYMPIC GAMES

The first Olympics were held in 776 BC at Olympia in Greece. This was a one-day event with just one race, a stadium (over 192 metres). Subsequently the games were held every four years and by the fifth century BC the event had become a major festival which lasted five days with 10 classes of contests. These were running (over distances from 192 to 4608 metres, with some of the races run in full military armour), pentathlon, jumping, discus, javelin, wrestling, boxing, pancration (a combination of wrestling and boxing), chariot racing and horse racing.

The athletics were integrated into a religious festival honouring Zeus, the chief Greek god. Warfare between the city states was always suspended for the duration of the Olympics. During each games 100 oxen were sacrificed, and the occasions became associated with enduring achievements in architecture, mathematics, sculpture and poetry.

All the games were held at Olympia. Only free men who spoke Greek could compete (not women, slaves or barbarians). Athletes competed for honour, but winners became lifelong heroes in their home cities which could be from as far away as Spain, Libya and Ukraine. When they returned home the winners could expect cash rewards and appointment to leadership positions in their cities.

The ancient games were abolished in 393 AD when (within the Roman Empire) the functioning of all idol-worshipping sanctuaries was forbidden.

Sources: www.olympics.org/uk/index_uk.asp, www.nostos.com/olympics

paid jobs which were their main occupations. Until 1961 top-flight footballers in Britain were decently paid only by a working class yardstick. Stanley Matthews and Tom Finney, and Bobby Charlton and the rest of the Busby babes in the 1950s, were making hardly better livings than they personally could have hoped for in alternative careers. Would they have been better players if they had been paid more? Sport is a challenge to the ideology of the market which claims that no other motivator can rival cash. Nowadays it tends to be taken for granted that professional players must be superior to amateurs either because the former are able to train and practise full-time, or because it will always be the best players, if any, who are paid. We no longer hear champions of amateurism arguing that the superior character of the amateur will always tell eventually in head-to-head contests. However, it is not clear that professional players are always superior. Since the First World War, professional football has certainly been stronger than the amateur game, but, prior to accepting payments to players in the 1990s, was rugby union in the UK inferior to rugby league in the players' fitness or skill levels, or as an entertaining spectacle? Sport is proof that people will push themselves to peaks of performance purely for the intrinsic satisfaction and the esteem which they attract. Sport (and the arts) also demonstrate how people will devote many hours, throughout their lives, to administering complex projects, without being paid, for just the same rewards as amateur players.

Sport and the state

The rapid and widespread popularisation of modern sports would have been impossible without strong and continuing support from governments. Generally, throughout the world, voluntary bodies have done most of the organising while governments have provided the facilities for amateur players. Governments have laid out playing fields, provided swimming pools and, in recent times, have built centres for indoor sports, and they have used education to introduce all children to sport. In England's secondary schools and universities where our original modern sports were invented, these games soon became part of the curriculum. Ever since then the British image of a well-equipped school has had the buildings surrounded by playing fields, and from the outset this 'model' was adopted in state education. Sport has always been a compulsory part of the school curriculum in Britain

Governments in other countries have been equally keen to promote sport. Why? Sport is congruent with all the public sector's special capabilities in leisure (see Chapter 4, pp. 54–7). Governments promote sport as a particularly worthwhile leisure activity: playing sport is believed to benefit both health and character, and it has been possible to make opportunities to play sport into, in effect, rights of citizenship. Governments have also been alert to the possibility of sporting excellence strengthening national identities and prestige. And, in recent times, governments have become aware that sport is (at least partly) a business and that national (and regional and local) economies stand to benefit if their teams and competitors gain a significant share of the global audience.

Participant sport

There are inter-country differences in exactly how governments support participant sport. In the Netherlands and Germany, and in some other countries of continental Europe, state support is channelled largely through voluntary sports clubs. So, after school, children go to their clubs to play sport whereas in Britain they have been more likely to stay behind to play sport extra-curricularly. Many continental schools use clubs' playing fields whereas in Britain clubs are more likely to use schools' sports halls and other facilities. In Britain local authorities provide public playing fields, swimming pools and sports centres which can be used by clubs. In the Netherlands and Germany clubs are helped to acquire and manage these facilities. There are pros and cons in all arrangements. In Britain there is believed to be a problem of young people dropping out of sport by failing to make the transition from school-based to club-based participation.

> Too many young people are lost for ever to sport because there is not a straightforward and attractive way, through local clubs, to continue playing after age 16.   (Department of National Heritage, 1995)

However, on the continent there is believed to be a problem of young people failing to join sports clubs (Deckers and Gratton, 1995). It is not that young continentals are abandoning physically active recreation altogether. The situation is rather that today's young people seem to be less 'clubbable' than their predecessors. They seem more attracted by recreational swimming, surfing, skiing and such like than by competitive club sports (see Scheerder et al., 2002). Education-based sports provision in the UK appears conducive to retaining in sport the increasing numbers of young people who remain in education up to age 18 and beyond, and public facilities that are available for general public use, on a pay-as-you-go basis, seem more congruent with present-day young people's and adults' lifestyle preferences than the stronger commitment involved in club membership.

Professional sport

In the UK state support has been directed overwhelmingly to participant sport. Governments have not regarded it as their responsibility to subsidise clubs that pay their players and attract paying spectators. These clubs have been expected to pay their own way. Governments in other countries have taken a rather different view. In US cities, major spectator sports are often played in publicly-owned stadiums which are made available to professional teams at zero or nominal rents (Crompton, 2001). Cities provide these facilities because they believe that there are public benefits in terms of the money and prestige that are attracted. It is different in Britain where professional football, rugby and cricket clubs have been expected to provide their own grounds. Other countries' governments have not hesitated when building prestigious national stadiums whereas Twickenham and Wembley have always been privately owned and financed.

Elite amateur sport

Government support, even for elite amateur sport in Britain, was extremely limited until very recently. Before the Second World War the administration of virtually all sport in Britain was not only non-commercial but also, at governing-body level, free of state intervention. At first this was simply because modern sports were created and developed independently. However, by the 1930s non-intervention had become more of a positive policy, demonstrating the purity of British sport and how Britain differed from communist and fascist regimes. For all practical purposes at that time, the UK government was indifferent as to whether or not funds could be raised to enable British teams to compete in the Olympics. The Football Association was arranging international fixtures, home and away, which attracted thousands of travelling fans, and the relevant government departments were being informed after everything had been set up (see Beck, 1999). At that time it would have been difficult for UK governments, even if they had wished to do so, to support sporting elites without favouring particular sports, clubs or competitors. Most sports and their clubs were aggressively independent. Things changed only after 1935 when the Central Council of Recreative Physical Training (renamed the Central Council of Physical Recreation in 1944) was formed. This body represents, and comprises, the governing bodies of all the main amateur sports, and from its beginning it became a channel through which (limited) state support could be channelled. However, until a Sports Council was created in 1965, most UK sport-governing bodies prioritised their independence. By then people were coming to believe that competitiveness at top-flight international level was impossible without some measure of state support. As explained above, from the earliest days of modern sport, the governing bodies had welcomed the promotion of their games in education, and the provision of swimming pools and playing fields, then indoor facilities. They have usually been willing recipients of public resources provided politicians and civil servants have steered clear of the sport's government. This, in fact, remains the position in UK sport today.

National sports systems

Other countries' governments have been far more interventionist. Britain's hands-off sports history developed because it was the first industrial nation and, initially, a *laissez-faire* one. Elsewhere economic and social modernisation have often been government-led, and these governments have frequently sought international sporting success as a way of boosting the prestige of the countries (and their political regimes). This was the policy of fascist and, for a longer period, communist governments. They all developed or adopted a similar system for producing sporting champions and some of the countries, especially the German Democratic Republic (see Box 6.3), were spectacularly successful.

Green and Oakley (2001) have noted that since the 1970s many Western governments have adopted their own (usually weaker) versions of the communist elite sports system. Since National Lottery money became available in the

BOX 6.3 THE GERMAN DEMOCRATIC REPUBLIC'S ELITE SPORT SYSTEM

The system had four principal features.

1 Scientifically organised selection of boys and girls in early childhood.
2 Best possible facilities and an organised, squad approach to coaching and training.
3 Support by highly qualified experts from all relevant disciplines. Thousands of scientists, physicians and trainers were involved. Anabolic steroids were used liberally. Athletes who questioned the use of drugs were told that compliance was a patriotic duty.
4 Efforts were concentrated within a restricted range of (particularly Olympic) sports.

Sport was supposed to nurture a socialist personality: disciplined, honest, imbued with collective spirit, and willing to defend the homeland. International success was intended to demonstrate the superiority of the socialist system over capitalism.

In practice most East Germans did not participate in organised sport, and the collapse of the communist regime in 1989 showed that it was desperately short of loyal citizens. However, the sport system was spectacularly effective in winning Olympic medals. In the summer 1988 Olympics (the last before the demise of the GDR) the country won 6.0 medals per million population. As a benchmark, in 2000 the UK won 0.5 (slightly more than the USA but slightly fewer than France).

Source: Green and Oakley, 2001.

mid-1990s (see Chapter 12), the UK has developed a National Sports Institute (a network of elite coaching centres) and has introduced World Class Performance Programmes (which contribute to talented athletes' training and travel costs). It is remarkable in an international context only that these interventions are so recent and so modest. Also, again thanks to National Lottery contributions, public funds are now being used to give Britain a set of prestige national sports stadiums – the Millennium Stadium in Cardiff, Glasgow's revamped Hampden Park, the 2002 Commonwealth Games stadium and associated facilities in Manchester (see Box 4.5, p. 57), maybe a rebuilt Wembley and an Olympic stadium to follow.

As quasi-communist methods of seeking national sporting success have spread around the world, the results have been less impressive than when fewer countries were involved (Green and Oakley, 2001). This will be partly because it is easier for talented young people in Western countries to decline to take part: both the rewards of success and the penalties of refusal are lighter than they were in the communist countries. More basically, there can be only one world champion per sport. So as more and more governments seek sporting success deliberatively, the results are inevitably diluted. Countries cancel out each others' efforts. This is why politicians are unwise to promise to deliver Olympic gold and football world cups. Indeed, as explained in the next chapter, it is not governments, but commerce, that is currently staging the most serious challenge to the traditional voluntary roots of our modern sports.

CONCLUSIONS

We have seen that our most popular sports were invented by amateur enthusiasts then placed under voluntary sector management. Remarkable though it may seem, these voluntary associations have remained in charge of most sports, including the very highest levels in some, while participation has risen to mass proportions all over the world, massive audiences have been attracted, and professional players hired.

We have also seen that governments have always taken an interest in sport. There are several reasons (in fact all the possible good reasons) why state backing for sport can serve a general public interest. Because the public regards sport participation as a particularly worthwhile use of leisure, government support can proclaim this regard. Opportunities to play sport can be made into rights of citizenship by providing facilities that are accessible to all. National sporting success can strengthen national identities and prestige, and national support can be expressed by governments enabling sports governing bodies to nurture elite competitors and by providing prestige venues for top-rank events, then ensuring that these are managed in the interest of the general sports public rather than run on a commercial basis.

However, we have noted that the state has been the main provider of sport only in the communist countries where civil society was extinguished. Some of these state sport systems achieved outstanding success in international sport which must have boosted the countries' international visibility and prestige, but we now know that this sporting success did not inspire enough loyalty among the countries' own citizens to save the regimes. In other countries the main role of the government in sport has been to provide facilities (playing fields and so on) for citizens to use. Mass levels of participation would never have been achieved without public playing fields, swimming pools and other facilities. Governments all over the world have also wanted to assist in the quest for international success in elite sport. Here their achievements have inevitably been mixed. Sporting success is a 'positional good'; it is impossible for everyone to win. The situation is akin to that in tourism; governments either assist their own competitors or the countries fall behind. In the long term, governments invariably learn not to expect too much from sport. It is not in their interest to take charge. In turn, sport communities learn not to expect too much from their governments, and that they have no need to depend entirely on them.

7 Sport: Commercial Inroads

Introduction

Commerce has always been interested in sport and its interest has intensified as the cash value of the sport industry has risen. There are lots of ways to make money out of sport. Players, newspapers, radio and TV stations, and gambling houses have led the way. However, it is difficult for either players, club owners or event promoters to organise the actual production of sport so as to make profits and pay out with sufficient reliability to attract stock exchange investors. In the following sections this is illustrated with reference mainly to football – the world's most popular sport – in which the control of the original voluntary governing bodies has been loosened but not yet broken.

We shall see that in a limited number of individual sports it is possible for the top players, but only the very top players, to organise and market their play so as to maximise their incomes. In contrast, it is still not clear that any team sports can be made into commercially viable spectacles. For grass-roots participants, individual exercise can be commercialised, but we shall see that commerce has absolutely no purchase over fun players' competitive sports. Commerce has made inroads, but this chapter will show that it has not become – nor is commerce likely ever to become – the lead provider in sport.

Losing control

Management by enthusiasts

The people who pioneered Britain's (and the world's) main sports did not expect to make money. This applied even in football where, very early on in Britain, the private company became the normal base for professional clubs. Other team sports with professional players, which have also attracted large crowds, have almost always operated as members' clubs. This has applied in UK county cricket and rugby union. In football, maybe on account of the game's mainly working-class support, the private company was considered a more suitable method to raise the capital necessary to build stadiums, and to accept responsibility for employing players and paying their wages. So most professional football clubs have always had private owners and shareholders. (Many share-owners in the early years, and again in the present day when football clubs have become public limited companies (PLCs), have been just ordinary supporters.) Needless to say, ordinary fans have never held controlling interests. There has usually been just one or a group of major share-owners, although even they have usually been fans also rather than merely money men. Until 1981 the rules of the Football Association limited dividend payments to 5 per cent of the shares' nominal value. Directors and other major (and minor) shareholders did not expect to make money. At best, they hoped not to lose – and they rarely did lose – their investments. The main reward for a substantial investment was a status position and an attractive hobby – access to directors' boxes and lounges, and the opportunity to play fantasy football, usually (and advisedly) alongside a team manager. At that time the money-value of football clubs was modest by present-day standards. In the 1980s Manchester United could still be bought for less than £10 million. Its value has subsequently exceeded £600 million. Huge capital gains have been possible. Who would not have been tempted? That said, most professional football clubs have still not become tempting investments. In 2001 Chesterfield (which had huge debts) could be bought for less than £10,000.

Football's maximum wage

Features of professional football in Britain that were condemned as out-of-date and abandoned during the second half of the twentieth century made sense in the context of a sport that was being run on a voluntary basis for the good of the game and for the people who enjoyed it as participants and spectators at all levels. Until 1961 there was a maximum wage. The justification was that in a team game all the players should be paid the same: the stars would perform for the glory (and they did). Differential payments were believed to be incompatible with team spirit. It seemed only fair that wage levels at all clubs should be similar because the players were doing identical jobs. Also, if the wealthiest clubs could pay the most, they would attract all the best players and become unbeatable. Remuneration was fixed at a level considered appropriate in view of the players' social origins (over-whelmingly working class) and what they might have earned in alternative trades. They were being recompensed for their loss of earnings rather than their market value to their clubs.

The maximum wage was abolished in 1961 under pressure from the Professional Footballers Association led by Jimmy Hill, a Fulham player. Pressure was also being applied by star players who were leaving Britain for other countries, mainly Italy, where they could earn considerably more. John Charles, Jimmy Greaves and Dennis Law had made this move. The labour market for professional footballers was becoming global. Most of the migrants returned after 1961. All the warnings issued when the maximum wage was abandoned have proved correct. We now have super clubs. Most top players are now 'mercenaries': only the fans continue to exhibit club loyalty.

BOX 7.1 PROFESSIONAL FOOTBALLERS: THREE GENERATIONS

The Summerbee family has produced three generations of professional footballers (and maybe more to come).

Between 1934 and 1949 George Summerbee played for Aldershot, Preston North End (a leading top division side at that time), Chester, then Barrow. George's maximum wage was £8 a week.

Mike Summerbee's playing career ran from 1958 to 1978 and took him from Swindon to Manchester City, then Burnley, Blackpool and Stockport. Mike was at Swindon when the maximum wage was abolished in 1961. It made no difference to Mike and his team mates: Swindon had no spare money. With Manchester City Mike won the Football League Championship, the FA Cup, the Football League Cup, the European Cup Winners Cup, and England international caps. His maximum pay as a footballer was £350 a week. At the time this was considered extremely high, which it was by pre-1961 standards.

Nicky Summerbee also began his professional career with Swindon. This was in 1987, on YTS pay. His first full professional contract in 1989 gave him £80 a week. Subsequently Nicky had contracts with Premier League clubs including Manchester City and Sunderland. He is among the first generation of British footballers to become financially secure for life – in other words, very wealthy – by playing football. In 2001 the average salary of Premier League footballers was £409,000 or £7865 per week (Magee, 2002).

Sources: Magee, 2002; Shindler, 2001.

Football's retain and transfer regime

Another traditional practice, which amazingly continues in football despite, it would appear, having been legally shredded, is the transfer system. This was instituted early in the history of the professional game. It created a mechanism whereby players could move between clubs to find their appropriate levels. The best players would move to the top division, but for strictly sporting rather than financial reasons because the maximum wage remained almost the same. The clubs and fans who were losing a player were recompensed. Overall, good players moved upwards and money flowed downwards to the weaker clubs. Every generation expressed astonishment at the astronomic levels to which transfer fees had risen, but in a sense the level did not matter because the money was retained within the game.

The transfer system could never survive a challenge in the courts. Slavery is no longer permitted. Employers in other sectors of the economy do not buy and sell staff from one to the other. For a long time football's transfer system was not brought before the courts. No clubs wished to challenge it. Any player who did so was likely to stall his career for years while a legal case took its course. However, in 1963 George Eastham, supported by the Professional Footballers Association, challenged the right of his club (Newcastle United) to refuse to release him (Eastham wished to join Arsenal) when his contract expired. Eastham, of course, won his case, so players could no longer be retained indefinitely, against their will, but the clubs agreed that transfer fees should still be paid (and settled by arbitration if necessary). The next significant legal challenge was the Marc Bosman case in 1995 which established, through a ruling of the European Court, that at the end of his contract a player could move without his former club receiving a transfer fee. Since then, at the end of their contracts, players have been free agents. They can move to the clubs of their choice that are willing to engage them. The practical outcome of the Bosman ruling is that much of the money that the wealthier clubs would formerly have spent on transfer fees has become available to offer attractive financial packages to star players. So, at the top end of the market, players earnings have rocketed. In 2001 the European Commission decided that, like other employees, sport players who wished to do so should be able to move between clubs although their existing contracts had not expired. The commission accepted that a system should be introduced to compensate a losing club, but at nothing resembling the level that transfer fees for top players had then reached. Amazingly, high transfer fees continue to be agreed despite there being no apparent legal requirement to pay. However, exactly as expected, top players' earnings have rocketed upwards once more (see Box 7.1) and young people's interest in careers in professional sport has increased (see Box 7.2).

Payments to players (as opposed to transfer fees paid between clubs) are a loss from the game. If more money flows out, more has to flow in. From where? At the end of all the chains of transactions are the fans who pay through admission prices at grounds or in television subscriptions. So the cost of being a football fan has risen steeply. Are they able to watch better players? Not usually. The concentration of top players at top clubs has continued. The top clubs now hoard so many world-class players that some spend entire games on, or do not even reach, the substitutes' bench, and no-one sees their skills.

BOX 7.2 RECRUITMENT TO PROFESSIONAL SPORT

Such is the appeal of careers in US professional sport that one-third of white, and as many as two-thirds of black, 13–18-year-old males convince themselves that they will be able to make livings from sport. The top USA colleges benefit from this. They act as nurseries for future professional sports players and national amateur squads, and offer sports scholarships to talented high school graduates. These colleges' sports players generate around one-fifth of the top sports colleges' total incomes. USA college sport attracts large live and TV audiences. The cost of the sports scholarships is covered many times over. The casualties are most of the scholarship winners. Very few leave their colleges with academic degrees, and very few become professional sports players. Out of the million or so who are the top high school and college American football players in any year, no more than 150 can expect to play professionally, and only four or five of these can expect their professional careers to last longer than a year (Brooks-Buck and Anderson, 2001).

There is a comparable situation in the 'academies' that are run by the UK's top football clubs. Every year thousands of schoolboy players attend to display their skills. No more than a dozen per club are selected to become full-time trainees at age 16. Very few are retained beyond age 18. The top clubs fill their teams with experienced, often imported, players.

Despite still being run by nominally voluntary bodies – the national football associations and their international federations – there is now a genuine players' labour market. This market has become more international than in the past, but it is still not literally global. Football remains embedded in different national cultures. English clubs tend to recruit foreign players with similar, reliable, cultural origins – from Scotland, northern Europe and Australia rather than from the Mediterranean countries and Latin America (McGovern, 2002). However, the internationalisation of the market for footballers has certainly increased player-power, and this has loosened the control of governing bodies.

Marketing the spectacle

There is now also a genuine market for the product – the football spectacle. Until recently clubs could only perform for, and draw income from, a club's own fans. This has changed. There is now competition among media companies for 'rights' to the product. This does not apply to most sports. Most are simply not tele-genic. Snooker, like football, is a lucky exception. Snooker was not invented by or for TV, but it has been developed into a major spectator 'sport' by television (see Box 7.3).

Sport has always received and welcomed media coverage. Its reader-appeal has always made sport valuable to the press. Sport sells newspapers. Sports themselves have benefitted from the publicity. So there has always been a mutually rewarding relationship between sport and the press in which neither side has normally paid the other. Broadcasting, in the era of European state monopolies (see Chapter 10, pp. 139–42), became part of this arrangement. Things began to change in Britain only when broadcasting competition, in 1955 from ITV, was introduced. The BBC–ITV 'duopoly' then competed by offering cash for the right to broadcast sports events. Needless to say, the most popular spectator sport, football, was the most sought

---

BOX 7.3 SNOOKER

Snooker has become a major 'sport' through television coverage. The game is said to have been invented by British army officers serving in India in 1875, but its breakthrough in the UK had to await the arrival of colour television. The one-frame BBC Pot Black tournament in 1969 started the snooker boom, but the really big breakthrough was in 1977 with the screening of the semi-finals and final of the World Snooker Championships from Sheffield's Crucible Theatre. The following year the BBC decided to show all 13 days of the championships and 7 million viewers watched Ray Reardon beat Perrie Mans 25–18 in the final. The pinnacle in TV coverage (up to now) came in 1985 when Dennis Taylor beat Steve Davies 18–17 in the final: 18.5 million viewers were still watching when the final ball was sunk at 23 minutes after midnight.

Only football now outperforms snooker in total viewer hours of sport on UK TV. Top players have benefitted enormously from the TV-led boom. In 1976 the total prize fund at the World Championships was just £11,000. In 2002 it was £1,615,700 with £250,000 going to the winner.

Sources: http://worldsnooker.com, www.thurston-games.co.uk

after and could command the highest prices. The sums which the BBC and ITV bid were modest only by subsequent standards. Their sports budgets were limited: by the government-fixed licence fee in the case of the BBC, by the sums that could be raised by selling advertising space on ITV, and by both broadcasters being required to maintain balanced programming.

Things changed radically in Britain only when satellite broadcasting began in 1989. By then the development of telecommunications had created a global market for media products, including sports events with global appeal. In 1989 British Sky Broadcasting became the sole satellite broadcaster to UK homes. Sky is not subject to the same constraints as the terrestrial broadcasters. Specifically, it is not required to offer 'balanced' programming (see Chapter 10, p. 143). Also, Sky's income depends on the number and level of subscriptions that it can attract from viewers. The size and composition of its audience then govern the rates that can be charged to advertisers. Sky is able to concentrate its spending on whatever products will sell subscriptions. These have proved to be, first, top sport, and second, recently released films. Sky uses approximately one-third of its total income to purchase sports broadcasting rights (Gratton and Taylor, 2000). Neither the BBC nor ITV has been able to match this spending power. In 1992 Sky acquired the rights to live-broadcast the new football Premier League's fixtures. The media money that they could command was, by then, a principal reason why the big clubs wished to separate themselves from the Football League. Sky has subsequently retained the right to broadcast live Premier League fixtures, and has bought the rights to other top sports. The price paid for football may now have peaked, but throughout the 1990s, at each new auction, costs increased. The creation of a second digital platform in 1998, originally Ondigital and subsequently called ITV Digital (see Chapter 10, p. 143), owned jointly by Carlton and Granada, presented Sky with a real competitor, and the prices paid for broadcasting rights in the most popular sports leapt upwards again. Then in 2002 ITV Digital collapsed having discovered that it had paid too much for the rights to live-broadcast Football League fixtures. The boom may now be over. Even so, popular sports, especially football, have received new money – substantial new cash injections. – from the media. The sport's governing bodies have been enriched, except that they have been obliged to pass on most of the income to the top clubs (whom the media wish to cover) who have used most of the money to further inflate top players' salaries.

New money

All major sports and sports events have benefitted financially from television's thirst for top sport, and the willingness of the TV companies to pay. Until the 1980s the Olympic Games was a loss-leader. There was little competition to host the games. Cities could hope to benefit from the publicity and goodwill which, they hoped, would follow, but it was always difficult to quantify these benefits. At the end of the twentieth century Montreal was still paying off debts incurred by the 1976 Olympics. Los Angeles in 1984 changed everything. These Olympics were said to have made money largely, though not exclusively, from the sale of television rights.

The rights to televise the summer Olympics were worth about US$50 million in 1976, but by the end of the century their value had soared to around $800 million (Airola with Craig, 2000). Ever since 1984 there has been strong competition to host the Olympics, and likewise the major football tournaments – the World Cup and the European Nations Cup (see Chapter 8, pp. 114–15).

Football's (and some other sports') voluntary governing bodies have seen little reason not to sell broadcasting rights to the highest bidders. They have been under pressure from the clubs that the media are most eager to cover. The top English and Scottish clubs have, in effect, broken away into premier leagues, with the acquiescence, though, in England, not at the instigation of the governing bodies (nominally in England still the Football Association). The superclubs constantly threaten to break away again into elite European consortia. They want to play in whichever competitions will maximise their incomes, and they want the maximum possible sums for media rights. These clubs claim, with justification, that this is necessary in order for them to match the spending power of foreign sides, otherwise they will be unable to match what the competition can pay for players in salaries and transfer fees. Needless to say, the same argument applies in every other country.

Media exposure on a global scale has created additional income streams for the top clubs. One is sponsorship. Two-thirds of all UK business sponsorship goes into sport (Gratton and Taylor, 2000), and the biggest sports and clubs (in terms of public exposure) get the biggest shares of this money. Businesses pay to have their names on clubs' shirts and around the edges of their pitches, and to be able to use the clubs' images in their advertising. Top sport has become, in some ways, a branch of the advertising industry (Whannel, 1986). A further stream of income has come from the sale of club strips and other branded products ranging from key rings to curtains. For clubs with global exposure via the media, this subsidiary income stream is now worldwide. The leading football clubs are global teams with fans all over the world. Gate receipts account for well under a half of Manchester United's total income. In 2002 Manchester United claimed to have 50 million supporters worldwide, including 1.8 million in Bangkok and 6 million in China, and a quarter of the UK's under-14-year-olds (Cassy, 2002).

Some clubs have opened further income streams by developing their grounds into stadiums-plus. The original Wembley Stadium which opened in 1923 was built in just 300 working days at a cost of £750,000. The new Wembley is costing over £700 million. It is possible, even in this day and age, to build large sports stadiums at a much lower cost. The City of Manchester Stadium, built for the 2002 Commonwealth Games (see Box 4.5, p. 57), cost just £110 million. Cardiff's Millennium Stadium cost £120 million. The budget for Liverpool AFC's proposed new 55,000-seat ground is just £70 million. The new Wembley will be bigger (90,000 seats), and Wembley is in London where everything costs more, but the cost of the new Wembley is inflated by the incorporation of restaurants, shops and conference facilities. The sports events are intended to attract users to the surrounding facilities. These ancillary facilities enable stadium owners to sell high-price hospitality packages at sports events: 17,500 of the best seats at all of the new Wembley's events are reserved for corporate customers whose payments will

---

BOX 7.4 HOSPITALITY PACKAGES

As well as a (good) seat at the event, these usually include food and drinks, and meetings with celebrities from the sport. Sometimes there are autograph and photo opportunities with the stars of the event. Sometimes small gifts (mementos of the occasion) are offered.

Prices vary according to the popularity of the event and, hence, the demand for hospitality. In 2002 the UK price list included the following (prices are per person):

- World Snooker Championships, semi-finals and final: £150–£200 per afternoon or evening session.
- FA Cup Final: around £700
- Football World Cup Finals (at UK hotels): around £200
- British Masters Golf, Woburn: £200 plus
- Superbikes at Silverstone: £350–£700
- The Derby: £245–£450
- Test Match, England vs India, at Lords: £300–£500
- British Grand Prix, Silverstone: £300–£950
- Cowes: £300–£950

Sources: personal research.

---

amount to 70 per cent of total ticket revenue (see Box 7.4). The non-sporting facilities are also expected to generate business in their own right. The enthusiasm of leading football, and some other high profile, clubs to enlarge existing stadiums, or move to new sites, originates not just from the desire to accommodate more spectators, in more comfort, and with better views, but also to generate or expand supplementary income streams.

Investing in sport

With its new income streams, some investors have decided that top sport can, in fact, be extremely commercial. The value of some football clubs spiralled upwards in the 1990s. By then the ceiling on dividends had become irrelevant. Investors are equally, if not more, interested in share prices and capital gains. In any case, many FA regulations can be side-stepped by legally separating a football club (like Manchester United) from its holding company. Some clubs have converted themselves into PLCs with stock exchange listings. This move makes it essential for them to pay dividends annually and to do whatever they can to maintain their share prices. Whether this strategy will work for the investors or for the clubs (in terms of playing success) is still unclear. Leisure businesses, from the music halls onwards (see Chapter 2, p. 15), have always been high-risk investments. In the early-1990s football clubs became fashionable investments and their capital value rose, but their value has since slumped. Most top continental sides are not businesses of this type. They are still run in something akin to the traditional British way; to boost the profile and prestige of private owners, nowadays multi-billionaires or multinationals rather than local shop-keepers. Most big European sides, despite their massive turnovers, are still not direct sources of income for their owners.

In the UK an outcome of all the above is that top football clubs and competitions are now run so as to maximise income. Admission prices are raised to whatever levels the market will stand. Spectator accommodation is allocated to those companies or individuals who will pay most. Fixture timings are switched for the convenience of television companies and their audiences who pay for their respective interests to be accommodated. Super-clubs have become more super than ever. Players' and managers' salaries have risen to levels that rival the earnings of top players in individual sports such as golf and tennis (see below), and other international entertainers.

There are still voluntary governing bodies in sport. Perhaps surprisingly, in view of the commercialised business that top sport has become, there are surprisingly few tales of outright corruption. Members of the International Olympics Committee have sometimes been given generous gifts, and five-star hospitality has become standard. Votes on hosting the Olympics may have been swayed on some occasions. However, the sites of football's top tournaments still seem to be selected through the kind of internal politics that has always occurred in sports associations (see Sugden and Tomlinson, 1998). For players, the rewards of success and the penalties of failure have risen, but it is naive to blame commercialism for phenomena such as drug use in sport. 'Doping' occurs at all levels. Even when they are just competing for the glory, players will do virtually anything to win. In view of the cash that is now at stake, there are surprisingly few stories of matches being fixed. When this happens it is still more likely to be a spin-off from gambling (see Chapter 12, pp. 169–70) than the greed of club owners.

The limited capabilities of commerce

There is certainly more money in sport today than there was in the past, but this applies equally to virtually all leisure industries. Spectators at football and other popular sports are paying more. As we have seen, the clubs have opened or widened additional income streams. Top players are paid more. However, these are not fundamental changes. The enlarged money flows have attracted investors but, in itself, more money does not amount to commercialisation.

Change always creates winners and losers. The losers in football include self-styled traditional fans who resent paying more for admission to grounds (if they are still attending) and to watch their sport on TV, and for their replica kits and other fan gear. They complain that club loyalty has been eroded among players, managers and owners, about fixtures being rescheduled to suit TV, and some deplore the demise of the old terrace culture (see Garland et al., 2000; King, 1998). But other fans obviously approve of the recent changes. There is more money in sport only because some people are willing to pay it. The benefits in UK football include upgraded stadiums. Attendances at top-flight soccer have risen. Stadiums have been made more welcoming to men and women. It is impossible to say for certain how crowd demography has changed because in the past no surveys were conducted. (This, in itself, is a change. Nowadays the industry wants to know its customers and what they think.) However, most observers detect an increase in the proportion of women in football crowds (Waddington et al., 1996; Williams, 1996), and entire ends of grounds are no longer dominated by young males. Football hooliganism may not have been eradicated but it has subsided. There is more football on TV. There are more big, exciting matches, and more people are watching them. The issue here is not so much whether these changes are good or bad (clearly, opinions differ), but the fact that, in themselves, the changes do not indicate that commerce has taken over even top-level sport.

It has always been possible to make money out of sport, and sport is now making more money than ever before for the media, for sports clothing and equipment manufacturers, and for the gambling industry. Top players' earnings have rocketed. But it remains difficult, and risky, to try to make money by producing and selling the actual sport spectacle. This is not impossible, but it is extremely difficult with most of the sports that were developed from a voluntary base from the nineteenth century onwards. Making sport commercial means organising everything so that investors' risks are minimised and their profits maximised. This is only possible if sports are designed and managed appropriately, and if the public can be 'educated' to appreciate the commercial sport spectacle. The requirements are always difficult to meet, and they differ somewhat between individual and team sports.

Individual sports

In individual sports the players are the most likely entrepreneurs. The top players need to form themselves into pools or circuits whose members compete wherever they can raise, then share out, the most money from live audiences, the media and sponsors. Circuits need to be open to new talent, otherwise competitor circuits are likely to be formed, which may in fact turn out to be best for all concerned because then there can be lucrative champion-of-champions (major, grand slam, unification) contests. Golf, tennis and snooker are run in this way. Boxing contests are arranged ad hoc. In Formula One motor racing the car constructors are the key players.

Commercialisation is possible, but, first of all, only in a few sports. Most sports cannot command sufficiently large media audiences day-to-day and week-to-week. Swimming, archery, pole vaulting, rowing and bowling are commercial basket cases. Second, and related to this, it is advantageous if the competitors can compete every day, throughout the year. This is possible in tennis and golf, but simply impossible for boxers and marathon runners. Third, audiences need to be 'educated' to support the sports rather than particular players or groups of players. Large daily media audiences have to be attracted by the sports themselves rather than just by particular stars (whose form and appeal can nose-dive rapidly). Fourth, even in the sports where commercialisation is possible, the pools of well-paid professionals are tiny: a few hundred golfers, a few dozen tennis players and motor racing drivers. In boxing it is usually necessary to become a world champion, preferably at heavyweight level, in order to make serious money. Fifth, the non-commercial layers in the relevant sports are not wiped out. They continue in their customary voluntary ways with more orderly hierarchies of local, regional, national and international competitions.

Team sports

Commerce makes some similar demands whether sports are played by teams or individuals. Once again, it wants only the best, the very top layers, so attention, wealth and talent become concentrated within super-clubs (Whannel, 1986). With team sports it is club owners, not individual players, who need to act as entrepreneurs and form themselves into circuits (leagues). There are most likely to be several leagues per sport, probably based in different regions or countries, but they compete for the same continental or global audiences. This makes it possible to organise champion-of-champions contests.

Commerce's requirements in team sports can be seen most clearly in the USA where, throughout their history, club owners have hoped to make money. A strong league needs to attract as many of the world's best players as possible but, because sports are interesting only if the outcomes are uncertain, it is necessary to ensure that the best players are not concentrated within a limited number of clubs. It may, therefore, be necessary to introduce rules governing player recruitment, exchanges, loans and transfers. Salaries need to be capped by collective agreement (among the club owners) in order to prevent the money attracted into a sport all flowing straight out into the players' bank accounts. Play-offs are exciting and attract large audiences, so when commerce rules there will be plenty of them. Play-offs may take the form of a series of matches (best out of seven, for example). There is no automatic relegation from commercial leagues: top earners are never expelled. Investors are not willing to stake everything on the vagaries of team performance. Owners may seek to relocate their clubs to different cities when doing so makes commercial sense.

There are signs of all these developments in European football, but we should note that North America's sports have not spread globally, and they have made few inroads in Europe, the world's other large market. In Europe there are serious obstacles to the commercialisation of team sports. As in individual sports, the audiences need to be educated to be attracted to the spectacle – the sport itself – rather than being committed long-term to just one team. They need to accept that their local clubs may have to sacrifice key players in the interest of maintaining competitive and entertaining sports spectacles: attracting a mass TV audience is only possible if people will switch on for the sport rather than watching only if their own teams are playing. In practice, European supporters have powerful club loyalties. They want their own teams to win. They expect club owners and managers to do everything possible to bring success. They do not expect star players to be transferred in the interest of keeping a league competitive. They expect owners to spend all their resources, sometimes more, in pursuit of glory. Owners (and their families) who resist may be subject to personalised hate campaigns. Fans demand that club owners and managers (and the players, if only temporarily) are committed to the success of their own teams. And the sizes of TV audiences vary considerably according to the popularity of the clubs that are playing. The number of viewers who will switch on for any football, or any rugby, is rather limited. Moreover, European 'investors' are willing to pour money into clubs where there is little hope of any profit, even in the long term. They simply refuse to quit and leave the market to stronger sides. Likewise fans will not switch loyalties. They stubbornly continue to support failing teams. They somehow keep clubs going whatever the circumstances and, as the case of Wimbledon AFC's move to Milton Keynes shows, they will definitely not countenance their relocation. Commercialisation may be easiest if sports are transformed into entertainment or art forms, as has happened with professional wrestling and ice skating.

Participant sport

This really is commercial no-go territory. The problem is not just competition from state-subsidised facilities. There is a basic incompatibility. In commerce you play if you are willing to pay. In sport you play if you are good enough. Selection for a team, or position on a squash ladder, depends on sporting ability. It is true that in many sports competition has been formally or informally restricted to social equals, but thereafter sporting criteria have applied. This is no good for commerce. Money has to rule throughout.

Exercise can be commercialised, and in the UK there has been a recent boom in commercial health and fitness clubs (see Box 7.5). Commerce has created new markets for exercise, but in doing so it has not eliminated, or even reduced the

---

BOX 7.5 HEALTH AND FITNESS CLUBS

In 2002 in the UK, commercial health and fitness clubs were opening at a rate of 100 per year. The industry was worth £600 million per annum in turnover and had six million adult members. Fifty multi-site operators were running around 2500 'clubs', and there was an unknown number of single-site operators (Audit Commission, 2002). Joining fees ranged from £40 to £550 and monthly subscriptions from £40 to £150. It is doubtful whether the clubs' facilities and personal trainers offer more in terms of fitness and health than could be achieved in people's homes, on the streets and in parks, or in local authority sports centres. However, the commercial sector knows that it must keep its facilities smart and up to date. Public sector facilities are more variable in quality. In 2002 41 per cent of all football pitches in England had drainage problems and 38 per cent had no changing rooms (Football Foundation, 2003).

There is a high rate of member turnover in commercial health and fitness clubs for which Sassatelli (1999) offers a plausible explanation:

> ... the more participants in fitness measure themselves against each other and a fantasized body ideal the less will be their capacity to continue attending the gym regularly. The more the desired objectives are perceived as vital, the more participants will feel inadequate...'

numbers playing, competitive sports (see Chapter 3, p. 33). There are limited commercial markets for sports that can be played by two, three and foursomes – squash, tennis and golf, for example – but even in these sports commerce cannot handle serious amateur competitions, and it has absolutely no purchase on large team sports. This is one reason why compulsory competitive tendering for the management of UK local authority sport and leisure facilities has made so little impact (see Chapter 4, p. 49). It has not led to an influx of private capital, commercial marketing, or increased participation. Commerce has displayed little interest. The plain fact is that European sport and commerce are poor bed-fellows. Some leisure activities are inherently non-commercial, yet they can be sustained in perpetuity because leisure provision has alternative 'engines'.

CONCLUSIONS

In the opening to Chapter 6, sport was presented as a test case. Are there limits to the expansion of commerce? Does commerce have the power to drive out other providers? Sport provides our first examples that, if governments decide that doing so serves a public interest, a leisure industry (such as the participant segment of sport) can be rendered non-commercial simply by offering a free-to-use or subsidised alternative. This is just one reason why commerce has little purchase on participant sport. It cannot compete with governments that are willing to create and maintain opportunities to play as rights of citizenship. Nor will commerce construct and run prestige sport stadiums. Thus sport vindicates a relaxed (third way) attitude to commercial inroads, secure in the knowledge that commerce's capabilities are strictly limited.

Sport also illustrates how enthusiasts can remain in charge of a leisure industry provided they maintain sufficient enthusiasm. It is possible for voluntary sports associations to be nudged aside by elite players in the limited number of individual sports in which there is sufficient media interest, but an awkward (for commerce) fact of this matter is that our modern sports were originally designed for the enjoyment of players and spectators and, in their historical forms, they are simply not commerce-friendly. Commerce needs to market its own sports (or near-alternatives such as individual exercise) for grass-roots participants. Spectator sports need to be redesigned so that spectators follow the sports rather than support specific teams or players. The problem for commerce is that spectators in most countries are hard to wean from Manchester United, Real Madrid and so on.

8 Events

Introduction

Attractions such as the Disney parks, Ayers Rock and the Eiffel Tower (see Chapter 5) are enduring, permanent fixtures. Events are different; they are discontinuous. They may be recurrent or one-off but they are always out of the ordinary. Historically most leisure events were primarily for the enjoyment of a local population – the church harvest festival, the school nativity play, the gardening club's annual display, the village summer carnival – but here we are concerned mainly with the (usually much larger) events that attract non-locals. Indeed, drawing in tourists (and their money) is now a principal reason why many events are staged. Throughout the world, ancient rites are being kept alive, and in some cases have been brought back to life, as tourist attractions. Other things have changed too. We saw in Chapter 7 (pp. 100–1) that not very long ago the International Olympics Committee and other international sports bodies had to persuade cities and countries to host their events. There is now intense competition. Indeed, attracting big events has become a prime aim in leisure policy of many national and local governments.

This and the two following chapters on the media place government leisure policies under scrutiny. This is not because events or the media are usually run by public authorities. Rather, what comes under scrutiny is the recent international trend towards governments treating leisure primarily as a business and subsidising, protecting or privileging what are basically commercial or voluntary sector ventures in the expectation that the countries, regions or cities will gain jobs and money. We saw in Chapter 4 that the underlying rationale is sound. Investing in leisure loss-leaders is among the public sector's special capabilities. The justification is always that the returns on the efforts and investments of others will be magnified and that there will be generalised public benefits. The problem is that all countries, regions, cities and villages are competing for a finite volume of business. What applies to tourism in general also applies to events. The basic case for public support has to be a business case. The rest of the public sector's special capabilities in leisure are not irrelevant, but hosting events has to be treated primarily as a business proposition. The crunch questions are always twofold: whether the public investment will pay off, and whether the benefits will flow to all, most, or just minority sections of the public who will contribute to the investment.

This chapter opens by defining events and categorising them according to their size and the types of activities on which they are based. The chapter proceeds to explain the growing importance of events in terms of the expansion of tourism, the globalisation of the media, and the awareness of present-day governments of the economic significance of leisure. Finally the chapter poses its crunch questions: are events really good business for the hosts, and exactly who gets the benefits?

Types of events

Events can be classified according to the kinds of activity on which they are based. Most are classified as based on either sport, the arts, other entertainments, the heritage, or food and/or drink. Events can also be grouped according to their size, usually measured by the numbers of people who attend. In these terms the biggest events are the sports megas. The summer Olympics is the biggest of all the sports megas and in recent decades each Olympics has been the biggest ever (see Toohey and Veal, 1999). These games involve all countries and all the sports that are played in most parts of the world. The games attract many thousands of competitors and officials, and far more spectators. Most individual sports have their own major events, and, of course, the biggest sports have the biggest majors. Football's World Cup is second only to the Olympics. In some respects – value of the TV rights, and total size of the TV audience – the football World Cup is now the leader. World regional contests such as football's European Nations Cup also count as megas. These are not just matches but tournaments which last for a month. Athletics has its own world, European and other international regional championships. Other sports – cricket, rugby union, rugby league, swimming, martial arts and so on – have equivalents. The bigger the sport, then the bigger the mega. In tennis the equivalents are the grand slam tournaments and in golf the majors. These are the events that attract all the star players and the most spectators. Obviously, some megas are bigger than others. Where should we draw the line? In practice the line is blurred. Did the World Student Games, hosted by Sheffield in 1991 (see Critcher, 1992), qualify as a true mega? Was the Commonwealth Games, hosted by Manchester in 2002, a real mega? Manchester 'won' the Commonwealth Games, having failed in two bids to become an Olympics host city. Most sports events do not aspire even to become majors let alone megas. Most Scottish Highland Games are still primarily local occasions, although nowadays they are also a part of Scotland's tourist industry. Visitors can admire kilted pipers and dancers, caber tossers and hammer throwers. Nowadays these events usually end with a games disco.

Arts megas are usually held in the same place on each occasion – the Edinburgh Festival of the Arts, and the Cannes Film Festival, for example. These events are attended by stars and huge crowds, and they generate immense publicity. The

Edinburgh Festival began in 1947 and is held during the second half of August. It was originally intended – as it still is – to be a celebration of the arts, to attract the very best artists in the world, and to achieve the highest possible standards, thereby enriching the cultural life of Scotland, Britain and Europe. Since 1996 modern and popular music have been part of the festival. The 2001 event offered 161 performances of opera, ballet, postmodern dance, drama, classical music, and so on. There is a simultaneous fringe festival which nowadays offers far more performances and involves more artists than the festival proper. Needless to say, as well as being a celebration of the arts, the festival is now a major highlight in Scotland's tourist calendar. Some arts events are partly trade fairs where deals are done: between film makers and distributors, theatrical groups and television producers, programme makers and broadcasters. The sports megas are always primarily contests; most 'trade' is done elsewhere.

High culture has its big events, and so does pop music nowadays. The pop industry's biggest events are not mere concerts but festivals which last for several days. Attending a pop festival has become a rite of passage in the transition to adulthood. These events date from the 1960s and, over time, they have become more numerous and, in some cases, bigger and bigger. One of the longest-running UK pop festivals is held at Glastonbury (see Box 8.1). However, one UK festival that lives on in the memories of many who attended was held at Knebworth in 1975.

BOX 8.1 GLASTONBURY FESTIVAL

This began as a two-day event in 1970 when Marc Bolan, Keith Christmas and others entertained a crowd of 1500 whose £1 admission fees entitled them to free milk from the farm as well as the entertainment. Admission was free at the 1971 festival when medieval music, poetry, dancing and theatre were added to the rock music, and 12,000 attended. There were no further Glastonburys until 1978 when 500 travellers converged on the site and an impromptu event was held. Then in 1979 a three-day organised event with Peter Gabriel, Steve Hillage and the Alex Harvey Band attracted 12,000 who paid £5 each.

The early Glastonburys were not really commercial affairs. The 'profits' went to charities: CND, Greenpeace, Oxfam and others. Also, throughout the 1970s and 1980s the festivals were arranged despite opposition from the local council and MP.

By 1987 Elvis Costello, Robert Cray, New Order and Van Morrison were attracting 60,000 at £21 a head, and £130,000 was donated to charities.

The 1990 festival is best recalled for ending with confrontations between travellers and security staff, which led to 235 arrests and £50,000 worth of damage.

1997 was the 'Year of Mud': attendance was 90,000 and admission £75.

In 1999, for the first time, the crowd exceeded 100,000.

In 2002 the entrance fee was £100.

The events are still raising money for charities: around £250,000 each year. But with a 'take' in excess of £10 million the festival has clearly become at least partly commercial. Interestingly, local opposition has now died down.

Sources: www.glastonburyfestivals.co.uk,
www.mystical-www.co.uk/glastonburyfestival/

Over 70,000 attended (a huge figure at that time). There were 10-mile traffic queues. Young people travelled in battered cars and camper vans, some hitch-hiked, others used public transport, and they came from all over Europe. They brought sleeping bags and tents, and enjoyed the open air, the beer, the joints, and, of course, the music which was provided by Pink Floyd, Linda Lewis, Monty Python, Steve Miller, Captain Beefheart and the Magic Band, and others. 'Knebworth' continued as an annual event until 1998 with Genesis in 1978 being another classic concert.

However, the all-time biggest (and arguably most successful) pop festival – an inspiration for all that followed – was Woodstock in 1969. This event actually took place in Bethel (NY). It was a three-day event. Tickets were $18 but in practice admission was free because 450,000 turned up and overwhelmed the site organisation. Those who attended recall the mud and empty stomachs, but also the happy smiling people, the peacefulness, the unadulterated freedom, and the great music which was provided by, among others, the Grateful Dead, Jefferson Airplane, Jimmy Hendrix, the Who, and Janice Joplin. Woodstock was documented on film. There have been revivals, with mixed success but neither was a patch on the original, on the 25th and 30th anniversaries of the original Woodstock.

The Munich Oktoberfest (see Box 8.2) is probably the world's best known drinking event, but there are many more of this type. All such events are simultaneously about tourism and something else – sport, an art form, beer or whatever. Most poetry, song, piano, wine, beer, garden and pop music occasions are aspirant rather than actual majors, or are still basically for local enjoyment, though what most have in common nowadays is that the events have begun to attract – or

---

BOX 8.2 OKTOBERFEST

This festival began in 1810 in Munich as a celebration of the marriage of Crown Prince Ludwig. The occasion was enjoyed so hugely that it was decided to commemorate the wedding annually. The wedding celebrations were followed by horse races. In 1811 an agricultural fair was added. Entertainers and beer sellers first appeared in 1818.

In 1880 the festival was switched from October to September for the warmer weather. Nowadays the 'Munich Beer Festival' lasts for 16 days and always ends on the first Sunday in October.

Horse racing was removed from Oktoberfest in 1938. Nowadays the beer is the star turn and each festival is attended by around 6 million thirsty souls from all over the world. There are giant beer tents (*festhallen*). Bavarian music rocks the air. There are dances, sideshows, roller coasters and other rides. Contests are held to see which waitress can carry the most full one litre beer mugs (the record is 21).

Oktoberfest is no longer celebrated only in Munich. There are similar festivals in many other parts of Germany, and in other parts of the world. In the USA the oldest and largest is the Milwaukee German Fest, first held in 1846, which now draws around 100,000 visitors annually.

Sources: www.bayernservice.de/e-bayernservice/e-oktoberfest.htm,
www.beerfestivals.org/archive/bt/munich_strong_beer.htm

the organisers hope to attract – large crowds and publicity. Events are definitely part of the present-day tourist industry.

The UK Sinatra Music Society holds its annual convention each autumn in Birmingham. This is not a mega-event or even a major. Attendance is usually under 1000. There are stalls where recordings and memorabilia can be purchased, the AGM, and, of course, a concert featuring you-know-who's music and songs. Chess, tiddlywinks and table soccer enthusiasts all hold conventions. These do not compare in scale with Edinburgh and Glastonbury, but the economies of most cities and holiday resorts (especially out of season) would stutter without a stream of such minor events plus business conferences (which usually mix work and leisure). When added together, the minors can be as important as individual megas, not least in creating a year-round, events industry.

Who wants events and why?

Mega-events have become the leisure industries' supernovas. The big megas grow ever bigger and more numerous. Arts and sports organisations, cities and countries, are eager to host them. They all want megas and, indeed, any events. This enthusiasm for events is less than 20 years old. How has it come about?

The expansion of tourism

There are three interacting reasons. First, as explained in Chapter 5, tourism has become the world's biggest, and its biggest growth, industry. More people are not just willing but eager to travel, and they have the time and money to make this possible, so there are more leisure travellers who can be pulled towards any special attraction, be this a site of natural beauty, a theme park or an event. Tens of thousands of sports fans will travel internationally to watch a single match even if the event is being broadcast live on television. Nowadays football's European Champions League Final is a reliable sell-out. Supporters treat these occasions as mini-holidays. Tournaments rather than just matches can attract fans from scores of countries who will stay for up to a month. Cities, even countries, become packed with tourists. Football's world and European tournaments are no longer played in empty stadiums. Nowadays tickets sell out well in advance of the events. Ticket allocation has become controversial. It seems that neither the hosts nor the visitors can get enough. Many fans are prepared to travel without tickets simply to be there and to share the atmosphere.

Sport governing bodies are keen to host megas because these generate revenue and publicity. So nowadays more sports than ever are organising world events. Specific sports are constantly inventing new international competitions. Football's initial world club championship was played in Brazil in 2000. Manchester United competed and was allowed to miss that year's FA Cup competition. FIFA, the organiser, hoped at the time that this event would be repeated regularly and that its profile and audience appeal would gradually increase. However, as already indicated, there is room only for a limited number of genuine megas. They compete against one another.

Countries and cities are as keen as sports and arts organisations to host megas and other events. The attraction is the same. Events, especially megas, mean money and publicity. There is always a boost to tourism. Sports events bring players, officials and spectators. They all spend money which flows into the local economy. The hosts may also hope for longer-term benefits. Host cities of megas are publicised worldwide. If first-time visitors enjoy the experience they may return. They may recommend a place to their friends. People who watch a mega on television may decide that it is a place that they really must visit. Hosting a mega is a way in which a place can gain a higher profile on the world map (see Roche, 1992, 2000; Street, 1993). Cities and countries are prepared to invest millions of dollars in bidding for a big mega, and this bidding itself raises the profile of the relevant sports or arts organisations, as well as the bidders (see Sugden and Tomlinson, 1998).

All this is possible only in the context of a booming and maturing tourist industry. More and more people are travelling from and to virtually all countries. Experienced leisure travellers are seeking something 'different' – a variation on the standard sun, sea or mountains. So, as explained in Chapter 5, the tourist industry has been developing a series of specialised market segments – city tourism, activity holidays, sex tourism. Sports and cultural tourism have become part of this menu. There are participant and spectator forms of sports tourism. Enthusiastic players take golf and tennis holidays. Amateur football, cricket and rugby teams arrange international (holiday) tours. In a similar way, fans will travel for a match, and in even greater numbers for a sports tournament. Cultural tourism exists independently of events. People will visit cities with histories and buildings from bygone ages. Florence, Paris and London have art galleries and museums that attract visitors. As Chapter 5 (pp. 72–3) explained, heritage is business nowadays. So are the high-profile performing arts. People flock to Verona every summer to watch the opera. Festivals act as a boost to cultural tourism and operate as magnets, drawing in tourists who might otherwise have gone elsewhere or at a different time.

It is the ability and willingness of the public to travel that makes events viable and commercially attractive. The number of people, and the amount of money, that can be drawn in has made all kinds of events (garden festivals, cup finals and the rest) more commercial than in the past. Oktoberfests (see Box 8.2, p. 111) and pop festivals are just two examples. In the 1960s and 1970s the cost of attending pop festivals, which were then very infrequent, had to be kept low because few fans could afford to spend expensive weekends away from home. In any case, the ethos of these events – part of the attraction to the fans who went and an inspiration of some organisers – was counter-cultural (see Box 8.1, p. 110). Pop and rock have roots in jazz (the music of oppressed black people). The early festivals were often explicitly pro-civil rights, against atomic weapons and against war (particularly the Vietnam War). The counter-culture was tolerant of drug use and pro-sexual liberation. Confrontations with authority were part of the pop festival experience. Event organisers had to appear (and often were) sympathetic. Organisation was typically ramshackle. Site perimeters were rarely secure and free entry was possible.

Everyone who attended was prepared to rough it. If the events were profitable (which they certainly were for some people, including most of the performers) appearances had to suggest otherwise. It is different today. Young fans as well as ageing hippies expect to pay and expect to be entertained in safety and in some degree of comfort.

Recurrent annual arts and pop festivals may not have the same pull as the Olympics but they have the advantage of being annual, so their booster value to tourism is repeated again and again. Different kinds of events attract different types of tourists, and their profiles, and their typical behaviour while visiting, especially their consumer behaviour, can be as important as sheer numbers in determining their value to the hosts. Single sports matches like football games may be of limited economic benefit to local businesses. Fans may simply arrive for the match and quit the area soon afterwards (see Nash and Johnstone, 2001). Visitors are more valuable when they stay overnight and spend money in the local hotels, restaurants and shops. High culture events are especially appealing (to potential hosts) because of the up-market visitors who are attracted. These crowds usually behave themselves and spend vigorously. Pop festivals and sports megas bring greater risks. Some sports, notably football, bring supporters who may drink heavily and fight with rival fans (and the local police) leaving immense damage and ill-will in their wake. British groups of young male spectator-sport tourists appear to behave in much the same way as they do on seaside holidays. They are likely to consume substantial quantities of alcohol and act out their everyday feelings towards foreigners. What is accepted (or tacitly tolerated) in Corfu easily becomes explosive in the context of a high-profile sports contest.

The media

The second engine which has inflated mega-events has been the globalisation and commercialisation of television. Globalisation has been crucial. It enables events to be broadcast live to a global audience simultaneously. Two-thirds of the global population now watches at least part of a summer Olympics (Henry and Gratton, 2001). All the main sports have now become global sports. Film and recorded music already had global markets. Sport has now joined them and its principal players have the same kind of celebrity status and earnings as film and pop stars. The commercialisation of broadcasting (see Chapter 10) has also been crucial. In Europe, one of the main world markets, event organisers are no longer faced by cartels of state broadcasters, all with capped budgets. There is intense competition for television rights and the bidders include broadcasters who can raise money through channel subscriptions, pay-per-view, and by selling advertising space at premium rates when the audience is guaranteed to be large with high-spending groups, notably young males, well-represented. Event organisers can raise substantial sums from the sale of television rights (see Chapter 7, pp. 99–102), and, once an event is being televised globally, additional income streams open. Businesses become keen to sponsor the events, specific sports, teams and players. The event organisers and local hosts benefit from all the secondary publicity that sponsors and their advertising generate. Images of the location are broadcast all over the world. The events themselves are publicised, at no cost to the organisers, by the media that are seeking audiences. Additional spectators may thereby be attracted, and there are likely to be longer-term enduring benefits from all the publicity, which are very difficult to quantify.

The big breakthroughs for the sports megas occurred during the 1980s. The 1984 Los Angeles Olympics was the first of these events to be declared a huge commercial success. Montreal, the 1976 Olympic host, was still bewailing its huge debts. Moscow in 1980 did not really try for commercial success. Then the Americans demonstrated how. All subsequent Olympics – Seoul in 1988, Barcelona in 1992, Atlanta in 1996, Sydney in 2000 – have been declared bonanzas by the organisers. In football's World Cup, Italia '90 was the breakthrough. The 1986 event had been switched from Columbia to Mexico because the original hosts were unable to provide the facilities that were required. Ever since then there has been keen competition to host this mega. Would-be organisers have needed to spend millions of dollars on their bids, where, previously, it was necessary to persuade a country to go to the trouble and expense.

The role of governments

Governments have been the third mega-driver. City, regional and national governments, virtually all of them, all over the world, are now alert to the economic importance of leisure. Once upon a time they set about developing their economies by investing, or attracting investment, in steel mills and shipyards. Now they want leisure businesses – dotcom retailers, media companies, shops, hotels and restaurants. How are these businesses to be attracted? One way is to host a mega and a stream of minor events which will draw in the people who will fill the hotels and so on. Governments are key players. They alone have the ability to orchestrate all the other interest groups. Governments provide organisation, speed up planning permissions, and are invariably required to invest public funds. Bidding for megas has become one of the highest-profile roles of the politicians who head leisure services departments. Manchester City Council was the lead player in the city's two unsuccessful bids for the Olympics. Eventually Manchester settled for the 'consolation prize' of the 2002 Commonwealth Games. Tony Banks resigned as sports minister in the 1997 Labour government to become the government representative on the 'team' which bid (unsuccessfully – Germany won) to host the 2006 football World Cup.

The public-at-leisure has become mobile. Every region's cities compete for shoppers and for the evenings-out market. So all cities want to image themselves as lively places which people will want to see, and where they will want to be seen. Countries are in a similar position. Tourism is the top leisure activity in terms of spending and present-day holiday-makers have a worldwide choice of destinations. At least, this applies to those who can afford to travel. Most of the world's people are not so fortunate but it is the holiday-makers with the most money that all countries are keenest to attract.

Voluntary sports and arts bodies find themselves in situations where logic more or less compels, or regulates, them to act as if they were commercial enterprises. If cities, countries and media companies are competing to host and broadcast the events, what can the organisers do but sell to the highest bidders? Governments are in a similar situation. If they want leisure business, then they need to compete. Failure to do so guarantees that the business and jobs will go elsewhere. Thus governments – national and local – are 'regulated' to act as leisure markets require. In turn, the governments must regulate their societies so that events can be accommodated. This means providing facilities, managing the environment and the local population, and supplying the workforce so that the events, together with the people who are attracted, can be treated in the manner that all concerned have come to expect. Thus the voluntary and public sectors become at least partly commercialised and, in turn, oblige their own dependants to act in commercial ways. When governments invest in facilities for economic, business reasons, they expect the managers of the facilities that receive state support to operate in a similar business-like way. Projects are judged on their business plans rather than the overall public benefits (including difficult-to-quantify benefits such as enlarging citizenship, and setting moral and aesthetic standards), that only state provisions can deliver (see Chapter 4, pp. 55–7). Public investment has to be channelled into high-profile facilities – sports stadiums such as Cardiff's Millennium, Glasgow's Hampden and the new Wembley. There are opportunity costs. The money might otherwise have gone into facilities designed for local users. So commerce rules, OK?

Who pays, who benefits?

Megas invariably require the 'investment' of substantial public funds. As independent businesses, facilities such as major opera houses and concert halls are nearly always non-commercial. This applies equally to athletics and cycling stadiums, and arenas for indoor events that are suitable for the limited number of international competitions that attract large crowds. These facilities are never constructed with money raised entirely by the private commercial sector. Likewise, it is always governments who provide most of the funding for any upgrading of transport that is necessary, and any new accommodation for large numbers of officials and competitors. Needless to say, all the government spending has to be paid for, in taxes, by the local population.

The case for events

It is possible to treat all this public outlay as investment. The spending is one-off rather than a recurrent cost. Whether it counts as investment in the normal commercial sense is controversial. It is likely, and always intended, that the income generated will exceed the sum invested. Income here is everything that is spent in the host territory by visitors – players, officials, media staff, spectators and anyone else who is attracted from outside. So is the investment repaid and a 'profit' achieved? Is this sound economics? There are costs, additional to the public sector investment, in hosting the visitors. Hotels and railways have to be staffed. The food and drink that visitors consume have to be produced or purchased. The visitors' spending is not all profit for the relevant businesses. True, but it can be argued that the costs to a hotel, for example, are income to the staff of the business. All the visitors' spending can be said to benefit the host community in so far as it is additional to the cash that would otherwise have been drawn in and, once in, it can ripple with multiplier effects throughout the local economy. So, whereas the new facilities and anything else that is specially constructed may not be profitable in themselves, there can be said to be general economic gains that justify the public outlay (see Gratton and Taylor, 2000). The immediate economic benefits are generated through the jobs that the initial investment, then the visitors' spending, create. Then the workers spend their wages which creates further employment for others, and the cycle is repeated. Some claim that the public investment that megas and other events require is almost always justified in these purely economic terms. This applies even if a tougher rule-of-thumb test is run. Increased spending by visitors boosts state tax revenues. In a country such as Britain around 40 per cent of the spending would end up in government hands via various taxes. If so, then provided visitors spend at least two-and-a-half times as much as the government invested, there will be a net gain to public funds. Airola and Craig (2000) estimate that, if attracted, visitors' spending at a summer Olympics would boost Houston's economy by US \$2.1 billion. They estimate that the multiplier would raise this figure to \$4.34 billion. These are huge amounts of money for any city. Then they estimate that the legacy (the boost to the Houston economy by visitors attracted in subsequent years by the publicity surrounding an Olympics) would be worth \$756 million a year. These sums dwarf the costs of the new facilities required to host the event. A super-stadium would not cost more than \$1 billion.

Then there are said to be further, less tangible, gains by the hosts. First, they can enjoy the events themselves. They can join the crowds in the concert halls or sports stadiums, or they can stay on the streets and enjoy the carnival atmosphere. Second, the facilities built for megas are subsequently available to host later events, and otherwise for use by the host communities. This applies to any new dwellings, upgraded transport, swimming pools and so on. Finally, the city or the entire country is said to benefit from the pride and prestige that accrue to a successful host.

The case against

The case against is easily stated but difficult to measure. Do we really hold South Korea in higher regard since the 1988 Olympics? Or Italy since Italia '90? Gratton and Henry (2001) conclude their review of recent evidence and experience of the use of sport in attempts to regenerate cities with the verdict that 'the potential benefits to social and economic regeneration of sport in the city have not yet been clearly demonstrated' (p. 314). They argue that the true megas, the world leaders, definitely pay in strict economic terms, but that the economic case for lesser events is not clear-cut (see Gratton *et al.*, 2001; Shibli and Gratton, 2001). Gratton and Shibli note how rare it still is for proper impact studies to be undertaken despite the modest cost (around £5000, if done by a UK university-based team). Maybe it serves some interests to continue to rely on speculation! The facilities built for megas are unlikely to be exactly what would have been constructed had they been designed primarily for community use. When Sheffield enhanced its swimming facilities in order to attract international events (such as the 1991 World Student Games) it was forecast that, with the attractive new facilities, there was sure to be a rise in participation in swimming by the local population. Actually, during the next 10 years there was no increase whatsoever (Taylor, 2001). The City of Manchester Stadium, built, mainly with public money, for the 2002 Commonwealth Games, has been virtually given away to a private company – Manchester City Football Club (who, admittedly, had to hand over their existing 1923 vintage ground in exchange for the 60-year lease). Do the local populations really enjoy the experience when their cities are taken over by tourists? Hall (2001) has queried whether the people of Sydney really did enjoy, or benefit in any way from, the 2000 Olympics.

> The irony is that government, which is meant to be serving the public interest, is instead concentrating its interests on entrepreneurial and corporate rather than broader social goals (p 180).

Who cares whether England hosts another football World Cup? Many fans are indifferent. They are able to watch the matches on television wherever they are played. Many will not want to pay extortionate prices to attend matches when they have no personal interest in the outcomes. The jobs created by megas are usually temporary. Is this the best way of boosting an economy? Building leisure facilities for use by the locals would not act as an equal economic stimulus because no new money from outside would be drawn into the territory. Megas, and tourism promotion more generally, perform better if the aim is economic growth. But to what extent should leisure policy be geared mainly to this? Workers would almost certainly prefer investment in export-oriented manufacturing or service industries which would lead to steady, never-ending flows of sales and therefore long-term jobs. That said, if such market opportunities cannot be identified – and if they were identified, then private investment would probably be forthcoming – then the leisure option is arguably better than nothing. Poor jobs are probably better than no jobs.

The alleged benefits to a host population-at-large can be queried, whereas some groups gain substantially from megas and other events. Hotels, restaurants and transport businesses benefit. They enjoy a one-off bonanza from megas. The event organisers, and the elite sportspersons or artists who perform, are among the principal beneficiaries. So are media businesses. These are the interest groups that are really keen for England to host another football World Cup or, better still, an Olympics, then a World Athletics Championship and as many additional events as possible. Bent Flyvbjerg *et al.* (2003) have argued that the promoters of multi-billion dollar mega-events have consistently, systematically and self-servingly misinformed parliaments and the public in order to get events approved: they have under-estimated costs, over-estimated revenues, under-valued environmental impacts, and over-valued economic development effects. Maybe the logic of present-day governments' situations leaves them with little option but to become partners of event promoters and other commercial leisure businesses.

When the modern holiday first developed tourism was concentrated within a limited number of holiday resorts, and exactly who benefitted was less of an issue. Tourism was usually the base of the local economy. Resorts did not want factories and office blocks which would lessen their attractiveness to holiday-makers. Within the resorts, virtually all residents benefitted either directly or via the economic multiplier. Things are different today. Tourists have dispersed. Everywhere wants them, including places where tourism is not the greater part or the base of the local economy. So the benefits are concentrated among people who own, manage or work in tourism and event-related businesses while all tax payers contribute towards any necessary infrastructure and cope with the inconvenience of influxes of visitors.

In practice present-day governments can and do query the benefits of events, and sometimes the expansion of tourism more generally. In 2001 the UK government decided not to fund the construction of an athletics stadium in London that would be suitable for the 2005 World Championships. Earlier, the UK government had assured the sport that such a stadium would be constructed. This debacle has reduced the chances of the UK hosting any future high-profile sports events. Such equivocation would be less likely if all such plans were grounded in proper leisure policies. At one time it was envisaged that a reconstructed Wembley Stadium would be the site of the 2005 World Athletics Championships, a future (football) World Cup, and even an Olympics. Then football decided that it was interested only in a football stadium, not a multi-use sports arena. The crunch question for the Football Association was whether such a stadium would make money. Top sport has become a big-money business (see Chapter 7). Yet high-profile events and facilities always need government money. In 2003 the UK government decided to back London's bid for the 2012 Olympics. It was estimated that this would cost Britain around £2.4 billion, roughly equal to all local authority spending on leisure in a year. The 'investment', if the bid succeeds, will be from various public funds (mainly the National Lottery) but, whatever the specific funds the public-at-large will pay. Will all, most or just a minority of the contributors benefit from a London Olympics? Governments are understandably hesitant to deliver huge subsidies when they know that other parties stand to make huge profits from the projects. There are grounds for governments to be forever cautious, but they also need a clear grasp of all the benefits (many of which are not strictly economic) that can be gained, and can only be gained, through state-funded leisure initiatives. The UK could have obtained a new national football stadium plus an international class athletics arena, and still had spare change from the total cost of the Millennium Dome (just over £1 billion).

CONCLUSIONS

This chapter has defined events and has categorised them according to their size (minor, major and mega) and according to the types of activities on which they are based. It has explained why the relevant bodies have recently become keen to organise and host events of all kinds. The growth of tourism, the global reach of the present-day media, and governments' sensitivity and responsiveness to the economic importance of leisure, have been responsible.

We have seen that, whatever the event – although the larger the better – any public sector cash investment is usually repaid. It may also be argued that supporting events can be entirely compatible with the public sector's special socio-cultural capabilities in leisure: setting standards (provided aesthetic and moral yardsticks play a part when deciding which events to support), extending citizenship (in so far as all sections of a population feel that they are benefitting), and boosting the prestige and identity of the host places and people. The big problem with public sector support for events is that while all sections of a population pay, and while most sections may derive some benefit, the economic benefits are usually heavily skewed. This applies to state support for tourism in general nowadays, but the dilemma is starker with events, and starkest of all with the true mega-events.

Third-way thinking is needed. This provides three ground rules. First, public investment in events purely for economic reasons can be justified only in regions or countries where tourism is the dominant industry. Other governments that compete for events (and tourism more generally) play beggar-my-neighbour and cancel out each other's efforts to capture larger shares of a finite volume of business. So, second, for most cities, regions and countries there must be additional socio-cultural reasons for using public money to attract and run events, and none of the public sector's special socio-cultural capabilities in leisure (setting standards, boosting prestige and identity, and extending citizenship) can be served by anything other than truly prestigious events. Third, anything created with public money should be managed in the general public interest. Stadiums and concert halls should be managed and performances should be broadcast so as to maximise access rather than to maximise the earnings of performers and event promoters.

9 The Media and Popular Culture

Introduction

The mass media really do provide important leisure industries. Television-viewing alone accounts for around two-fifths of all leisure time. All governments have media policies; inevitably so, because the media are such an important part of people's lives and they are also big business. Nowadays Britain is just one country where it has become impossible to understand the government's media policies except in terms of encouraging further growth in the industry and gaining as large as possible a share of the global market. The manner in which the media have been developed by commerce has inspired some of the fiercest critiques of commercial leisure provision, most notably by the Frankfurt School and subsequent critics of postmodern consumer culture. Since the media are among the largest leisure industries, they offer an important test for critiques of commerce. All over the world, except under communism and fascism, state policy has always been to leave the regulation of the media primarily to the market. The main exception was broadcasting in European countries where it was treated, originally, basically as a public service. However, in recent times European broadcasting has undergone extensive commercialisation. Most governments have stood aside or even encouraged commercial 'invaders'. In 1980 around three-quarters of all European TV channels were public service. By 1995 over three-quarters were commercial (McCullagh, 2002). Why have governments stood aside? They have done so largely for business reasons. They realise that excluding or fettering commerce could cost trade and jobs. Present-day broadcasting offers some of the clearest illustrations of what is at risk if commercialisation is resisted or restricted, and also of what is vulnerable when public authorities withdraw from leisure provision.

There is a parallel between sport and the media, and this parallel is just one instance of a theme – commercialisation – that is present in all this book's chapters. One difference *vis-à-vis* sport is that most of the media – print, film and recorded sound – were developed commercially from the very beginning, but, as already mentioned, in Europe broadcasting was the big exception. Third-way thinking presumes that there are benefits in allowing commerce to do whatever it can and that critics of commercial popular cultures are mistaken. Simultaneously, the third way requires politicians and those who advise them to decide which, if any, of the public sector's special capabilities in leisure can and should be operationalised via media policies. Public service broadcasting and other media run as public services have capabilities that are simply beyond commerce. Access can be offered to all citizens. Publicly approved standards of news and entertainment can be upheld. The losses, if public service broadcasting dies, will be especially severe in the UK because the BBC has been a world leader in setting standards – a true prestige earner. The problem, with which all governments must grapple, is how to retain the benefits of public service media while allowing maximum scope for popular commercial products which widen people's leisure options and simultaneously create swathes of new jobs – better jobs overall than in most of the leisure industries.

This chapter proceeds by outlining the historical development of the media. It then introduces the searing criticisms of the commercial 'culture industry' delivered by the Frankfurt School and its successors. Criticisms of the critiques are then presented, leading into a rounded examination of the character of present-day popular culture and the commercial businesses that are its main suppliers. The roles of governments and the public sector, and the fate of public service broadcasting, are then examined in detail in the following chapter.

Development

We speak of mass media when a communicator can reach an audience beyond the scope of 'live' sight and sound. So, the mass media are capable of reaching large audiences, and the audiences are created by the media. Audiences are not usually from any specific neighbourhood, social class, church or any other organisation. The media create their own viewer, listener and reader groups. These may be drawn unequally from the various socio-demographic groups, but the audiences are not co-terminous with any previously existing formations. Communication is basically one way. This remains the case despite so-called interactive television. Live phone-ins and studio audiences are carefully managed. The audience may write or phone in or email or post messages on websites. During some programmes digital viewers can select camera angles or player-cams, or partisan commentators at sports events. Even so, it is still necessary for newspapers and broadcasters to conduct market research before they have any firm idea about an audience's size, social composition or its reactions to a message. The telephone is interactive. The internet may be used interactively (as in chat rooms). Television is still basically just one way.

Print was the first medium of mass communication. William Caxton invented the printing press in 1478. Thereafter it was possible to mass produce books, magazines, pamphlets and newspapers, but the circulations were usually tiny by present-day standards. In Britain the 'popular' press was created towards the end of the nineteenth century. The *Daily Mail*, Britain's first popular newspaper, was founded in 1896 followed by the *Daily Mirror* in 1903. These were daily newspapers with national circulations which were read by people in all social classes (but mainly the working class). By the end of the nineteenth century advances in printing technology and the availability of cheap paper for newsprint had been joined by the telephone and the telegraph, railways and a literate population to make mass circulation (in the modern sense) newspapers viable. Newspapers have always been regulated primarily by competition. Newspaper owners and editors claim that this gives readers a choice of opinions. To an extent this is true, but by the First World War competition from the mass circulation dailies had all but wiped out more radical publications with smaller readerships (Curran, 1977; Lee, 1976).

By the end of the nineteenth century the basic technologies already existed on which additional mass media are now based. Recorded sound, moving pictures and wireless had been invented, but the uses to which these inventions would be put remained unclear. Before the First World War short movies were being shown to paying audiences in fairground booths and in high street store-type premises and subsequently in grander film theatres (see Box 9.1). Then, Hollywood began to produce feature length movies. Sound was added before the end of the 1920s and by then picture palaces were being opened throughout the world and the age of Hollywood had started.

Sales of gramophones and records began to take off after the First World War when radio began to develop. By then discs played on turntables had replaced the revolving cylinders which carried the first recordings (see Box 9.2). The gramophone was among the new range of consumer goods sold by department and mail-order stores. Worldwide sales of recorded music have grown fairly steadily ever since, although internet piracy may cause a more serious and lasting downturn in legal sales.

BOX 9.1 MOVING PICTURES

In 1888 W K L Dickson, assistant to Thomas Edison, created the kinetograph which made short moving pictures. These were intended to be shown peep-show style in a kinetoscope. However, the French were the first to lay on a theatrical performance of a moving picture. This was in Paris in 1895. The French had developed a superior and lighter camera, the cinematographe. Edison followed quickly and displayed a film to a New York audience in 1896. Up until the First World War, European film-makers were every bit as inventive and successful as their American counterparts. In 1907 London's first film theatre opened, and by 1910 London had around 300 of them. This new leisure industry was then expanding rapidly.

America established a decisive lead only during the First World War when Europe was pre-occupied with other things. Before the end of the war, America was producing 'full length' feature movies which were attracting large audiences to picture houses. Soon afterwards Los Angeles became the main US centre of moving picture production. Its attractions were the sun and the varied landscape.

The first sound picture was *The Jazz Singer* (1927).

Sources: www.thomasedison.com, www.precinemahistory.net

BOX 9.2 RECORDED SOUND

Thomas Edison invented the phonograph in 1877. The sound was reproduced from rotating sheets of tinfoil.

In 1893 Emile Berliner produced the first disc with a recording on just one side, to be played on a hand-driven gramophone.

The double-sided disc was patented in 1904, and by 1923 the gramophones were mechanically driven and all the recording companies were using these technologies. A mass market developed during the 1920s when radio created a mass demand for a new type of popular music.

The original record with one number on each side was joined, after the Second World War, by extended and long-playing discs. Cassette tapes and CDs have subsequently become the recorded music industry's main products. The video-tape and subsequently the digital video-disc (DVD) have made it possible to add pictures to the sound, and these have also become alternative ways of distributing films.

Sources: http://memory.loc.gov/ammem/berlhtml/berlhome.html, www.ovationtv.com/artszone/programs/bigbangs/berliner.html

---

From the start, films and recorded music, like the press, developed as commercial leisure industries. Broadcasting developed rather differently in Britain and most other European countries. From the outset it was subject to much tighter state regulation. The British Broadcasting Company was formed in 1922 by a group of radio manufacturers who had decided that the way to make money out of radio was to sell receivers to households, and to broadcast programmes that would create a demand for the equipment. Almost immediately the British Broadcasting Company was granted monopoly rights and subjected to state regulation. It was nationalised, and became the British Broadcasting Corporation (BBC), in 1927. Radio was regarded as a natural monopoly because air space was limited and, in any case, governments at that time were concerned about the anticipated power of the new medium. They believed that broadcasters, by speaking directly into all the nation's homes, would be able to shape people's tastes and opinions. The use of radio and other media by the totalitarian governments in Nazi Germany and Stalin's Soviet Union in the 1930s appeared to endorse these concerns. Broadcasting, it was believed, would be dangerous if left in private hands, or if broadcasters were under the pressure of market competition. There were fears that broadcasters would pander to a 'lowest common denominator'. The UK's BBC was to be a more responsible 'paternalist', but politically neutral, broadcaster. John (Lord) Reith, the BBC's first director-general, wanted broadcasting to educate, inform and entertain the whole nation free from both political interference and commercial pressures.

Broadcasting developed differently in America where there was less fear of the market and deeper reservations about anything that looked socialist. In any case, the sheer size of the USA meant that there was no danger of a single broadcaster being able to command the entire population. Thus from the outset, in America, broadcasting was a commercial business, funded by advertising. There have always been public service slots within the USA's commercial channels, public service programme makers, and even entire public service radio and TV channels funded by non-profit organisations and state sources, but in America they have always operated within a basically commercial industry. In most European countries, in the early years of broadcasting, this situation was reversed. Commerce had wedges within what was basically a public service. 'Light' commercial-type entertainment was not allowed to dominate the air-waves. However, the radio did enable its star entertainers to become household names throughout their countries, and rich by the standards of the time. In Britain the radio elevated to stardom the likes of Kenneth Horne, Jimmy Edwards, Peter Sellers, Tony Hancock and Wilfred Pickles (see Box 9.3).

Radio broadcasting quickly became a huge success not just in Britain but all over the world. Take-up was rapid in the economically advanced countries. Over a million ten-shilling (50 p) radio licences had already been sold prior to broadcasting commencing in Britain in 1922. During the 1930s in Britain the wireless became standard domestic equipment. This was the age of radio. In Britain television broadcasting, by the BBC, commenced in 1936, was suspended during the Second World War, then resumed afterwards, and the television set rapidly replaced the radio as the staple source of family entertainment and news. The age of television had commenced and has lasted up to the present day.

Throughout their development all the mass media have adapted to and influenced one another. During the second half of the twentieth century all the other pre-existing media were obliged to accommodate the dominant position of television. Radio lost its truly mass audience and has adapted by filling niches that television cannot, or fails to, fill: in-car entertainment, local news and gossip, and continuous music, for example. Radio has adapted so successfully that by 2001, in Britain, total listening time exceeded total TV viewing time. Radio has staged a truly remarkable recovery. From its birth, recorded music has depended on the radio to

---

BOX 9.3 *HAVE A GO*

This weekly, live and unscripted BBC radio show ran from 1946 until 1967. The host was Wilfred Pickles, the first man on the BBC with a regional (Yorkshire) accent. Wilfred Pickles began as an amateur actor, made his first broadcast in 1927, then became an occasional announcer for the BBC. In 1946 he was invited to compere *Have a Go*, and both the show and its compere were instant successes. Wilfred Pickles fought successfully against all the BBC's efforts to make him use bland received pronunciation.

Basically a quiz, with a top prize of just £1.05 at first, *Have a Go* travelled the length and breadth of Britain. Violet Carson (who became Ena Sharples in *Coronation Street*) was the show's resident pianist until 1953.

Have a Go was one of Britain's most popular radio shows ever. It regularly attracted audiences of 20 million. In its 20 years the programme travelled 400,000 miles. It never went to anywhere twice and received enough invitations to have kept going for 1500 years.

Sources: www.whirligig-tv.co.uk/radio/
www.thisisbradford.co.uk/bradford_district/100_years/1948.htm

broadcast and create a demand for new releases. These industries support one another rather than compete. The cinema, like the radio, lost most of its earlier mass audience to television. In Britain there were 1.35 billion cinema admissions in 1951 which had declined to just 53 million in 1984 (the low point to date). The film-making industry has adapted by producing for television, or for the cinema with a view to video then television distribution. Cinema houses have been redesigned, scaled down and divided into multiplexes, to cater for smaller, sometimes specialist audiences (of foreign and 'art' films, for example) which may be neglected by terrestrial television. As radio and subsequently television became the public's main sources of news, the press adapted either, in the case of the tabloids, by concentrating on sport, entertainment and news about other media, especially television, or, in the case of the broadsheets, by providing news coverage and comment in greater depth than radio and television. Newspaper sales have declined during the 'age of television' but in Britain three-fifths of all men and a half of all women still read a national daily. However, UK adults spend an average of just 6 hours a week on all types of reading whereas they spend over 3 hours each day watching television (BBC, 2002). We should note that newspaper readers are still reading the paper versions despite the newspapers now being published, and available free-of-charge, over the internet. This is an instance where the internet could, but will not necessarily, replace other media. It is possible, but not inevitable, that people will soon obtain all their entertainment, news, music and films via the internet (see Chapter 10, pp. 148–52).

The production of popular arts

All the present-day popular arts have been created by or with crucial assistance from the mass media. It is their mass delivery that enables these arts to become popular in the present-day sense. These arts are all distinctively commercial products. Neither the voluntary nor the public sector of the leisure industries could produce them. It is not just that the entertainment is popular only against commercial criteria; the art forms will be produced only under commercial pressures. Music is a good example.

Two conditions must be met before popular music will be produced. First, there must be media of mass communication, and the radio has always been crucial for the pop music business. Throughout the world, radio has always been, and remains, the place where new releases are most likely to be first heard by the people who are most likely to become purchasers (London and Hearder, 1997). The radio enables releases to be popularised quickly across a country and, nowadays, all over the world. Of course, music was popular before radio, but the artists of that era performed to live audiences and usually had local reputations which occasionally spread further afield. These artists were able, and were expected by their audiences, to perform much the same programmes year after year. The second condition is that there must be a product which can be sold for profit. At first this was sheet music, but before the Second World War this had been overtaken in value by sales of recordings – initially 'records', then also tapes, later CDs, and this list will continue to need updating repeatedly.

The Frankfurt School

All the leisure industries have critics. Commerce attracts criticism wherever it spreads. Some criticisms are specific to, or have arisen in response to, particular leisure industries such as sport. Tourism has been accused of degrading environments, debasing local cultures, and locking host populations in dependency relationships. We shall see in later chapters that restaurants, the drinks industry and gambling all have critics. Likewise, the popular arts have always attracted fierce criticism, especially from people who credit themselves with higher tastes. Popular culture is dubbed lowbrow and accused of drowning out superior products. However, the most searing and enduring attack on the popular 'culture industry' originates with the Frankfurt School.

The critique

The Frankfurt School is the name given to a group of 'critical theorists' who all worked at the Frankfurt Institute for Social Research in the period following its foundation in 1922. The key writers on the (capitalist) culture industry were Theodor Adorno, Walter Benjamin, Max Horkheimer and Herbert Marcuse. They were Marxists, but not party-liners. Rather, they set out to rectify what they perceived as weaknesses in Marx's own work and in the Marxism of their time. The outcome was a new approach to sociological analysis called 'critical theory'. Here we need not review the entire approach except to note that the Frankfurt School highlighted the importance of culture instead of presuming that, even in the final analysis, the economic base determined everything else when analysing the capitalist society of their time. With the rise of fascism the members of the Frankfurt School found Germany inhospitable, and relocated to New York. The institute returned to Frankfurt in 1949 and remained there until it was formally closed in 1969.

Up until the First World War, Marxists had explained (to their own satisfaction) why revolution was inevitable in capitalist countries and why there would not be long to wait. By the 1920s free-thinking Marxists were asking why there had been no revolutions in the most mature capitalist countries. They realised that Russia was not the place where, according to Marx's theory, the revolution should have begun. All the answers given by Marxists to the 'Why no revolution?' question have recognised that the working class has not been held back solely by its need to subsist and political repression. They have identified additional, more subtle, processes whereby workers are made willing prisoners. Lenin himself, in his theory of imperialism, argued that by exploiting colonies the colonising countries were able to allow their own workers to enjoy standards of living in excess of the subsistence level to which Marx believed they would be confined. A set of ideas, which were labelled 'the embourgeoisement thesis' in the 1950s, argued that by conceding improvements in living standards, and encouraging workers to seek further gains, the proletariat could be locked into a basically exploitative capitalist system. The Frankfurt School joined in these debates by identifying additional processes whereby the willing imprisonment of the working class was accomplished. In their view, the 'culture industry' that capitalism produced played a crucial role. The members of the Frankfurt School were responding to post-First World War developments such as radio broadcasting, Hollywood and the popular music that was then cascading from 'Tin Pan Alley' (see Adorno and Horkheimer, 1977). They were influenced by their experience in Germany, but no less so by what they experienced as the superficial and, in its own way, equally oppressive mass culture of America.

The Frankfurt argument is that capitalism's culture industry is run for profit and operates so as to maximise profit. The key to this is to learn quickly from experience what works – the kinds of plots and stars who draw audiences into cinemas, and the singers, lyrics and melodies that sell – and to repeat each successful formula again and again with only minor variations. What works is invariably simple and easily understood. The cultural products can therefore become popular objects of mass appeal very quickly. So people will queue to see the latest film and will flock to buy the latest recording by a popular artist. Their interest in each product is soon quenched, but by this time a similar but slightly different product will be on the market to repeat the cycle. Operating in this way maximises sales and profits, but the Frankfurt School went on to examine (or to speculate about) the effects on audiences. They claimed that audiences were distracted from their woes and socialised into passivity; that entertainment was the new narcotic. (Marx had argued that religion was the opium of the people.) The Frankfurt School alleged that it was the capitalist culture industry that tamed potentially rebellious workers and turned them into compliant citizens. Adorno believed that popular music itself, through its repetitive composition, affected consciousness and acted as a form of social control (DeNora, 2003).

> The power of the culture industry's ideology is such that conformity has replaced consciousness ... the total effect of the culture industry is one of anti-enlightenment ... it impedes the development of autonomous, independent individuals who judge and decide consciously for themselves.
>
> (Adorno, 1996, pp. 90–2)

The Frankfurt School recognised, as Marxists would, that these outcomes were not inevitable and that the cycle could be broken. Walter Benjamin, in particular, realised that giving workers free time placed capitalism at risk (see Rojek, 1997). Workers had time to develop their own organisations – trade unions and political parties, for example – and to reflect on their condition. They could educate themselves in evening classes, or less formally in their own arts and sports organisations. The Frankfurt School was aware of the voluntary sector and how workers had organised themselves into sports teams, brass bands and such like, developing social bonds and skills that were susceptible to politicisation. This remains the leisure policy agenda of some socialists (Tomlinson, 1990). However, the Frankfurt authors were, and all their successors have been, aware that the capitalist industries have been winning the battle for workers' attention.

The Frankfurt School did most of its innovative thinking between the 1920s and the 1940s, but it was not until after the Second World War that most of their work was translated into English and other languages and became widely known throughout the international social science community. By then the culture industries were growing from strength to strength, which made the arguments more relevant than ever. In the 1950s and 1960s consumer society and consumer culture were developing rapidly. Against this backcloth, a new generation of scholars built on the Frankfurt theory to develop a critique of the 'postmodern' consumer society into which workers are said to be bound, not so much through the relationships of production as by relationships and cultures of consumption. French writers have referred to the 'culture industries' rather than 'industry' in recognition that the industries are less unified and more complex than the original Frankfurt analysis suggested. However, basic features of the Frankfurt position have been retained by some of these authors – the Marxist base, and the view of popular culture as oppressive. Jean Baudrillard (1998) contends that amid the profusion of goods and services that advanced capitalism has produced – goods surrounded by consumer culture – the distinction between the image and any underlying reality breaks down and simulations can become reality for all practical purposes. So people become imprisoned in a hyper-reality. People relate to characters in television soap operas as if they were real people. The symbolic associations of certain commodities – jeans and trainers, for instance – are said to be as important to the purchaser as the object's practical uses. The present-day bounty of goods, all with attractive images, is said to give the appearance that everyone is happy. Individuals who feel otherwise are likely to believe that they are odd exceptions and that their failure is due to their own inadequacies rather than pathologies of the socio-economic system.

Neil Ravenscroft et al. (2001) have employed this thinking in their analysis of the movie-house industry in Singapore, where, as in other parts of the world, the standard outlet is now the multiplex. In Singapore these are typically located in shopping malls. Cinema-goers have a choice of films and arrival times, and going to the cinema, and being in and around the multiplexes, is intended to be a wholly pleasurable experience. We are told that people do indeed experience choice and pleasure. However, Ravenscroft and his colleagues argue that the cinema-goers' scope for choice is really quite narrow. All the Singapore multiplexes are likely to be offering the same batch of films at any single time, and all the films are products of the market economy. People's freedom and pursuit of pleasure are wholly contained within the over-arching structures of their society.

There are several key arguments in this neo-Marxist critique of the so-called culture industry or industries and the popular cultures that they manufacture. First, capitalism needs consumers as surely as it needs workers; a consumers' strike would be just as crippling. Second, as capitalism expands and basic needs are satisfied, people must be persuaded to consume a new array of non-essential cultural products. Third, in practice it proves far easier to make people want to consume than to want to work, so people become enslaved by consumerism – incorporated into the capitalist system. Capitalism gives, or appears to give, people the things that they want. Even if they are not content, it makes them feel that they ought to be.

Once people become part of this system, no alternative may be even imaginable. Thus the system can become hegemonic, experienced as an unquestionable fact of life, like the weather.

Objections

What are we to make of this critique? Some of its points are clearly correct. The popular music, cinema and broadcasting industries do seek, then repeat, winning formulas. What is successful is invariably simple and therefore easily appreciated by a mass audience. However, the fact that some of the thesis's observations are sound should not seduce anyone into digesting the whole package. Also, changes in the 'culture industry' over the last 60 years need to be taken into account. Arguments that were justified in the 1920s and 1930s have sometimes been overtaken by subsequent developments.

There are five serious objections to the Frankfurt arguments. First, capitalism cannot win: it loses both ways when viewed through Marxist spectacles. Capitalism would be condemned if, in spite of the possibilities opened up by its technologies and productivity, workers were given no more leisure time than was strictly necessary to re-create their labour power, and wages which covered no more than their basic needs. Capitalism is also condemned if it provides more free time, and higher incomes, so that workers can indulge additional wants. All societies are systems of interdependent parts, so it is inevitably the case that each part will in some way contribute to the maintenance of the whole. A key Marxist observation – that the consumer aspirations which are both stimulated and satisfied by capitalism, and which give advanced capitalism some of its distinctive characteristics, are among the reasons why the system endures – is true, but also truly unremarkable rather than a crushing indictment.

Second, the wares offered by the culture industries are not quite as standardised as the Frankfurt School claimed. (Note that such claims have not been made by subsequent writers on the culture *industries*.) It is true that cultural production is industrialised, up to a point (see below, p. 135) and that successive products remain faithful to their brands. But the film industry has more than one story-line. Similarly, there are many types of commercial popular music, more so today than in the 1920s and 1930s. Kiddie-pop is different from the various kinds of 'serious' rock. All the popular musical genres of the present day and earlier decades, including rock's predecessor, now called easy listening, remain available. Consumers are not only able, but are required, to be discriminating.

This leads into the third criticism. Consumers are more active than the Frankfurt writers envisaged, and their activity extends beyond deciding which brand of entertainment to passively absorb. Early studies of the printed media's political influence discovered a two-step flow of communication: from the media into primary groups where messages are filtered and evaluated, then to individuals. Television is received in a broadly similar way. Households do not just watch whatever happens to be on. Channels are chosen, sometimes argued over, by household members, and likewise the events and characters in soap operas and dramas (McCullagh, 2002; Morley, 1986). In the 1960s a group of sociologists at Birmingham University's Centre for Contemporary Cultural Studies explained how, in post-war working class youth cultures, the kids on the streets, from teddy boys to skinheads, had actually created these styles and, in doing so, had given new connotations to the commercial products (Hall and Jefferson, 1976). David Rowe (1995) has argued that all popular cultures are, at least potentially, subversive. Capitalism will feed whatever tastes are profitable – popular music with psychedelic messages or which celebrates revolution, for example.

Fourth, the commercial culture industry has not operated like a steamroller, obliterating other kinds of leisure provision. This is still a vibrant voluntary sector and extensive public provision. Local dramatic and operatic societies are still performing. High culture is not in decline (see Chapter 13). Commerce has certainly not achieved a total take-over. Moreover, if we scan the full range of commercial leisure provision, we see much that is not keeping the population passively amused and entertained. Rather, commerce also provides environments (bars and restaurants, for example) in which people can make their own leisure experiences (see Chapter 11). It is only commerce that is prepared to offer a minimal service on which consumers can then build, provided the service pays. Chapter 4 explained that public provision is likely to prove sustainable in the long term only if there are transparent public as well as private benefits. The voluntary sector always wants some of its users to become participants in the associations rather than just visitors seeking private pleasures. Commerce does not have these limitations.

Fifth, capitalist leisure provision is not hegemonic. People are aware of public and voluntary sector alternatives. Some are aware that the former socialist countries were largely free of commercial temptations. Western populations were not converted by what they knew about the socialist way of life, or by what they glimpsed when they spent holidays in those countries. In contrast, communism collapsed partly because the populations demanded access to Western lifestyles. What they sought was not wholly a mirage. Since 'the reforms' commenced, the Western way of life has entered their own countries. Most people are still too poor to avail themselves of most of these new consumption opportunities, but, having seen them close-up, their appetites have been strengthened rather than extinguished (see Roberts et al., 2000).

To repeat, aspects of the Frankfurt School's analysis of how the pop business maximises profit were not only basically correct in the early years of Tin Pan Alley and Hollywood but remain basically correct today in certain sections of the industries. Record producers discover which artists, melodies and lyrics are popular, then release endless similar numbers. Each release is 'plugged' until it becomes a hit or is abandoned quickly if it flops (as has always happened to most releases). Hits have brief periods of popularity while the recordings are purchased. All who are likely to purchase usually do so quickly, after which the number drops out of the charts and is replaced by a similar product. This formula maximises sales and profits. The same principles apply to popular TV programmes and 'blockbuster' films. All the popular present-day arts depend on the mass media to achieve their popularity. Radio, TV, films and the printed media are the sources of popular culture. They all 'manufacture' popularity in basically the same way. Popular soap operas present endless sketches by the same characters, in the same places, confronting the same batch of problems. Game shows, comedy series and individual entertainers use the same formula. Film-makers produce repetitions of the *Rocky*, *James Bond*, *Terminator*, *Star Wars* and other successful genres. Hit formulae and artists are screened repeatedly. Every time it is basically the same, but just a little different.

Popular culture today

There are other constants in the culture industries. Producing cultural products commercially has always been high risk. The Frankfurt School somehow overlooked this rather basic fact. Most products flop, and most revenue is generated by a relatively small number of hits. This applies in films, music and books. Production costs tend to be high relative to reproduction costs, so really big hits are extraordinarily profitable (Hesmondhalgh, 2002). However, much has changed since the early days of Hollywood, recorded music and radio. Technology has provided video, the internet, fibre optic cable and satellite communications. Sounds and pictures now travel around the world more rapidly than ever before. Consumer choice has widened. There are now hundreds of television and radio channels to surf. There are more record labels and types of pop and rock. It is unrealistic for most producers to try to satisfy everyone. Mass markets have splintered and products have to be aimed at specific market segments.

In a sense, consumers have always been part of the cultural production process. Their record purchasing, cinema going and radio listening have told the industries what to produce. Producers have always needed to be streetwise. Once upon a time they may have relied on intuition and personal social networks. Nowadays they commission market research. Suzanne Schulz (2002) has explained how, in the high street fashion trade, designers, merchandisers and buyers debate what to produce with reference to an image of 'our lady', the target customer group. This 'accords customers a central role throughout the selection stages and hence puts fashion production and consumption into a dialectical relationship'. Even so, there is a far from perfect match between the public's actual tastes and the flow of output from the popular culture industries.

Measuring popularity

Explanations of the types of music, films, soap operas and so on that are produced in terms of the structure and operations of the relevant industries are far more successful than attempts to match the products to audience characteristics (see Frith, 1978, 1988; Negus, 1999). This is rather important. It shows that the industries are neither responding to nor shaping popular taste in a direct and simple way. It shows that the consumers of the popular arts are able to form and preserve their own judgments. Hit records are popular only according to the industry's criteria – sales during the last week. The industry tries to convince us that its hits are our top 10, 20 and 40, but there are other ways of measuring popularity. A 1998 opinion poll which asked a representative British sample for their all-time favourite performers resulted in a top five of the Beatles, Sinatra, Presley, Queen and Elton John. Robbie Williams was ranked 85. Another way of measuring popularity is how many times a composition has been recorded. *Stardust* and *Rudolph the Red Nosed Reindeer* both score highly on this criterion. A further measure of popularity is all-time sales. *White Christmas* is still at, or near to, the top of these lists (see Harker, 1978). Likewise, audience size during the last week is just one way – much publicised by the industries – of measuring the popularity of films and TV programmes. These are the industries' preferred way, but not a particularly objective way, of measuring popular appeal. Every individual will have a favourite TV programme that is no longer being broadcast.

It is noteworthy that the non-commercial branches of the culture industries rarely produce popular genres. Amateur choral societies rarely stage pop concerts. Drama societies rarely perform soap operas. Their repertoires are more likely to be middlebrow than highbrow but they tend to avoid 'pop'. This will only be produced by commerce, and both the breadth and depth of its popularity are suspect. Performers' enthusiasm alone is unlikely to prove sufficient to sustain production. This is why popular music and films will probably cease to be produced if people are allowed to give them away via the internet. If they have to work for the love of their arts and reputations alone, artists are unlikely to create popular entertainment as it currently exists.

Uses of popular music

Critics of popular music are mistaken if and when they imagine that the flow of releases resembles the way in which purchasers listen to the music: that one week people are fanatical about one number and have switched to something else a week later. Purchasers' behaviour corresponds to the charts only in their radio listening whereby they keep abreast of the scene. The charts are taken-for-granted knowledge among most groups of young people. They expect their peers to know what has been released and who is in the charts, while also expecting anyone aged over 15 to express disdain for all mainstream pop. Purchasers do not buy whatever happens to be number one. They have their own favourites and compile collections accordingly. This is what they play for themselves – their own all-time favourites – when they are alone or, since the advent of the Sony Walkman and its competitors, while walking down the street or on public transport.

Fans of particular types of music and performers may form clubs which act as grapevines on who is playing where, the latest underground releases and so on, and hold meetings at which they can compare their favourite numbers, rate other artists and types of music, and enjoy their own sounds in the company of others who share the taste. Recorded music is a self-servicing product. Once acquired, it can be played in any place, at any time of the owner's choosing. Commerce excels in providing goods with which, and environments where, people can entertain themselves. In a similar way, viewers put TV programmes and films to their own uses. They decide which soaps to follow assiduously and which characters to identify with. They thereby become personally involved in the stories. Viewers of game shows test themselves against the on-screen competitors. Consumers of popular culture are less passive than the Frankfurt School originally suggested.

With music, as with holiday packages and venues for going out, commerce has proved its ability to design attractive but simple products which people can put to their own uses. Individuals, groups of friends and more formal clubs do this with popular, and other, musical genres. So do other businesses. High street shops play background music which links their product ranges to the audiences and whatever meanings and broader lifestyles have become associated, on a socio-cultural level, with the types of music in question (DeNora and Belcher, 2000). Particular recordings, and types of music, may be adopted by followers of a particular sport or team, leading to cross-overs and fusions between music-based and other cultures (see Redhead, 1993).

Types of pop

Nowadays one really needs to be aged over 70 to believe that it is all the same. The Frankfurt School exaggerated the extent to which the culture industry emits standardised products. The fact is that there are dozens of popular standards and none are stable. The analysis of the Frankfurt School may have been a reasonable interpretation of how the 'culture industry' operated in the 1920s and 1930s, but the entire scene has changed since then. The long-playing recording rather than the single has become the main product. Most purchasers, like holiday-makers (see Chapter 5, p. 68), appear to have become much more sophisticated. They now have definite preferences for particular kinds of music and performers. They also have a wider choice of record labels and radio channels. In the long term, commercial markets do not homogenise. All providers distinguish and target, and thereby help to create or consolidate, separate market segments and niches. The map of popular music is complicated. Every teenager (and older people, if they try) will map the field differently. That said, there is now a distinct variety of kiddie-pop, often played by boy- and girl-bands, which is just one part of the mainstream pop (Top 20) scene. Mainstream is a benchmark against which most teenagers define their own more sophisticated tastes in more serious kinds of rock (Railton, 2000). Who says that it is more serious? It is just the performers and their audiences. Individuals are usually especially keen on a particular genre or a trend within one, or a certain performer of drum and bass, one of the retros, technos, metals, garage, goth, acid, house/dance compilations, reggae and so on. Nowadays the audiences for all the popular arts are selective. No-one can keep abreast of everything that is offered. In culture, as in other markets, commerce offers a huge variety of 'brands'.

It is true that the recording industry is dominated by its majors. Just five companies (Vivendi-Universal, AOL-Time Warner, Sony, EMI/Virgin and Bertelsmann) are responsible for roughly 80 per cent of worldwide sales. They are not all well-known (see Box 9.4 for a profile of Bertelsmann). All these businesses are in fact multimedia conglomerates, and they all operate all over the world. Nowadays popular culture is global. That said, none of the majors has just one product line. They need stakes in all the genres if they are to remain majors, and they must constantly recruit new talent and absorb smaller 'independent' record companies (see McDonald, 1999; Smith and Maughan, 1997). Most of the independent record companies, or 'indies', are linked to the majors via licensing, franchise and distribution deals. Cultural workers move freely between their industry's major and minor sectors (Hesmondhalgh, 2002). Exactly the same applies to TV broadcasters and film-makers. Pop conglomerates need to be flexible. Cultural production simply cannot be fully industrialised. Creative staff have to be given some autonomy, which is compatible with small and large enterprises' need for flexibility. At present all media businesses are having to learn to live with the internet. It may have been declared illegal for third parties to give away their products but this does not prevent it happening. At any time it is estimated that over 100 million music tracks are posted on the web and are available for free downloading. Then there are the more conventional forms of piracy – the illegal copying and selling of discs and tapes. The internet has serious (potentially disastrous) implications for the manufacturing and distribution chains in the popular culture industries. If the majors discover that they can sell directly over the

---

BOX 9.4 BERTELSMANN AG

Bertelsmann AG is an international media corporation with over 9500 employees and a 2001 turnover of over €3.5 billion. Bertelsmann has more than 200 separate record labels, including:

Arista Records	La Face Records
BMG Classics	RCA
Buddha Records	RLG
J Records	

Its recording artists include:

Christina Aguilera	Santana
Alabama	George Winston
Toni Braxton	Westlife
Whitney Houston	Pink
Kenny G	Will Young
Andy Lau	Gareth Gates
Alicia Keys	

In 2001 Bertelsmann departed from the traditional record industry strategy of splitting its staff into separate labels. Staff are now divided by musical genre: dance, pop, R&B, and so on.

Source: www.bmg.com

internet (as is most likely, eventually) what will happen to all the record shops, disc manufacturing companies and distributors? Maybe the majors themselves will be bypassed and artists will sell directly to the public via the internet.

The immense variety that is marketed (and this applies to fashion clothing as much as to other popular art forms) makes commercial products, and the meanings associated with them, excellent building blocks for constructing or expressing an individual identity. Young people do not listen to and purchase whatever everyone else likes. They make individual choices so that they can 'stick out' and express their individuality (Miles, 2000; van der Poel, 1994), albeit, in most cases, within the limits defined as acceptable among their associates. The point of relevance here is that only commerce, with the variety of products that it offers, allows such numerous variations in individuality to be expressed and thereby helps to create, or consolidates, individual differences and sensitivity to them. Voluntary and public sector provisions are simply less malleable.

Clubbing

In recent years 'clubbing' has probably been the definitive youth, or young singles, leisure activity. They nearly all do it at some time or another, and members of older age groups simply do not understand the club scene which was created in Britain in the late-1980s and early-1990s inspired by holiday experiences in Ibiza and other Mediterranean resorts, and preceded by impromptu open air or warehouse raves (see Critcher, 2000). Clubbing confers a collective identity. Among other things, it enables the 30- and even 40-somethings who go to be classed as 'young'. There is a common experience of getting ready, going into town, on to a club, then exiting later. The club scene is highly differentiated (see Malbon, 1999; Thornton, 1995). Particular venues are associated with particular genres of rock. Particular DJs, and nights of the week, establish their own reputations and crowds. The clubbing experience is one of intense sociality. Everyone is friendly, loving the music and very likely using the same 'substances'. These scenes are extremely fluid. A particular crowd can form and disintegrate within months. Rather than expressing the identities of groups of clubbers who are already bonded by their similar family and neighbourhood backgrounds, music-based sub-cultures create their own communities, or proto-communities as they are sometimes labelled to distinguish them from more enduring formations (see Bennett, 2000). Neither voluntary nor public leisure providers can offer true functional equivalents.

CONCLUSIONS

This chapter has traced the development of the mass media from their origins in technologies that were mostly invented towards the end of the nineteenth century. We have seen that commerce was the main motor that developed the new technologies – printing, radio, moving pictures and recorded music – into major leisure industries. Perhaps not surprisingly, given the breadth of their appeal, commerce's uses of these technologies has led to harsh criticism, most notably from the Frankfurt School and later critics of commercial consumer culture.

Some of the critics' points are valid, but this chapter has shown that some distinctive features of commercial media products can be regarded as strengths. The commercial media offer a variety of products that consumers can put to their own varied uses. Commerce has not standardised everyone's tastes. It has not eliminated voluntary sector cultural production. We still have amateur drama and operatic societies, and unpaid rock bands perform in public, interacting directly with their audiences and thereby establishing local reputations. Commerce has not and cannot steamroller governments aside. There is no need for those who dislike the products to try to suppress commerce. The big policy issue, featured in the next chapter, is how to enjoy the benefits of commerce and public service media simultaneously.

10 The Media: Recent Developments

Introduction

The recent developments in this chapter are all based, at least in part, on the latest wave of new technology. This has given us new items of leisure equipment, such as the mobile phone and the PC, and new play areas in cyberspace. The same new technologies have wrought change in publishing, film and recorded music, and they are creating a revolution in broadcasting.

This chapter opens with an overview of the relationships that have prevailed in Western countries between the mass media and governments. Western governments have usually left media regulation to the market plus the industries' own self-regulation bodies such as the British Board of Film Censors and the Press Complaints Commission. Rather than the state being empowered by the media, there has been more concern about the power of media 'barons', including their ability to use their wealth and media influence as springboards into political careers.

European broadcasting used to be the big exception to the absence of government control. Thus a distinctive type of public service broadcasting, exemplified by the BBC, was brought into being. This chapter outlines the main features of 'traditional' public service broadcasting, then explains how and why European broadcasting has recently been transformed from a public service into basically another commercial industry. We shall see that this has been a result of terrestrial competition, satellite, cable and digital broadcasting, and globalisation. The outcomes are that consumer choice has been extended and state control has been eroded. The costs and benefits of this transformation are then discussed.

The final chapter section deals with how information and communications technology (ICT) may revolutionise our leisure, or how it may be assimilated into established patterns. We shall see that much is likely to depend on exactly who, if anyone, takes charge of cyberspace. Will it be commerce? Up to now cyberspace has been a risky place to invest. Will governments take charge? Or will this new technology give a boost to civil society?

The state and the media

Governments have always had media policies even if and when the policy has been one of non-intervention. They need to regulate access to broadcasting air space because a free-for-all would negate everyone's interests. There are other reasons for governments to take some interest in all the media. One of the principal reasons is the actual or potential political influence of the media. Newspapers were the first truly mass media and some of the early 'press barons' (newspaper owners) were explicit in their desire to sway public opinion and thereby governments. The response of Western governments has been to leave the press 'free' and to rely on competition between newspapers to prevent any single publication from exerting undue influence. Indeed, the existence of a 'free press' is often regarded as a litmus test of whether a country is genuinely democratic. However, this is a viewpoint propagated by the press themselves. The arguments ignore the unlikelihood of 'free' newspapers opposing a 'free' enterprise market economy.

Films and recorded music have always been produced primarily for profit rather than to propagate political messages, but politicians have sometimes been nervous that these media could be infiltrated by dissenters, intent on subtly indoctrinating the public. Hence the post-Second World War campaign by Senator McCarthy to identify communists and exclude them from Hollywood. There are repeated moral panics about the lyrics in particular kinds of popular music which are variously regarded as promoting promiscuity, rebellion, racism and xenophobia.

Researchers who have tried to measure the political influence of the media have usually found it difficult to detect any short-term effects, such as during election campaigns. They have discovered that people are most likely to expose themselves to views with which they are pre-disposed to agree. Otherwise they may ignore or discount what they hear and read. Films and song lyrics may be enjoyed purely as entertainment. Likewise it has proved impossible to establish any causal link between media portrayals of sex and violence and how people behave in their everyday lives (McCullagh, 2002). Most media researchers have now abandoned the search for direct effects and have concentrated, on the one hand, on how reality is represented, or framed, by the media, and, on the other hand, how the messages are understood and interpreted by their audiences. The significance of these research topics must be diminished by the absence of clear evidence of media effects, but this has not prevented media studies from becoming one of social science's boom areas. All that said, it is likely that the media have long-term drip-drip effects which are difficult to measure precisely because they are long-term, and over a long period it is impossible to prevent other influences contaminating any measurements. For example, it is likely, though impossible to prove, that persistent press criticism, combined with stories of sleaze and personal misdemeanours, has weakened the public's trust in politicians. Nowadays our knowledge about the wider world is nearly all filtered through the mass media, mainly television. Distortion is inevitable. Television likes stories which are photogenic and especially ones with 'human interest'. Stories which unfold day to day are 'news' whereas developments which extend over months or years receive less attention.

BOX 10.1 MEDIASET, RAI AND SILVIO BERLUSCONI

Media ownership, control and political influence has been a particularly high-profile issue in Italy during Silvio Berlusconi's periods as prime minister. Berlusconi is Italy's richest man. His personal wealth is estimated at well over $12 billion.

Following careers as a cruise boat crooner, and then a property developer, Berlusconi launched three commercial television networks in Italy in the 1980s, extended his media interests into publishing, and in 1986 he became president of the football club, AC Milan.

He founded the political party Forza Italia and was elected prime minister of Italy in 1994. From 1996 to 2001 he was leader of the opposition. In 2001 he again became prime minister as leader of the Casa Delle Liberta coalition.

As controller of Italy's largest commercial broadcaster (Mediaset), plus the state-run RAI, prime minister Berlusconi controlled 90 per cent of Italy's TV market. At the same time, his brother was editor of *Il Giornale*, a daily national newspaper, and Berlusconi himself owned the companies which controlled one of Italy's leading advertising agencies plus Italy's biggest book and magazine publisher.

Sources: press files.

Whatever the facts of these and similar matters, Western governments have never sought to nationalise the press, recorded music or film, or to somehow turn them into instruments of state policy. It must also be said at this point that media proprietors' principal concern is usually to make money, and they may regard it as commercially expedient not to offend governments. Very early in its history, in 1912, the British film industry created the British Board of Film Censors with the aim of reducing the likelihood of state regulation. The media may also practice self-censorship as a commercial tactic. The media businesses controlled by Rupert Murdoch have been instructed to exclude features and opinions (including those of Chris Patten, the last governor of Hong Kong), that are considered likely to annoy the Chinese government so that the Star satellite can continue to beam broadcasts into China (and expand its number of channels in the future). There are dangers of media sycophancy as well as subversion (see Box 10.1).

Public service broadcasting

From its inception in the 1920s, broadcasting in Europe was treated differently from the other media. The limited airspace at that time made competition inappropriate (or so it was believed). There were fears (maybe exaggerated) of the power of the spoken word broadcast directly and simultaneously into all of a nation's homes, and there were also fears about the influence of broadcasting on public taste. The outcome was that broadcasting developed within a regulatory framework which produced a distinctive type of public service broadcasting (see Burns, 1977). This has three key features, all of which soon became hallmarks of the UK's BBC.

The first key feature is political neutrality. As explained in Chapter 9, the BBC was made a nationalised monopoly UK broadcaster in 1927 and was required to keep out of politics. Until the mid-1950s this was interpreted by the BBC as requiring it to abstain from discussion or commentary, as opposed to factual news reporting, on any matters which were before parliament. Elections were not covered except to report that they were taking place. The parties' campaigns and policies were broadcast only in the slots allocated for party political broadcasts. This changed with the advent of commercial television in 1955. Commercial TV companies were licensed on terms which required them to observe a public service code which included political neutrality, but this was interpreted as requiring balance rather than abstaining from independent editorial coverage of political events and issues. The BBC followed suit very quickly. Since then politicians have been subjected to probing, even aggressive, interviewing techniques. All politicians who hope to get on nowadays need to be good on 'the box'. Political journalism has become more investigative. Coverage of politics has been made more entertaining by the competition for viewers, but with the cost, some argue, of considerable 'dumbing down'.

It is necessary to point out here that, although UK broadcasters have been expected to remain politically neutral and to offer balanced coverage of domestic politics, the BBC has been expected to act (overtly or covertly) as spokesperson for the UK government when broadcasting to the rest of the world. The BBC World Service is, in fact, funded by the Foreign Office, not by the licence fee, and in times of war all UK broadcasters (and the press) have been expected to report UK government versions of events as the correct versions. This applied during the Second World War, the 1982 Falklands War, the Gulf War in 1991, the Kosovo War in 1999, the war in Afghanistan in 2001–02 and the Iraq war in 2003. That said, the broadcasters have not always complied with governments' expectations. In times of war governments can be annoyed when broadcasters attribute versions of events to the government's own spokespersons rather than simply reporting them as objective truth.

The second key feature of public service broadcasting has been 'balanced' programming. Broadcasters have not been permitted to pack the schedules with the most popular programmes measured in terms of listening and viewing figures. When broadcasting began there were fears that the use of sex and violence to shock, titillate and entertain would deprave public morals and behaviour. There were fears that broadcasters would pander to the 'lowest common denominator' and thereby degrade public taste, and that the availability of in-home round-the-clock entertainment would nurture passive rather than active citizens. Once again, the fears appear to have been exaggerated. As noted above, it has been difficult to establish any short-term links between the amounts and types of sex and violence that people watch on screen (television and cinema) and their behaviour in the rest of their lives (see Eysenck and Nias, 1978; McCullagh, 2002), but as with politics there may be long-term drip-drip effects. Television has made less difference to participation in relatively active out-of-home leisure than to radio, cinema and theatre audiences. People do not watch whatever happens to be on but view selectively according to their varied tastes. Despite this, until recent times broadcasters (who transmit into people's homes) have been given far less latitude than film-makers to portray sex and violence, and they have been required to cater for minority tastes; to cover high culture, and a wide range of sports, for example, and to schedule news and documentary programmes during peak listening and viewing hours. In its early years the BBC believed that its mission was to raise the level of popular taste and culture. Its post-Second World War radio programming envisaged listeners graduating from 'light' entertainment to the more serious 'home' service or to the highbrow 'third programme'. These aspirations have now been abandoned but we still have a 'hierarchy' of national BBC radio channels – 1, 2, 3 and 4. News, documentaries and high culture have retained prime time slots in the BBC's TV schedules despite their relatively low viewing figures, and, up to now, the licences of commercial terrestrial broadcasters have required them to emulate the BBC in this respect.

The above features of its broadcasting – the quality of its drama, arts programmes, news and current affairs coverage, and its editorial impartiality – are responsible for the high international regard which the BBC now enjoys. It is a British institution that has won, and up to now retained, worldwide admiration: a genuine national asset.

The third key feature of public service broadcasting has been its accessibility to all sections of the population. Terrestrial analogue commercial television has been free-to-view for all viewers. The commercial channels have been funded entirely by advertising. Reception of television broadcasts has been conditional on payment of a licence fee, and people have needed to purchase radio and TV sets, but these costs have never risen above a level consistent with more-or-less universal access. Popular radio programmes in the 1930s and 1940s, and the most popular television programmes subsequently, have been viewed by high proportions of all adults. Twenty-four million people – at the time the largest ever audience for a single UK TV programme – watched the BBC's Christmas edition of *Only Fools and Horses* in 1996. Such television programmes have arguably been the main components of a common culture (what everyone knows and can talk about to each other). Access to broadcasts has been, in effect, a right of citizenship.

From public service to commercial industry

All the aforementioned features of public service broadcasting are now at risk, and could (but will not necessarily) be swept away entirely by ongoing changes in the broadcasting industry. European governments have been losing their ability to operate broadcasting as a public service. This is partly because, as the European Union, they have collectively decided to follow America in adopting competition as the best regulatory framework (Collins, 1999). Europeans used to snigger at the Americans who had a choice of dozens of TV channels, all filled with rubbish. Now they are importing this choice into Europe.

Terrestrial competition

In the UK the weakening of state control began with the birth of commercial television in 1955. BBC radio already had limited competition from overseas commercial stations (mainly Radio Luxembourg) which was joined in the 1960s by so-called pirate stations broadcasting from vessels just outside UK territorial waters. Luxembourg and the pirates specialised in popular music: at that time the BBC was refusing to dedicate an entire channel to the hit parade.

Commercial television was introduced into the UK in 1955 under pressure from would-be broadcasters and advertisers. The Conservative government at that time was sympathetic to these demands and by the 1950s it was known that other countries (notably the USA) had lived with commercial broadcasting without either democracy or levels of popular taste collapsing. So in 1955 the BBC and ITV began to compete for audience share, but this competition was within a public service framework which remained in place when additional channels – BBC2 in 1964, then the advertising-funded channels 4 (in 1982) and 5 (in 1997) – were launched. Advances in broadcasting technology and the rising demand for advertising space had made additional channels viable. This was also the context in which commercial radio broadcasting began in 1973 then steadily expanded.

Satellite, cable and digital broadcasting

Satellite and cable broadcasting, coupled with digital technology, has probably dealt a death blow to public service broadcasting as known up to now. Sky began satellite broadcasting in Britain in 1989, and commenced digital broadcasting in 1998. Viewers with digital receivers or 'boxes' and satellite or cable connections now have access to hundreds of television channels. By 2003 over 50 per cent of all UK homes had multi-channel television. The additional channels to which they had access accounted for around 20 per cent of the total audience. Both figures have risen steadily since 1989 and are expected to continue to do so. Up to now, most UK households with multi-channel television have received their transmissions by satellite (from Sky), but ultimately cable transmission's technological edge could prove decisive. Cable can carry more information more cheaply. Fibre optic cable has 250,000 times the capacity of ordinary telephone wire (Crisell, 1999). A second UK digital platform, using terrestrial wavelengths, was created in 1998: Ondigital which was renamed ITV Digital in 2001. This platform was owned jointly by Carlton and Granada, already the two largest UK commercial TV broadcasters. ITV Digital collapsed in 2002. It had failed to attract enough subscribers and viewers to pay for the 'content' that it had bought. The price paid to broadcast the Football League's fixtures had proved excessive. The platform was subsequently awarded to Freeserve, a company formed jointly by Sky and the BBC. Like other terrestrial broadcasts, the programmes from this platform are free to viewers (who must purchase special 'boxes'). Digital television has not been a 'licence to print money'. Up to now, in the UK, Sky has been a commercial success, but neither the main cable companies nor rival digital broadcasting platforms have made profits.

Expansion of the industry

One outcome of the above developments has been a massive expansion of the broadcasting industry. There are now many more companies making many more

---

BOX 10.2 VIACOM INC

This is a US-based entertainment company, operating throughout the world, worth around $80 billion.

Viacom has interests in:

1. *Cable TV*: MTV (available in 384 million households in 140 territories), Showtime, Nickelodeon (available in 300 million households), VH1, TNN, CMT, and BET (Black Entertainment Television).
2. *Conventional TV*: CBS (which has 200 affiliated stations), UPN, and the Showtime networks.
3. *TV production*: Paramount Television (which has 55,000 hours of programming in its library).
4. *Radio*: Infinity (which has 184 radio stations).
5. *Music*: Famous Music (holds 100,000 copyrights).
6. *Advertising*: outdoor sites across North America and Europe.
7. *Movies*: Paramount Pictures.
8. *Cinemas*: Famous Players (884 screens in Canada), United Cinemas International (868 screens worldwide).
9. *Theme parks*: Paramount Parks (five North American parks which attract 13 million visitors annually).
10. *Video*: Blockbuster Inc, Paramount Home Entertainment.
11. *Publishing*: Simon & Schuster (brings out 2100 titles annually).

Source: www.viacom.com

---

programmes. People are not watching any more television (in terms of total time) than in the 1970s but they are paying a lot more for what they view. Broadcasting is now the base for some of the world's biggest companies. Media conglomerates are not new (see Murdock and Golding, 1977) but the giants of the media industries (such as Time-Warner/AOL, Disney, Viacom, Vivendi-Universal, Bertelsmann, and News Corporation) are now bigger than ever and have stakes in television, radio, newspapers, magazines, books, films and the internet. Nowadays these businesses operate on a global scale (see Box 10.2).

Media businesses are not sluggish bureaucracies. Broadcasting is part of the present-day global economy's 'wild west'. The multinationals buy in most of their material. They are divided internally into units, all of which are expected to be innovative profit centres. If any fail, they are likely to be closed down or sold off, or placed under new management. The giants of this industry seek maximum flexibility. They are at the cutting edge of new technology. The industry has a large number of freelance workers, with people coming together in temporary teams to work on specific projects. The industry has plenty of good jobs, but precious little secure employment. Many occupations in the industry are still untitled (such is the pace of change). There are no set qualifications for entry or routes to the top. Workers forge their own careers and establish personal reputations in the industry. Creative technologists, and technologically competent creatives, are at a premium. The work is typically both exciting and stressful. Broadcasting is an extreme example of work in leisure. The risks are high but there is the prospect of spectacular gains and rapid career progress (see Dex *et al.*, 2000; European Commission, 2001).

Consumer choice

Another outcome of the wider choice of channels is that broadcasters have less influence over what people actually view or listen to. Audiences have more choice. They can do their own scheduling. Even 'balanced' programming on all channels would not ensure that viewers' diets were balanced. The video-recorder has added to viewers' ability to watch what they want, when they want.

Broadcasters have lost influence over what people view, and public authorities, which answer to governments, have been losing control over what is broadcast. Satellite, cable and other broadcasts to subscribers are not subject to the same public service requirements as the UK's 'traditional' terrestrial channels. It is difficult, probably impossible, to set standards of taste and decency for material that is beamed in by satellite (or transmitted via the internet). It may be illegal to download child pornography, but can it actually be prevented? With cable and satellite broadcasters able to extend the limits and to concentrate on the most popular types of programmes, the 'traditional' terrestrial channels have demanded similar freedom in order to protect their shares of the audience. So 'unpopular' news programmes have been pushed beyond, or to the fringes of, peak viewing hours, and documentaries now concentrate on issues with viewer appeal, especially sex.

Future developments in communication technology are likely to merge the PC, the TV and the internet in some way or another. It is expected that before long viewers will be able to call up information, entertainment, music and shopping catalogues of their choice whenever they wish. An end result of all this is certain to be a further erosion of 'traditional' public service principles.

Globalisation

Another outcome of commercialisation is that more of what is available for people to view is of foreign origin. This is less of an issue in the UK than in most other countries. The UK has one of the world's stronger television production industries, and state policy is geared to maintaining this position. Elsewhere the entertainment and news to which people have access is increasingly sourced outside the viewers' countries. The USA is the world's main production site. America began its cultural colonisation of the world with Hollywood films (see Hoggart, 1957), and television has steadily enlarged American influence (Boyd-Barrett, 1977). Nearly all the programmes that are popular in most European countries are of American origin (Collins, 1999). More and more people throughout the world are able to watch the CNN, NBC or BBC versions of world events rather than their own countries' news. In a similar way, football fans are able to watch the English Premier League or the Spanish or Italian leagues, rather than their domestic football competitions.

However, the fact that people are able to do something does not mean that they will necessarily do it. In all countries the most popular TV programmes are produced locally (Hesmondhalgh, 2002). The USA has a larger slice of the global film market than any other producer, but the American share is well under 50 per cent. India actually produces more films per year than the USA. Cultural imperialism has become more difficult to achieve as more and more countries have developed their own broadcasting industries. There are new exporters. For example, Latin America exports *telenovelas*. Australia is now the source of some soaps that are watched all over the world (*Neighbours*, for example).

That said, given an increasingly competitive context, it is understandable if governments respond by trying to ensure that their home-based media businesses gain the largest possible shares of the global market. Doing otherwise would neglect one of their special capabilities in the field of leisure. Television may or may not still be a public service, but nowadays it most definitely is big business. In practice, the search for global market share has become the main aim of UK and European Union media policy. The old public service principles are being quietly sidelined. All UK households are being encouraged to go digital. The analogue signals will be switched off as soon as possible. This will enable the government to auction off the analogue wavebands to other commercial businesses like telephone companies. However, the main prize is putting the UK at the forefront of the digital revolution, creating a strong domestic market for equipment manufacturers, programme makers and broadcasters, and other service providers, thus making the UK an attractive base for the companies. Of course, hospitable financial and cultural regulations are also important. There is in fact a strong case for prioritising economic objectives in media (and other leisure) policies. Media businesses have some of the best jobs in the leisure industries. All countries want them. Anthony Giddens (2001, pp. 483–4) has noted that:

> placing limits on who can own what, and what forms of media technology they can use, might affect the economic prospects of the media sector. A country which is too restrictive might find itself left behind – the media industries are one of the fastest growing sectors of the modern economy.

Costs and benefits

The BBC, as it has existed up to now, is certain to become a casualty. Some people – mainly in commercial media companies – have been asking why everyone should pay a licence fee for the BBC to replicate what is already available on other channels (game shows and soap operas, for example). Competitor broadcasters object to subsidised competition, and eventually viewers with a widened choice of channels who rarely watch the BBC are likely to agree. The BBC could become a public service broadcaster in a new (or rather North American) sense of offering non-commercial products to minority audiences. This development would be applauded by the BBC's commercial competitors. BBC radio, with the exception of Radio 1, has taken this route. It concentrates on classical pop, classical music, local news and serious talk programmes. BBC television could follow suit except that the Corporation suspects that the public will eventually prove unwilling to pay the licence fee to run channels that most people never watch. The BBC believes that it must continue to make popular programmes if it is to retain general public support (and its licence fee). In this case the BBC will be condemned for not being different – for just replicating what commercial broadcasters offer. But the option of being very different – emphatically uncommercial – is equally hazardous. Will support for, or acquiescent payment of, the licence fee continue if the BBC's audience share dips below, say, 15 per cent? If the BBC continues to broadcast commercial-type programmes there will surely be arguments for it to raise its money in the same way as the commercial channels by charging subscriptions to viewers or carrying advertising. The BBC has needed to enter the digital age and to increase the number of channels in order to protect its market share. Filling more channels means spending more money which means raising the licence fee. How long will it be before fee-payers object to higher charges to fund broadcasts that they never watch? If advertising on its main channels and viewer subscriptions are introduced by the BBC as additional income streams (advertising is already carried on some BBC satellite channels), there is sure to come a time when the licence fee is phased out and a government of the day decides to privatise, that is, sell off, the BBC. Instead of funding a state broadcaster, the government might subsidise specific public service programmes or channels carried by other broadcasters. The end of the BBC in its present form is in sight, but not necessarily the end of all public service broadcasting.

There are costs attached to any change, including the changes that are currently occurring in broadcasting, and these costs extend far beyond people paying more. There is already less potential to use broadcasting to express a clear moral and aesthetic order: clear limits of taste and decency, and a hierarchy of tastes which insists that certain less popular programmes, measured by audience figures, deserve prime air space. It is possible for people to approve of prime-time news programmes even if they themselves do not watch them, just as non-ramblers can be in favour of a public right to roam. However, it will remain possible for governments, if they wish, to retain taxation-funded public service channels with round-the-clock news coverage, plus documentaries and arts programmes which would never attract enough viewers to be commercially viable.

Broadcasting is no longer a pillar of citizenship – everyone having access to all broadcasts. In the new commercial world of broadcasting viewers get what they pay for. However, there is nothing to stop governments maintaining free-to-air channels carrying a full range of programmes (although these would not include the most popular programmes which would be sold to commercial channels), or assisting the poorer sections of the population to pay channel subscriptions.

Broadcasting's ability to create a common culture – programmes that virtually everyone watches and which then become the currency of small talk and political debate – may also be lost. Maybe there will be no repeats of *Dallas* and *Cathy Come Home*. Or maybe there will still be programmes with mass appeal (see below, p. 150).

In any event, here we see yet again that the voluntary, public and commercial sectors are not just alternative delivery mechanisms. The media provide further examples of how the sectors differ in what is provided.

What deserves highlighting is that all the costs are threatened or are actually being incurred only because enough people are willing to pay for the increased viewer choice and the commercial products. As with the types of holidays, evenings-out and gambling (see Chapters 11 and 12) that it has created, in broadcasting commerce is adding to people's leisure options. As indicated above, it will be possible, if governments and the wider public wish, to retain a diluted form of public service broadcasting: programmes or even entire channels that maintain 'standards', to which everyone has free access, and to ensure that prime time viewing schedules on these channels contain some 'unpopular' news, current affairs and arts programmes. Such a public service wedge would be a minority 'ghetto', but the majority might approve of its existence, courtesy of public funding, just as non-users can approve of publicly-funded open spaces and sport centres. Minority programmes and channels could remain a source of national prestige and identity. That said, it will probably be necessary for future governments to look to other public leisure (or alternative) services to create a common culture and the kind of national citizenship that used to be sustained by everyone having access to all broadcasts. Leisure policy-makers need to identify the best means, which will always change over time, of achieving what they alone can do. The new broadcasting system could, over time, develop a new form of global citizenship through the films, entertainment and sports events which attract large numbers of viewers all over the world. However, the really big prize for heading the march into the new digital age is jobs – good quality jobs. All countries want these. Any country will incur costs if it decides to opt out of the age of commercialised multimedia, multi-channel, terrestrial, satellite and cable telecommunications. Programme-makers, channels, writers and technicians will base themselves elsewhere. This is the principal reason why the age of traditional public service broadcasting is ending.

New technology

Uncertain future

A cautionary tactic of present-day writers is to observe that everything may change very soon. Information and communications technology (ICT), which itself develops at a bewildering pace, is the assumed catalyst. Note, however, that the caution is invariably that things 'may' rather than 'will' change. Books are still being published which shows that some people remain confident that 'shelf life' is not an outdated concept. Moreover, even if we could be confident that ICT will change our leisure, it would still be impossible to forecast exactly what the changes will be. The current situation is comparable to radio, moving pictures and recorded sound at the beginning of the twentieth century. The basic technologies had then been created but no-one knew how they would be used.

Up to now, forecasts of ICT's impact have needed several revisions. In the 1970s the silicon chip made the personal computer (PC) viable and it seemed possible that before long everyone would become amateur programmers and use this technology to monitor their personal cash flows, close and open the curtains, and switch heating and cookers on and off. It soon became evident that the domestic PC was being used mainly to play computer games. Games are still a huge and expanding, innovative and fiercely competitive industry. However, in the early-1990s the internet became operational, and this is the application of ICT which, at present, looks most likely to transform lifestyles. Future uses of the internet may be rather different from those to date. In 2002 the number of mobiles overtook the number of landline phones in operation throughout the world. It is possible that before long the most common way of accessing the internet will be via a hand-held device and the typical heavy internet user will no longer be a home-based 'anorak'.

So far it looks as if some leisure activities, and the corresponding industries, will be basically unscathed by ICT. People's enthusiasm for travel is not diminishing (Urry, 2001, 2002). The same is true for participant sport and exercise. Demand for live entertainment has not declined. The hospitality industries have not lost customers. In contrast, it seems likely that more and more people will obtain recorded music and maybe films online. This may be done legally, for payment, or illegally and free. Who knows? Online gambling is most likely to increase (see Chapter 12, p. 168). There may be less use of betting shops, fewer cash sales of lottery tickets, and fewer football pool coupons mailed or collected, whereas casinos and horse race tracks seem less likely to suffer. Businesses and private consumers are most likely to do more shopping online. Window-shopping practices may or may not change: people may continue to gather 'market intelligence' in traditional ways while making actual purchases via the web (see Chapter 11, p. 160). Many people may make personal selections of evening viewing from the thousands of programmes that are now available on hundreds of channels. This may be the future, but not necessarily.

By the end of the twentieth century a half of the UK population, and 70 per cent of 16–24-year-olds, had already used the internet at some time or another (Russell and Drew, 2001). Between 2000 and 2003 the proportion of households with home access to the internet rose from 30 per cent to 47 per cent (Russell and Stafford, 2002; www.statistics.gov.uk). If this growth rate is maintained, internet access will soon become as common as the telephone, but maybe this will not happen: by 2002 the growth rate had slowed in those countries where the highest proportions of the populations were already using the internet. It appeared that nearly everyone who wanted to do so had already gone online (Eurescom, 2002). Nevertheless, there is a decade's experience of children and young people who have grown up with the internet and mobile phones. For them the internet is not novel: it might as well always have existed. First world countries are not at the forefront of all these developments. The Philippines claims to be the world's texting capital. Its population cannot afford computers but they can afford mobile phones. Young people in the Philippines are avid texters. Batan (2002) found that 337 out of the 407 Manila university students in his survey had mobile phones. On average each user was receiving 22 text messages, and sending 22 messages every day, nearly all to and from friends. They were spending a quarter of their personal incomes on pre-paid mobile phone cards. What were the messages about? They were mainly greetings, keeping in touch, and replying to messages. Is this trivia? Batan claims that a new subculture, with new kinds of links, networks and connectivity, is spreading. On the basis of their Australian research, Wearing and Foley (2002) have claimed that the mobile phone, which enables users to remain 'in touch' wherever they are, and enables them to be seen to be actually or potentially 'in touch', has given young women a new sense of security and increased their willingness to go out alone. Jam Feng-chien Lee (2002) claims that important developments are occurring in internet chat rooms. These have their own rituals and rules. Visitors need to learn how to chat. The normal rules in the rooms used by Taiwan's young people include no erotica, no abuse and no foul language. Offenders are simply thrown out. The chat room is another site where new kinds of social relationships appear to be forming. The maturation of relationships is time-compressed. Closeness can develop quickly. Fast replies are read as indicating sincerity. Highly personal questions are often asked near to the beginning of a chat relationship. Anonymity in a public place (the chat room) appears to encourage both emotionless and reckless emotional behaviour. Research among 9–16-year-olds in the UK (see Batty, 2002) has found that 58 per cent of young chat-room users chat about sex (at least sometimes). Ten per cent say that they have met face-to-face with people initially befriended in chat rooms. The character of sex offenders, and their strategies, appear to be changing. The 'dirty mac' brigade is being ousted by younger computer literates who download from the internet and, in the case of paedophiles, try to ensnare children in this way.

So new technology could bring about a sea change in personal relationships. But remember, in many countries most young people are already internet and mobile phone users. Given this, the continuities over time in young people's uses of leisure are surely as remarkable as the changes. Even when they could change, they may prefer to stick to familiar ways. As noted in Chapter 9 (p. 126), most people still buy newspapers even though these can be accessed free online. Rather than investing valuable personal time, or trusting software to select their preferred films, singers, comedy shows, sports, teams and events, people may prefer to stick to 'routines' and to trust a limited number of preferred channels to select their evening viewing. So there may continue to be some programmes – light entertainment and major sports events – that the 'entire nation' watches. Who can tell? In 2002 a new UK TV audience record, estimated at 30 million, was set for a single programme, England versus Brazil in the football World Cup.

Drivers

Technology is never neutral. There may be such a thing as pure science but applications are always developed by or for people with particular interests. It is normally assumed nowadays that uses of new technology will be commerce-driven, and it is certainly true that commerce can be relied on to identify any ways of making money out of whatever technology is operative. There is money in new technology for hardware and software businesses – everyone must have heard of Microsoft and Bill Gates. There is money for the telecom businesses that sell in real time online, and for the servers who supply addresses to users and direct messages to and from these sites. There are profits to be made from making and distributing live and recorded pictures and sound. Internet commerce can also be profitable. Transaction costs are minimised which gives these businesses a market edge while fierce competition from easily accessed competitor sites drives prices down. It is still unclear whether the ultimate winners will be from the new generation of dotcoms (such as lastminute.com) or longer-established household names (such as Tesco). Note, however, that there have been plenty of dotcom failures, and digital TV platforms have crashed, like the UK's ITV Digital in 2002 (see p. 143). Only a tiny proportion of websites are profitable, although most are not meant to make money.

Up to now governments have not attempted to take charge and turn the internet into a public service. Their main concern in Europe and North America has been to expand their own territories' shares of the industry. Technology and, indeed, economic life have leapt ahead of the nation state. National governments can try to create favourable conditions for high-tech investors. They can make it illegal to manufacture, distribute, receive and download particular materials, but up to now governments have not developed effective policing systems. Film and music companies must rely primarily on their own technological ingenuity to combat piracy. However, there are an increasing number of ever more powerful supra-national agencies such as the European Union, North Atlantic Treaty Organization (NATO), the International Monetary Fund, and the World Trade Organization. There is now a standing international court. Maybe, some time in the twenty-first century, there will be a global internet regulator, which is empowered to confer global rights of citizenship (access to particular kinds of information and entertainment) and to impose universal standards of (alleged) truth, taste and decency. However, unlike national governments, the single global regulator will probably be unable to strengthen the global population's sense of identity and related prestige.

There is a third possibility, a potential third way. The anarchy of the early years of the internet may not prove temporary. Text language and the rules of internet chat have been developed by users, not by governments or commerce. US commentators have tended to regard ICT as a threat to civil society, and it does appear that heavy internet users in North America engage in less face-to-face interaction than other citizens (Kraut et al., 1998). North America's first internet generations appear to have contained many 'anoraks' who have immersed themselves in virtual communities in which they have been able to create virtual identities for themselves. ICT does appear to be enabling Americans to 'sign up and pay' rather than engage in any 'real' civic or political activity (Putnam, 2000; see also Chapter 3, pp. 32–3). However, America is neither everywhere nor necessarily the world leader in all respects. In Europe there appears to be a reaction to the fact that the constraints in cyberspace are at least as severe as those encountered anywhere else (Miah, 2000). Internet users in Europe are not escaping en masse into virtual reality.

One Swiss study has found that internet users in that country have larger social networks and engage in more face-to-face interaction than non-users (Franzen, 2000). Just as real travel remains necessary in order to enjoy the tourist experience, so face-to-face contact is likely to prove irreplaceable. International firms congregate their headquarters in global cities largely because top executives find that they need personal contact in order to develop trust relationships with colleagues, and with suppliers and customers in cognate businesses (Sassen, 2000). Texting and the mobile phone seem less likely to replace than to add a new dimension to, and maybe facilitate more frequent, face-to-face encounters. The new technologies are most likely to change the character of voluntary associations in some way or another but could leave them stronger than ever. Maybe, with ICT, civil society will roll-back both commerce and the public sector. Who knows? Any such development is more likely to start in leisure than anywhere else.

CONCLUSIONS

This chapter has examined how the latest technologies are changing some of the major leisure industries. Some older industries such as broadcasting are being transformed. Some are being enlarged: this also applies to broadcasting. Some entirely new kinds of industries, such as those based on the internet, have been created.

One really big change – big in the sense that it affects most people's everyday lives – has been the transformation of broadcasting, especially in those countries where it was formerly basically a public service and has now become another commercial leisure industry. This chapter has explained how and why this has come about, and has identified the costs and benefits. Some of the costs appear inevitable whereas others are subject to political choice, but at present there appear to be more grounds for pessimism than for optimism over the likelihood of retaining the benefits of the older public service broadcasting.

The most important fact about the final impact of the latest generation of new technology is probably that at present it is impossible to know for certain what it will be. There are amazing new possibilities which may or may not become actualities. This chapter has suggested that what eventually happens may depend greatly on who takes charge of cyberspace. Will it be commerce or political actors? Or will civil society retain the upper hand?

11 Hospitality and Shopping

Introduction

Why bracket these industries? Eating, drinking, sleeping and shopping are all ordinary common or garden activities. They are necessary for self-maintenance, like washing and grooming which do not feature in this book, although they could, because these are further examples of commerce's ability to develop the commonplace into leisure industries which offer appealing uses of our time and money.

Hospitality is what we might offer to friends and relatives who come to visit – food, drink, accommodation and maybe entertainment either bought in or self-produced by camcorder. The hospitality industries commodify and commercialise these services. The accommodation part of hospitality is subsumed within tourism in this book (see Chapter 5), and entertainment is considered with media (Chapters 9 and 10), so here we are concerned only with the refreshment parts of hospitality. Eating and drinking are favourite activities on nights-out. Drinking alcohol is second only to tourism in terms of money spent. Like eating and drinking, certain types of shopping have been made glamorous rather than chores; most definitely leisure.

These industries have plenty of critics. It is said that commerce persuades people to shop and consume excessively, until they drop deep into debt. The food industries are accused of promoting unhealthy eating and cajoling people to eat so much that they become overweight. One branch of the leisure industries persuades people to eat more fulsomely while another persuades them to diet and equates thinness with health and beauty. The drinks industry is blamed for accidents, illnesses, premature deaths, work absences and crime. The restaurant trade is the womb of the McDonaldization thesis which ranks alongside the arguments of the Frankfurt School (see Chapter 9, pp. 127–30) as a particularly biting critique of how commercialisation, beneath the glitz, is blighting people's everyday lives. This chapter begins by presenting the McDonaldization thesis. Criticisms of the thesis follow. The subsequent chapter sections deal with shopping, then drinking. They explain how commerce has confounded its critics and has made these activities appetising and, in the case of alcohol, low risk for most people.

This chapter and the next (on gambling) deal with uses of time and money that fall within leisure's 'grey' zone. These are not topics that are included automatically in texts and courses on leisure. Even so, these chapters are crucial to this book's overall third-way stance. They illustrate why we should welcome commerce's ability to devise appetising uses for our leisure time and money; why our gut instinct should be to liberalise rather than to regulate and, when regulating, to be guided by commerce's own inclinations. This is where the third way overlaps with the libertarian right position (see Chapter 1, pp. 6–7). The third way differs by making equally strong cases for the voluntary and public sectors.

Dining out and the McDonaldization thesis

Is the McDonaldization thesis a joke? No, George Ritzer, an American sociologist, is deadly serious. People speak about an earlier Fordist era. Ritzer has selected the business which, in his view, best exemplifies the present time. The McDonaldization thesis has been developed in a series of books and articles which Ritzer has written during and since the 1990s (1993, 1998, 1999, 2001). McDonaldization is:

> the process by which the principles of the fast food industry are coming to dominate more and more sectors of American society as well as the rest of the world.   (Ritzer, 1993, p. 1)

Rationalisation

Ritzer believes that Max Weber was broadly correct about the modern era becoming, above all else, an age of rationality. This means being systematic, cold and calculative in selecting the best means to achieve an end – profit in the present instance. Alternative means are compared. Relative costs and returns are calculated carefully. A good or service is then provided in the most efficient and effective way. Improvements are sought constantly but they have to be justified rationally, otherwise no deviations from what is known to work best are permitted. The key principles of McDonaldization are efficiency, calculability, predictability and control. Weber thought that the outcome of progressive rationalisation would be mammoth bureaucracies. Here Ritzer disagrees and nominates McDonald's as exemplifying the actual outcome of rationalisation.

McDonald's is a USA-based restaurant chain which now has branches all over the world. Everyone is sure to have heard of McDonald's (see Box 11.1). It is basically the same menu everywhere with very limited local variations. The burgers are always the same size and shape, and are cooked to the same specifications. The premises – the backrooms and the counter equipment, the furnishings and the decor – are always recognisably McDonald's. All over the world the staff wear the

---

BOX 11.1 MCDONALD'S

Ray Kroc had mortgaged his home and had invested his life savings to become the exclusive distributor of a five-spindled milkshake-maker called the Multimixer. In 1954 he heard about McDonald's hamburger stand in California which was running eight Multimixers. Kroc put the idea of opening several restaurants to Dick and Mac McDonald. At first Kroc's plan was to make money by selling Multimixers to the restaurants. Fortunately for Kroc, he offered to run the restaurants in order to get the idea started.

The first McDonald's restaurant opened at Des Plaines in 1955. The first day's revenue was $366.12. This building is now a McDonald's museum.

McDonald's is now the world's largest food-service retailer with more than 30,000 restaurants in 121 countries.

Source: www.mcdonalds.com

---

same uniforms. There is a standard division of labour among the 'crews'. They are all trained to issue the same McDonald's greeting and to wear the same McDonald's smile. Enter a McDonald's anywhere and you know what you will get. There have been few changes over time. The company has discovered a formula that works and is sticking with it. So, for customers, McDonald's is dead predictable. Prices depend on local costs but are always 'value for money'. Yet, Ritzer claims, McDonald's offers not only food and drink but also an enchanting experience. Go through the door into a McDonald's and you leave behind outside, drab, mundane everyday life.

McDonald's has achieved all this without becoming a mammoth bureaucracy. The business is centralised. Nowadays the latest information technology enables the performance of every branch to be monitored by the centre from day to day, even from hour to hour. The centre knows exactly how every single branch is performing, and it knows what is selling, and can order fresh supplies so that they arrive in time, every time. Every McDonald's uses local suppliers, but the supplies have to be made according to McDonald's standard specification, and suppliers receive their instructions from the centre. So McDonald's achieves its standardised and predictable service without employing armies of managers.

McDonald's was not the first fast-food business. Fish-and-chip shops have a longer history of selling fast food to eat in or to take away. McDonald's was not even the first fast-food restaurant chain. It was years behind Wimpy and decades behind UCP, which stands for United Cattle Products. Their restaurants flourished in Britain when tripe was a popular dish before and after the Second World War. McDonald's stands out because of its extraordinary success. The name is recognised all over the world, like Coca-Cola which is not a restaurant chain but bears some resemblances to McDonald's (see below, p. 158). Most towns and cities in Western Europe and North America now host at least one McDonald's and have done so for several decades, and towns and cities across the rest of the world are fast following suit. There were long queues when the restaurants first opened in Moscow, Warsaw and other East European cities in the early 1990s, and the crowds are still there at peak times. If they cannot afford to eat in, young people hang around outside. McDonald's has become a symbol of consumer culture and the Western way of life more generally.

The claim that society is being McDonaldized (Ritzer's first book on this subject was titled *The McDonaldization of Society*) is a response to the extent to which the model is being copied. McDonald's has acted as an exemplar for many other businesses. There are now many other fast-food chains selling burgers, pizzas, kebabs, chicken and so on. We have Wendy's, Starvin' Marvin's, Garfunkel's, Little Chef, Happy Eater. The model has now spread beyond fast food. We have branded pubs such as, in Britain, Wetherspoons and Wacky Warehouse. As with McDonald's, customers know what they will find inside – the beers and the food menus. There are similar developments in other branches of retailing: brands such as Tie Rack, Sock Shop and Knickerbocker which may operate in high streets, railway stations, airports or as shops within larger stores. No matter what the location, the range of goods is constant. There are even wider applications of the McDonald's model. In the USA chains of hospitals and clinics offer a standard tariff of treatments. Higher education is displaying symptoms. Degree programmes are divided into modules of standard weights. Leading brands – the universities – franchise modules, so wherever in the world students enrol they receive the same course materials, recommended reading, and do the same exercises. Ritzer claims that present-day society is fast becoming one where people can leave one standardised service only by stepping into another.

Despite the success of the business, McDonaldization has few academic supporters. Ritzer claims that his intention in highlighting the process is to stimulate a search for ways of resisting. Weber feared that we would become prisoners of large bureaucracies and wrestled with the problem of how to prevent this. In a similar way, sociological conferences in the 1990s debated how to resist McDonaldization (see Smart, 1999). It seems strange that our freedom could be threatened by what at first sight appears an innocuous business. The core problem inherent in McDonaldization is said to be the ultimate irrationality of rationality. Humans have the ability to act rationally but by taking this to extreme lengths we can dehumanise everything. So work is deskilled and even consumption may eventually become routine and boring.

> Rational systems inevitably spawn a series of irrationalities that limit, eventually compromise and perhaps even undermine their rationality.
>
> (Ritzer, 1993, p. 121)

This is the core criticism. Another is that:

> Consumers are led to believe that they are operating freely when, in fact, great effort has been made to control their actions without them being aware of it.
>
> (Ritzer, 2001, p. 8)

Things that apply to McDonald's itself will not necessarily apply in all McDonaldized businesses. The food does not have to be unhealthy. There is no need to sacrifice quality for quantity. The workforces in supplying companies need not be low-paid. Customers need not park their own trays. A McDonaldized operation must simply identify the core features of whatever it is providing, then create them as efficiently as possible, calculate the best way, then stick to it and make everything 100 per cent predictable. This will always require strong managerial control, which will usually be achieved by relying on technology rather than human judgement.

One of Ritzer's problems has been the success of his own branding. Had his first book on the subject been titled 'The Rationalisation of Consumption' it is just possible that it would have received less attention than *The McDonaldization of Society*. However, McDonald's was never intended to be more than an example. Rationalisation is the master trend (so Ritzer and his supporters claim). In his later books Ritzer has brought rationalisation to the fore and concentrated on other examples – the Disney parks, Las Vegas, cruise ships, casinos and shopping malls. Their common feature, according to Ritzer, is that, like McDonald's, they not only rationalise consumption but try to keep customers visiting by maintaining their enchantment, which is difficult when goods and services are standardised.

It is partly, but not only, the rationalisation – the standardisation – that keeps customers visiting McDonald's, or sailing with the same cruise line. People are willing to book with a cruise company, or into a hotel chain, because they know what the accommodation will be like, what entertainment will be offered, and the range of food. Likewise visitors to any Disney park know what they will get. Rationalisation takes much of the risk out of spending. One problem, for the businesses and the customers, is that the experience is likely to become boring. It is true that even the McDonald's restaurants continue to be enchanting places for successive cohorts of children. The stream of customers never ends. However, by age 15 customers are likely to have become disenchanted. McDonald's will have become routine. How can businesses retain customers throughout their lives? Ritzer argues that businesses can rationalise not only enchantment but also re-enchantment. They are said to do this by constantly offering spectaculars and extravaganzas as well as best ever, truly unrepeatable bargains. These always seem to be available. Shops put on fantastic displays with more lights or more fireworks than have ever been used before, anywhere. Present-day spectaculars include so-called implosions wherein normal boundaries disappear. People are able to mix shopping, gambling and a bit of sport, all in one hotel. At a single event they may spend their past, present and part of their future earnings. They can experience tropical environments, the wild west, white-water situations or a nightclub in any place, any time of the day or night. They move across an archipelago, not just from one rationalised consumer setting to another, but from one spectacular to the next (so Ritzer claims), with the spectacles having to become increasingly exciting in order to retain their interest.

Can this cycle continue? Ritzer sees no reason why not. The process is not displaying signs of exhaustion.

> I conclude that while McDonald's will eventually grow less important and may even disappear completely, and the label McDonaldization will become increasingly less important as a result, the underlying process of rationalization will continue apace, or even accelerate.   (Ritzer, 2001, p. 3)

However, Ritzer (1999) notes that some groups are excluded from the consumer extravaganzas by their poverty and believes that, eventually, their frustration could threaten the consumer society.

Why Ritzer is wrong

To begin, none of the elements that make up McDonaldization are novel. Actually Ritzer has never claimed that McDonaldization is an outcome of very recent trends. Rather, he presents McDonaldization as the latest outcome of a process of rationalisation that began with the birth of modernity. So why invent new vocabulary if so-called McDonaldization is just a stage (and not necessarily the final stage) in a long-term process, another outcome of rationalisation? In some ways, Ritzer's thesis has been a victim of its own success. The brand name is better known than the actual theory. Far more people will have heard of McDonaldization than will have read Ritzer's books. The standardisation of products was a hallmark of Fordism. Ritzer himself recognises this. Henry Ford's discovery was that, by standardising products, costs and prices could be lowered, which boosted sales to a level which made it worthwhile to invest in the production lines from which standardised products would roll. Branding, too, has a long history. It is ages since the personal reputation of the local butcher and grocer was replaced by reliance on brand names as our guarantee of quality. Likewise spectaculars and extravaganzas have been used for over a century to attract crowds to fairgrounds and emporiums. Crowds came because the world's strongest man or the fattest woman was to be displayed. In recent times technological advances and the sums of money available for investment have enabled spectaculars to become even more spectacular. Present-day marketing techniques and technologies allow not just the same product, but an entire consumer service to be replicated throughout the world. Branding has now become so vital that the names of some businesses are their only significant assets. For example, Coca-Cola itself does not manufacture any drinks: the corporation just sells, and controls the use of, its name.

The big mistakes in the McDonaldization thesis are three-fold. First, despite the talk about McUniversities and so on, McDonaldization is a phenomenon of commerce. It is the quest for profit, not straightforward rationalisation, that creates restaurant chains such as McDonald's and their kin. Second, even within the commercial sector of the leisure industries, McDonaldization is confined to specific, and really quite limited, segments. It is impossible to McDonaldize sports spectacles. Modern sports are more rational than their predecessors. The games are governed by clear and detailed rules. The fields and time limits of play are clearly defined. Methods of scoring should leave no room for doubt. Even so, what happens during a contest is far from entirely predictable. Heritage, too, is not susceptible to full McDonaldization. Cultural products, whether highbrow or lowbrow, cannot be McDonaldized. Commerce may always try to repeat a winning formula, whenever possible, but even then the outcome will not always resemble a restaurant chain. The result of the next football match or the next popular song is not 100 per cent predictable. 'Frankfurtisation' (see Chapter 9, pp. 127–30) is not exactly the same as McDonaldization. Third, even if all commercial goods and services were McDonaldized (which will never happen) the same process would not apply to the consumers' lifestyles.

Ritzer is wrong about the McDonaldization of society. Actually it is very difficult to select any business that is representative of the present age. Should it be McDonald's? Or should it be Las Vegas or Disney? There are not many Las Vegases or Disney parks. Indeed, their attraction is precisely that they are so out of the ordinary. Few people can be more than once-a-year visitors. Is the true emblem of our age a cruise ship, an internet-based business, or a shopping mall or precinct? A case could be made for all these candidates. They may all exhibit rationalisation, but they are still very different from each other. My own nomination would be a supermarket. An outstanding feature of the present time is that consumers have so much choice. There are so many different restaurant chains, holiday packages and so forth, and the chains and brand names do not have the market to themselves. In all consumer services there are hundreds of small independent companies. This certainly applies with restaurants (see Warde and Martens, 2000). It applies in the holiday trade also. The recorded music business has giants but most dance music, which has been extremely popular in recent years, is compiled by small local companies, some of them one-person businesses (Hesmondhalgh, 1998; Smith and Maughan, 1997). Commercial leisure markets are different partly in the sheer number of small operators who are trying to carve out niches. Many of these businesses rely on flair and enthusiasts' know-how rather than marketing science. Most of the businesses are fragile. They are vulnerable to economic downturns and shifts in fashion but there is a constant stream of new entrants (see Berrett *et al.*, 1993; Butler, 1978; Hodgson, 1988).

Globalisation is one of the most-used words in present-day social science. The word is new but not the trend itself. There have been world empires and religions for over a thousand years. Now it is true that goods, fashions and music spread more rapidly than ever before, and that more people are travelling, doing it more often, and going further afield, but the outcome is not that every place ends up with exactly the same shops, restaurants and so on. Even McDonald's varies its menus slightly by adding dishes to suit local tastes. In India there is no beef in McDonald's burgers, because Hindus believe that the cow is sacred. Every location offers a unique combination of the global and the local. The music may be the same, but its meanings vary. Performers and their audiences find meanings in sounds and lyrics by making their own connections with local events and places (Bennett, 2001). The outcome of globalisation is not a single global village but rather a network of villages, all with distinctive characters.

Commerce does not standardise even what it makes available, and it cannot standardise people's lives. Rather, commerce extends choice. By making available so many possible combinations of goods and services, commerce enables consumers to develop individualised lifestyles. In every leisure field in which it operates, commerce offers variety. Consumers have far more choice today than in the pre-McDonald's era. In addition, commerce does other things that no other type of leisure provision can replicate. It provides a distinctive consumer experience, that of being served, it stimulates people's wants, it makes access simple, and it offers goods and services that are undemanding, thereby widening its markets. No-one has to go to McDonald's. Indeed, it is always possible to avoid the entire commercial sector. There are always voluntary or public sector alternatives. This applies with holidays, places to eat and drink, and music to listen to. Commerce does not remove its competitors. It adds options, as illustrated in previous discussions of tourism (Chapter 5) and popular music (Chapter 9). The market sector offers a wealth of goods and services that no other kind of leisure provision can match.

It is true, as Marxists point out, that by developing lifestyles that involve the consumption of commercial goods and services, people become bound into and, in a sense, prisoners within, the global market economy. But we are prisoners by choice. We can opt out if we wish, although that is unlikely. Those who are still outside are keen to get in. This applies to the populations of countries that are still emerging from state socialism, in the third world, and the poor in the economically advanced societies.

Shopping

Is shopping a leisure activity? When asked how they feel about shopping, members of the public often say that it depends on the type: that the weekly trip for food and other household goods is different from shopping for clothes, cosmetics, gifts, furniture, videos, DVDs, CDs etc. However, the boundaries are fraying, if not disintegrating, as supermarkets become hypermarkets and locate to shopping precincts (malls) or retail parks where batches of purchases can be loaded into a car before returning at a leisurely pace to the stores. Supermarkets themselves are introducing more and more specialty lines. Mood music and controlled temperatures can make even the journey down the grocery aisles into a pleasant excursion.

In practice, feelings about shopping differ from person to person. They range from love to hate. Women are over-represented among the lovers and men among the haters (Campbell, 1997). Most leisure activities, football for instance, elicit equally varied reactions. Shopping is different in that all households have to do it. Although people could do more and more shopping online, thereby saving time, in practice they are spending more time at the shops – up by roughly 50 per cent in Britain since the 1960s (see Roberts, 1999a). Shopping is what people are most likely to do on their days off work and when they go for days out. Tourists can be relied on to shop. In the 1990s relaxation of Britain's Sunday trading laws rapidly transformed Sunday into a major shopping day. Car parks at retail precincts were soon jammed and congestion at nearby motorway junctions has become a normal Sunday motoring experience.

Shopping for pleasure is not new. Walter Benjamin (a member of the Frankfurt School, see Chapter 9, pp. 127–30) wrote about the shopping arcades that had been constructed in nineteenth-century Paris and other European cities (see Rojek, 1997). These were smart, up-market places. The customers were all well-to-do. However, the working class at that time experienced comparable pleasures in the markets and in the streets which were filled with shops, stalls, buskers and organ grinders. At the end of the working week people experienced the pleasures of spending. The spread of department stores in major cities during the inter-war years made the excursion into town a highlight of the weeks before Christmas, and maybe at Easter and Whitsun. Shoppers would amble through the stores before deciding exactly what to purchase. The profusion of goods, all so close, available to touch, was a dreamland of the era.

The present-day equivalents are the out-of-town malls and retail parks which cater for the car-borne. Their architecture makes its own statements. These are the cathedrals of today – cathedrals of consumerism. Look what the malls contain. There are so many kinds of shops – large and small, specialist boutiques and general department stores. Present-day shopping precincts have everything that one could possibly desire within walking distance. There are bars, restaurants, very likely a movie multiplex, even a casino. The places cater for day-time and night-time interests. One can merge into the other. There are children's play areas and places for everyone to relax. And, of course, there is the mood music, and the controlled temperature – very important in places where outdoor winters are intolerably cold and/or summers unbearably hot. Some shopping complexes incorporate hotels and night clubs (see Box 11.2). It is possible to visit for a weekend and never go outdoors. Malls have become favoured sites for teenagers who want somewhere to hang out and to meet friends. The presence of groups of teenagers is sometimes regarded as troublesome, but it appears that most young people spend at least some of the time shopping (if window shopping is included) (see G Lowe, 2002). When they are at home watching TV (and the adverts) and when they are 'out', today's young people are likely to be learning to link leisure with buying.

It is convenient to have everything in one place but, as noted above, the new retail venues are not leading to a decline in total shopping time. People have more money to spend than in the past, and they are devoting more time to spending it. Some older marketing aids have survived – shopping catalogues for instance. More people are buying online. Some viewers switch on the TV shopping channels. All this appears to be in addition to, rather than instead of, actually going out to shop.

These retail developments are products of a rational mentality. They are located and designed so as to attract the maximum possible number of shoppers, and to induce them to spend as much as possible per dollar invested. However, although very likely to contain one, the malls, precincts and retail parks themselves cannot be described as McDonaldized. Each development has its own character – a unique mixture of shops, restaurants and so on. They can be used flexibly, at times of their

---

BOX 11.2 MALL OF AMERICA

In 1982 Minnesota's professional baseball and football teams moved from Met Stadium to downtown Minneapolis. This released 78 acres of land just one-and-a-half miles from the airport.

In August 1992 the Mall of America opened its doors. This is North America's largest retail and entertainment complex. It has:

- 520 stores
- 12,000 employees on site
- Over 35 million visitors a year
- Attractions which include Camp Snoopy (roller coaster and other rides), Underwater Adventure, LEGO Imagination Centre, Cereal Adventure, Jillian's Hi Life Lanes (bowling), NASCAR Silicon Motor Speedway (indoor stock cars), Rainforest Café, Café Odyssey, America Live (4 night clubs), and General Cinema (14 screens).

Tourists account for 40 per cent of all visitors. For every dollar spent in the Mall, two or three dollars are spent outside on petrol, lodgings, food, transportation etc.

Sources: www.mallofamerica.com, www.bloomingtonmm.org/mallofamerica.asp

---

own choosing, by consumers who plot their own itineraries. Singles, couples, families, young and old; everyone is catered for. The success formula here is not to standardise the experience but to offer a range of sale-points so that all groups of consumers can use the facilities according to their own desires.

Note that only commerce is able to develop shopping into a leisure activity. Under communism in Eastern Europe shopping was a chore. There were always shortages, and it was necessary to queue for virtually everything. This was also 'rational'. There are always many different things that can be equally rational: so many that very little is explained. What is rational depends on an actor's objectives and power, and on the social, cultural, economic and political contexts.

Going out for a drink

The types of holidays that people take nowadays are modern commercial social inventions, and likewise the out-of-home eating and drinking that most people enjoy. Here commerce has adapted, modernised and civilised traditional forms of recreation (eating and drinking) and situations (inns and ale houses). Commerce has made the activities harmless for the vast majority of customers. As this has happened, state controls have been relaxed, state revenues have benefitted, and going out for a meal and a drink have become popular pastimes in virtually all sections of the population.

History

In Britain the popularity of eating out has been achieved only since the Second World War. Formerly only the wealthy dined out regularly. Others may have paid for catering while on holiday and on very special occasions, though even celebrations at christenings, weddings and funerals were very likely to be self-catered. Before the First World War, out-of-home drinking was disreputable. Nineteenth-century social reformers had set about curbing this aspect of the 'dark side' of leisure. Levels of consumption declined steadily throughout the nineteenth and early twentieth centuries. Consumption levels in pre-industrial (merrie) England and elsewhere have still not been surpassed (Silcock, 1977). Prior to the Second World War, consumption was depressed steadily by higher taxes, laws governing licensing premises and opening hours, the legally enforced separation of the sale of alcohol from most places of music and entertainment, and campaigns for temperance. Pure water supplies, and the growing popularity of tea and coffee plus soft drinks such as orange squash, also played a part in the decline in alcohol consumption. Drink was believed to be a major cause of poverty, although at the turn of the century the famous poverty surveys of Charles Booth (in London) and Seebohm Rowntree (in York) had shown that unemployment, low wages and large families were the main sources of working-class hardship. Campaigns for temperance were fiercer in northern Europe and North America than in other Western countries. The USA actually prohibited the manufacture and sale of alcohol products for a period between the World Wars and thereby gave an enormous boost to organised crime (see Box 11.3).

Since 1945 alcohol consumption has recovered, more so in Europe than in North America. Per capita consumption in Britain doubled between the 1950s and the early 1980s (see Smith, 1982). Since then the overall level of consumption has been stable, albeit with slight ups and downs from year to year. There is fierce competition between different manufacturers, beverages such as alcopops and other RMDs (ready-mixed drinks), and brands (of bottled beers and so on) for shares in a static market. However, there are no signs of consumption tailing off. By the 1970s

---

BOX 11.3 PROHIBITION

At midnight on 16 January 1920 the eighteenth amendment to the constitution put an end to all importing, exporting, transporting, selling and manufacturing of intoxicating liquor in the USA. The results were:

- Alcohol consumption increased. Bootleggers smuggled liquor into the USA or produced their own. Illegal speakeasies replaced legal saloons. By 1925 there were over 100,000 speakeasies in New York alone.
- Crime increased. The liquor business fell under the control of organised gangs who bribed or otherwise overpowered the authorities. In large cities homicides increased from 5.5 to nearly 10.0 per 100,000 of population. Rivalry between gangs led to gangland killings at a rate of around 400 per year. The most famous bootlegger was Al Capone who operated out of Chicago. He was responsible for one of the most gruesome gangland killings – the St Valentine's Day massacre in 1929.

Prohibition ended in 1933.

Sources: http://prohibition.history.ohio-state.edu/, www.cato.org/pubs/pas/pa-157.html

---

BOX 11.4 DRINKING OURSELVES TO DEATH?

In the UK:

- 27% of 11–16-year-olds drink at least once a week.
- 27% of adult men and 37% of male 16–24-year-olds drink above the recommended safe weekly limit of 21 units.
  15% of adult women and 23% of female 16–24-year-olds, drink above the recommended safe weekly limit of 14 units.
- A quarter of all adults, and two-fifths of 16–24-year-olds, engage in 'hazardous drinking' which is accompanied or followed by loss of memory, injury, or failing to do what was expected of them like turning up for work the next morning.
- 1 person in 13 is alcohol dependent.
- Estimates of the number of deaths in which alcohol plays a part range up to 33,000 a year.
- One in six people attending accident and emergency hospital departments has alcohol-related problems or injuries. Every year there are 28,000 hospital admissions of patients suffering from alcohol dependency or poisoning. Alcohol is estimated to cost the NHS £3 billion a year.
- One in seven people killed on the roads, and 1 in 20 of those injured, are involved in drink-drive accidents.
- In 40 per cent of violent crimes, the victims say that the perpetrators were under the influence of alcohol.
- Sixty per cent of employers say that they experience problems (absenteeism or poor performance, for example) due to employees drinking.

Sources: Alcohol Concern, *The State of the Nation: Britain's True Alcohol Bill*, www.alcoholconcern.org.uk, 12.2.02; S Boseley, 'Alcohol problem inflicts £3 bn bill on NHS', *Guardian*, 1.3.02, p. 3.

---

commerce had made drink respectable. There are still opponents (see Box 11.4), but alcohol has now become a normal, indeed expected, part of most leisure occasions which involve social intercourse. It has also become acceptable within sections of the population where it was previously uncommon, namely, women and young people. The Liverpool Cavern where the Beatles played in the early 1960s was dry. A few years previously, skiffle groups had launched their careers in coffee bars. It was not until the 1970s that alcohol was thoroughly assimilated into Britain's youth cultures. Alcohol products are now available in most places where people gather for recreation or entertainment. Beers, wines and spirits can be purchased at any supermarket, along with other groceries: sales for consumption off the premises are no longer restricted to a limited number of 'off-licences'. Breweries sponsor football teams. They make donations to political parties. No-one's reputation appears to be blemished. The drinks business is no longer shady.

Making alcohol acceptable

Alcohol consumption in present-day Britain is slightly beneath the European Union average. Luxembourg is top. The UK adult population consumes an average of 7.5 litres of alcohol a year. It is claimed that the British drink differently; bingeing and getting drunk instead of spreading consumption in a glass of wine or beer at most meal times. Staggered consumption will be preferable if the aim is quiet town centres. If the aim is merriment, drinking so slowly that the effect is hardly noticeable will seem pointless. The Scandinavian countries, Sweden and Norway, have the lowest levels of alcohol consumption in Western Europe (under 5 litres per capita per year). In Ukraine, a vodka country where, as in Russia, alcoholism is considered a serious problem, consumption averages just 1.2 litres per year (*Guardian*, 21 February 2001). How can this be possible? The official statistics will be under-estimates: they do not include home-produced drink. However, the main fact of this matter is that in market economies commerce succeeds in increasing the amount of alcohol consumed while diminishing unwanted side-effects.

The traditional (pre-industrial) way to drink was to carry on until one fell asleep. This continued under communism in Eastern Europe where there were no pubs and very few restaurants. People usually drank, if they did so, in their homes, in private, or, in some cases, in parks or on the streets. Commerce has civilised drinking, and what was formerly the Western way of drinking is currently spreading in Eastern Europe (see Roberts *et al.*, 2000). Commerce wants people – most people, preferably all people – to drink, and to do so regularly, which is only likely if drinking can be made harmless and therefore socially acceptable. The owners of bars, cafes and restaurants do not want customers to become drunk and disorderly, or too ill to continue to work and sustain their leisure spending. The 'rules of drinking' enforced informally upon themselves by customers (and proprietors) may approve of 'getting merry' but not out of control. Hence the tolerance of young people's alcohol consumption: the majority in present-day Britain consume alcohol regularly in licensed premises before reaching the age at which this becomes legal (see Sharp *et al.*, 1988).

Britain is in fact the European leader in levels of alcohol consumption, and likewise of tobacco and the use of other drugs, by 15–16-year-olds (*Guardian*, 21 February 2001). Parents condone teenagers drinking (but not necessarily their use of tobacco or other drugs). Most children learn to drink at home (Sharp *et al.*, 1988). Parents know where their teenage children go on Friday and Saturday nights. Everyone knows who the fun pubs are for. Judged from the behaviour of present-day young people, it seems unlikely that the character of a 'good night out' will change dramatically among the next generation of adults. One study found that young people who were going 'down town' regularly for their nights-out were spending close on two-fifths of their total incomes on these occasions (Hollands, 1995). Despite claims of student poverty since the phasing-out of maintenance grants in the UK, between 1995/6 and 1998/9 student spending on essentials fell by 5 per cent while their spending on other items (including alcohol) rose by 25 per cent (Callender and Kemp, 2000). Impoverishment is usually accompanied by a declining proportion of all spending being allocated to non-essentials. Clearly, their pleasures are important to young people. Most say, when questioned, that it would be a totally unacceptable restriction to be deprived of their nights-out (Hollands, 1995). Ninety per cent of Britain's young adults drink alcohol at least occasionally; 80 per cent go to pubs, and 50 per cent to clubs, at least once a month (Hollands and Chatterton, 2002).

The attractions of restaurants and bars

Levels of spending on out-of-home eating and drinking are remarkable when we bear in mind that, when questioned, the majority of people say that the main reason why they visit pubs is not for the drink but for the company (Wilders, 1975). They go out to socialise on neutral territory. Commerce provides the venues, covers the costs, and usually makes a handsome profit, by selling food and drink. This does not mean that commerce is persuading people to consume things that they do not really want, though considerable sums are spent on promoting alcohol sales. The public is obviously willing to be seduced. We like the moods that alcohol can induce. People need to eat and can do so relatively cheaply by purchasing foodstuffs at supermarkets and consuming meals at home, but going out has special attractions. One is relieved of the need to prepare the food and to clear up afterwards. In a restaurant there is a choice of dishes, many more exotic than standard domestic fare. Everyone in a party can select their own dishes: there is no need to have a set meal. People are willing to pay for this experience and commerce provides the opportunity. Of course, there are risks, especially in recreational drinking (see Box 11.4, p. 164). People surely cannot be unaware of the hazards. Most people try to avoid them, but we all know that there will be some casualties. We know that driving a car exposes us to risks but, as with alcohol, we obviously find the risks acceptable, outweighed by the benefits.

There is plenty of McDonaldization in out-of-home dining and drinking, just as there is in the holiday trade, but in all these leisure industries there are several major chains, the bigger players all have several brands which are updated regularly to keep abreast of changing tastes and fashions, and there are many independent operators. The net effect is that consumers have a wealth of choice. The variety in the 'packaging' is remarkable when we bear in mind the similar basic commodities that all the packages contain. Cities with booming night-time economies have not just particular bars and restaurants, but entire streets and precincts, which cater for specific tastes and types of customers. In Newcastle-upon-Tyne there are venues for those seeking a traditional (working class) night out, students, gays, and the young rich who are to be found in up-market, 'classy' places, very likely located close to waterfronts (see Chatterton and Hollands, 2001). People do not have to always go to the same place. They can experience different scenes on different occasions, or even during a single evening. By virtue of where they go and where they are seen, people can be identified, and they can identify themselves (maybe only temporarily), as particular kinds of people.

The licensed trade is highly responsive to its customers' varied interests. During the era of televised sport the trade has created environments where people can enjoy the spectator crowd experience. Some football fans claim that nowadays pubs are the places where they can best express their support. Hence the crowds that fill pubs to watch international soccer fixtures. Many of those concerned are able to watch at home, if they prefer. During the 2002 World Cup pubs became crowded for matches with morning kick-offs – very early morning kick-offs in some cases (Weed, 2003).

Nightlife has plenty of critics: the health lobby occupies one flank, and on another there are those who detect and deplore McDonaldization. Robert Hollands and Paul Chatterton (2002) complain about 'a lack of real consumer choice and diversity in spite of the increases in designs and branding, and continued social and spatial segmentation due to market segmentation'. They object to 'gentrified nightlife environments [that] consciously sanitise and exclude the poor and disenfranchised', and to big corporations which are accused of 'spatially squeezing out independent entrepreneurs'. They conclude that, 'Nightlife, then, rather than being a post-modern panacea of creativity is increasingly packaged as something which happens to people, rather than something which people participate in and shape'. Yet Hollands and Chatterton's own research in Newcastle-upon-Tyne has documented the wealth of choice available to consumers in mainstream scenes within which there is an up-market exclusive end, traditional venues, and alternative places which cater for specific tastes in music or particular kinds of people such as gays (see Hollands, 2002). If ungentrified and unsanitised places are being squeezed out of prime city centre sites, this can only be because more consumers will visit and pay more for the gentrified and sanitised alternatives, and it is not self-evident that there really is less 'participation' in chain pubs than in independent bars.

Holidays and evenings-out both illustrate that commerce is not just a method of delivery. The products are distinctly commercial. Neither the voluntary nor the public sector could replicate them. They could not replicate the variety: the choice of meals, drinks and settings in different types of bars, cafes and restaurants, sometimes with and sometimes without background music. Nor could any other provider replicate the commercial experience of being served. We should note that in creating these leisure opportunities commerce has not eliminated anything else. It has widened people's options. No-one has to go on a commercial holiday, to a pub or to a restaurant. They do so because, given the choice, this is self-evidently how they prefer to use some of their time and money. Why criticise any of those involved?

CONCLUSIONS

This chapter opened by presenting the McDonaldization thesis, then proceeded to explore what people find attractive about shopping and out-of-home eating and drinking. Commerce has an army of social science critics. One of their battalions has taken on the hospitality trade. Exponents of the McDonaldization thesis complain about consumption being programmed, standardised, drained of real choice, spontaneity and creativity. The truth is precisely the reverse. The leisure provisions discussed in this chapter demonstrate commerce's unique ability to transform necessary activities into appetising uses of time and money. Rather than featuring in the case for the prosecution, these leisure industries vindicate commerce. The alcohol trade also shows how, with an activity which is inherently risky, commerce has been able to expand the market while containing, rather than magnifying, the risks (for most customers) within acceptable limits. We shall see in the next chapter that this applies equally to gambling.

12 Gambling

Introduction

Gambling is a huge global industry. It has become one of the more trans-national leisure industries. Nowadays people do not need to travel or telephone in order to place a bet in another country; this can now be done easily and cheaply via the internet (see Gaming Board for Great Britain, 2000). In 2001 the UK government abolished its 9 per cent tax on betting shop and similar stakes (which punters could avoid by placing bets online or by telephone with overseas-based bookmakers) and replaced it with a 15 per cent tax on the firms' gross profits. Following this change, UK bookies' turnover rose by 40 per cent. This gives an indication of the amount of gambling that is internationally footloose nowadays. Online gambling has become a UK business success story. The UK is expected to take half of the total European interactive gambling market (Bulkley, 2003). Most present-day governments are keen to attract the business and the UK government is succeeding. Foreign gamblers are often particularly welcome. In some countries (including South Korea until 2000) admission to casinos has been restricted to foreign passport holders.

Gambling used to be an adult activity that took place legally only in heavily regulated premises. All of a sudden technology has brought it into people's homes. By 2001 one per cent of all adults in Britain were gambling on the internet every week, and globally online gambling accounted for £21 billion out of a total turnover of £638 billion. By 2003 nearly two dozen gambling channels were available to Sky's 7 million UK digital subscribers.

This chapter opens by acknowledging that the inclusion of gambling in a book on the leisure industries may raise some eyebrows. Gambling has certainly been among our shadier uses of leisure. The chapter continues by explaining how gambling's seedy reputation owes much to its heavily regulated past. Until the 1960s in Britain, and in most other countries, there were precious few opportunities to gamble legally. We then see how, since the 1960s, the industry has been progressively liberalised. One of the reasons is that the business proves highly lucrative not just for the promoters but also for the host governments. The chapter continues by explaining how and why the UK introduced a national lottery in 1994 and concludes by discussing the short-term and likely long-term impacts. These include a further massive expansion of the industry, and we question whether that is cause for alarm.

A shady business?

Gambling is a topic that is as likely to be covered in books on crime as in books on leisure. It is a moot point whether its shady reputation is inherent in the activity or a product of the legal restrictions which were in force in the nineteenth and early twentieth centuries in most of Europe and North America, and which resulted in most gambling involving some breach of the law.

Gambling is certainly a strange business. Persuading people to part with money usually involves handing over something of equal value – food, drink, accommodation, transport or entertainment. In gambling people part with cash for virtually nothing. In the UK they play the National Lottery, exchanging cash for mere strips of paper, and sometimes queue for the privilege. They give money to casinos in exchange for being allowed to place counters on gaming tables. Gambling is so strange that its existence disturbs some people. It can be a dangerous business unless properly regulated, but what we have learnt in recent times is that stringent state control is not necessarily the most effective way to minimise gambling.

The basic costs of running a gambling business can be modest. Betting shops are spartan. Casino equipment is not expensive. Starting up in the business need not require a huge investment or a highly-developed esoteric skill. Yet gambling can be extraordinarily lucrative for the promoters. The ground rule in all commercial gambling is that the house always wins. Some punters win, many more lose, but the house always comes out on top. The odds guarantee this. Of course, the industry likes to pretend otherwise. Bookmakers moan when a favourite romps home, and it is claimed that a man really did break the bank and close the main casino in Monte Carlo. The fact is that punters never put the bank out of business. This is not allowed to happen.

Gambling's shady reputation stems partly from the business being so lucrative. Yet, as far as basic know-how and investment are concerned, the trade can be easy to enter. Profits can be huge for a modest outlay. These profits are at risk if anyone opens a rival betting office or card room across the street. So all proprietors have an interest in discouraging competitors, and in unregulated markets they need to protect their own premises, staff and customers. Throughout the world, when it has not been prohibited, governments have decided that gambling is too dangerous an activity to be left entirely to the market. They have decided that gambling businesses should be licensed to ensure that proprietors are of good character and remain well-behaved, but this immediately opens the possibility of the police, politicians and state officials being corrupted because promoters are often prepared to pay generously to obtain and to keep their licences, and to prevent competitors fouling their space.

Customers need to be policed by gambling houses, which may appear to have an interest in offering almost unlimited credit. What do they lose if someone is allowed to continue playing the tables and losing on IOUs? The house loses nothing if the customer defaults but can gain substantially if the punter pays up. In order to discourage gambling houses from enticing punters to stake more than they can afford to lose, governments (as in the UK, though not in most parts of the USA) may decide that gambling debts should not be recoverable through the courts, which means that gambling businesses which are liberal with credit need their own ways of persuading debtors to pay. In practice, gambling houses which are operated by legitimate businesses usually prefer to be extremely cautious in offering credit, and they certainly have no intention of resorting to strong-arm tactics. They know that this would be bad for business. These practices are common only when gambling is forced into the shade, beyond the law. Legitimate gambling businesses' main problem customers are those who try to cheat, and those who demand and would gamble on credit without intending to pay up, or knowing full well that, in the event of them losing, they would be unable to pay. Houses do not need to cheat: 'fair' play guarantees that the house always wins. Another problem for the industry (whether shady or legitimate) is that punters can win substantial sums by fixing the result of a sport event or colluding with casino or betting office staff. Anything that is the subject of gambling is liable to be corrupted – boxing, football and cricket matches – because the sums at stake (and which can be offered as bribes) are so huge. The gambling industry has an interest in keeping sports clean and may be unable to rely on the governing bodies. It also needs to make sure that its own staff are clean. The necessity for these measures ensures that gambling retains a shady reputation.

There is a 'science' of gambling. This is not a punters' science: there is no way in which most of them can win. The 'scientific' evidence shows that they must lose. Rather, the industry has its body of 'scientific' knowledge, or trade know-how, on how to maximise profits. The key is usually not to retain a high proportion of the sums staked but to persuade more people to play, or to persuade people who play to stake more. First, the possibility, however remote, of a 'big strike' – a mega-prize – entices punters. Britain's National Lottery, football pools and bingo halls all know that jackpots lure players. Combination bets enable horse-race punters to hope that one day will be their really lucky day. Second, there needs to be a flow of smaller prizes, reinforcers, to reassure punters that they can win, and motivate them to continue playing. Gaming machines need to pay out regularly. The house still wins in the end. Punters will usually stake back any modest winnings. Third, the sums staked should be variable to suit customers with different means and who need to risk different amounts in order to kindle excitement. Fourth, it helps if a game can be linked with a 'good cause' however small the proportion of the total stake that flows in that direction.

The gambling industry and its analysts distinguish between soft and hard gambling. In soft gambling there is a cooling-off period between gambling events, as in weekly football pools and the UK's twice-weekly National Lottery. Hard gambling is when play is continuous, and when it is possible (though not inevitable) that punters will be carried away in attempting to increase their winnings or to recover their losses. The casino is the hard gambling situation *par excellence*, and the betting shop or any informal card school can become one if people remain *in situ*, staking bets for hour after hour, maybe throughout the night. Hard gambling is generally considered particularly dangerous. The public is said to need protection from its own weaknesses. So hard gambling places may be made difficult to access – members only, no advertising, invisible from the street – or uncomfortable – no food or drink, especially alcohol, maybe no music and just spartan furnishings.

State control

Until quite recently most modern-age governments tried to discourage gambling. Britain was no exception. Prior to 1960 most types of gambling were illegal in the UK. Most gambling had been made unlawful during the nineteenth century when it was believed to be a cause of poverty. As a matter of fact gambling was not a major cause of poverty, but it was true that most people could not really afford to deflect any of their income away from essentials. If they did so, it was considered preferable that they should choose 'rational recreation'. The rich, as well as the poor, could be impoverished by gambling. Some obviously (so it was believed) needed to be protected from their own weaknesses. Perhaps most fundamentally, gambling has been regarded as incompatible with the values of modern societies. People are supposed to succeed by studying, gaining qualifications and skills, then by working hard. Life is not supposed to be a lottery.

Until 1960 the legal forms of gambling in Britain were on-course betting at horse-racing and greyhound tracks, the football pools which a limited number of companies were allowed to operate, and charity raffles. These had to be licensed and in practice this meant that the prizes were modest and entering was more akin to a donation than the pursuit of wealth or excitement. It was also possible to place telephone bets on horse and greyhound races. There were no betting shops, no casinos, no gaming machines (except for amusement), and no bingo for cash prizes. Premium bonds (with which, in effect, savers gamble their interest) had been introduced in 1957 amid much controversy.

There were several problems with this tight control regime. First, there was a great deal of illegal gambling. Bookies' runners accepted bets on street corners, and collected from and paid out at most industrial workplaces. Informal (illegal) betting on cards, dominoes, darts and snooker was taking place in pubs and clubs throughout the country. Many voluntary societies were operating illegal raffles (just for fund-raising purposes). Hence the argument that it would be preferable for the law to be liberalised so that the gambling which seemed inevitable could be properly regulated (see Clapson, 1990). In more recent times the same case has been argued for cannabis and other recreational drugs. A second problem was said to be the unfairness that people with telephones, who were considered creditworthy by bookmakers, had more opportunity to gamble than the rest of the population. There was a third problem. Countries which had liberalised their gaming laws had

---

BOX 12.1 LAS VEGAS

Nowadays Las Vegas describes itself as the most exciting and entertaining city in the world. It is the place where you can see amazing re-creations such as erupting volcanoes, the Eiffel Tower, and the Sphinx of Egypt. In 2002 the artists appearing in Las Vegas included Little Richard, Oasis, Alanis Morissette, Elvis Costello, The Who, Wynonna, Paul McCartney, Tom Jones, Paul Anka, Britney Spears, Al Martino, Cleo Laine, Art Garfunkel, Frankie Avalon, Neil Sedaka, Debbie Reynolds, Natalie Cole, Tony Bennett, Glen Campbell, Ray Charles and Connie Francis.

Yet in 1930 Las Vegas was basically just another small railroad town with a bit of mining and some agriculture. Its population was a mere 5165. Then in 1931 gambling was legalised by the State of Nevada and the City of Las Vegas issued six gambling licences. It was only after the Second World War that lavishly decorated resort hotels were built and top-name entertainers began to be attracted. Thus by 1960 tourism and entertainment had become the largest employers and the population had risen to 64,405.

Major corporations then began investing in huge hotel/casino complexes. In 1995 the population was 368,360 and further expansion (to 2 million eventually) is envisaged. In the mid-1990s employment was growing at a rate of 18 per cent each year. It is jobs that drive the growth of population. Gambling has made Las Vegas a booming city.

Sources: www.vegas.com, www.ci.las-vegas.nv.us/

---

discovered that doing so attracted large sums of money into their territories. The main states which had trail-blazed were Monaco (capital Monte Carlo) and Nevada (where Las Vegas is situated) in the USA (see Box 12.1). Subsequently many other places have followed suit. In the USA these include some Indian reservations whose populations have become wealthy by the simple device of opening a casino.

The UK's laws were liberalised by the 1960 and 1968 Gaming Acts. Since 1960 the UK has had betting shops where bets can be placed on horses, dogs, elections, football matches, the weather, and virtually everything else where the outcome is uncertain. These Acts also provided for casinos to open in a limited number of locations (major cities and tourist destinations), for clubs to operate cash-prize bingo, and for gaming machines to be installed in licensed premises and a limited number of other locations. These machines have subsequently become a significant source of income for the site owners. Universities could solve their financial problems if they were permitted to install them. The 1960 Act also authorised charity raffles. Later, scratchcards were permitted. Since 1968 a Gaming Board has supervised and licensed the entire UK gambling industry. Private lotteries (among people at a particular workplace, for example), and small society lotteries (for fund-raising and/or members' entertainment) have been exempted from control and have thereby been legalised. However, all types of legal gambling have remained surrounded by numerous restrictions. Under the post-1960 regime, cash bingo and casino games could be played only in 'clubs' and membership could not be awarded instantly. Would-be players had to wait for at least 24 hours. The intention was to prevent impulse gambling. None of the gambling businesses were allowed to advertise, although pools firms circumvented this by publishing press notices of their pay-outs. The actual gambling in casinos and betting shops had to be invisible from the street in case the innocent were tempted in by the excitement. There were additional restrictions: no use of credit cards, no alcohol, and spartan accommodation in betting shops to discourage punters from lingering. An effect of some of these restrictions was to accentuate the distinctive atmosphere in gambling 'dens' – punters cut off from the outside world, in environments where everyone is part of the culture.

After the 1960s' liberalisation, independent researchers, in addition to the industry, began to study in detail exactly how people gamble. It was found that, even in hard gambling situations, most punters remain 'in control'. They decide in advance how much they are prepared to spend at bingo or in a casino or on a visit to the races. They hope to win but expect to lose. They pay for the chance of riches and for the thrill – the excitement that envelopes a horse race, a round of golf, or a game of cards or bingo when money is at stake (Dixey, 1987; Neal, 1998; Saunders and Turner, 1987). Most players stake no more than they can afford to lose but enough to make the events exciting. Some people become addicted to gambling – unable to withdraw from gambling situations, or to pass a betting shop without placing a bet. As with alcohol, the only remedy appears to be complete abstention. The proportion of the population that can be described as addicted is tiny. 'Reckless' gambling is more common, where punters are carried away by the excitement and end up losing more than they intended (see Oldman, 1978). However, most punters avoid this risk by following set routines. Betting shop regulars usually stake the same amounts on each visit and on each race, and use the same bets (Bruce and Johnson, 1992, 1995; Filby and Harvey, 1988, 1989). If they lose, which is what they really expect, punters can still feel that they have enjoyed a good afternoon or night out. Camelot, the firm that has operated the UK's National Lottery since 1994 (see below, pp. 175–7), estimates that less than one per cent of the population are 'problem gamblers'. However, in the USA the National Opinion Research Center (1999) puts the proportion of 'pathological' and 'problem' gamblers at 2.5 per cent of all adults, and estimates that they account for 15 per cent of all lottery and casino receipts. Also, in the USA 1 per cent of adults define themselves as 'professional gamblers'.

So is it possible for punters to win? Professionals obviously think so. It is possible, by 'counting', to beat the casino at blackjack (pontoon), but the industry defines counting as cheating and anyone suspected, because they are winning too regularly, is required to leave. It is possible to win at horse-race betting but this requires detailed knowledge of the racing industry from published information (and maybe tips from trusted insiders). One needs to know things about which most punters are ignorant, like the horses whose recent form is a poor guide to their true potential, and which have been trained to peak condition for a particular meeting. A point to note here is that these professionals are trying to perform better, on average, than other punters and thereby win more than they lose in the long run. They are not really taking on the bookies. The industry is fireproof except when punters manage to break the rules, for example, by doping a favourite, or somehow intervening in the industry's flow of betting information and thereby fixing the odds.

As well as offering thrills, gambling locations are theatres where punters can role play, acquiring reputations for being cool, calculating, gregarious or aloof. Punters attribute what are really chance outcomes to skill, knowledge and judgement (Oldman, 1974). They may emulate professionals and study the form of horses and football teams in detail. They work out systems for placing bets on horses and in casinos. Some study lottery numbers that have come up in the past, in various combinations. Regulars are usually interested in each other's tactics and systems. Similar processes have been observed among teenagers who play for-amusement arcade machines (see Fisher, 1993). There are 'arcade kings' who play to win and attract attention, 'machine beaters' who play to win without an audience, and 'rent-a-spacers' who simply want to be with friends. Like going for a drink, gambling can be a great social occasion. Company intensifies the excitement at a casino, at bingo, or during a day at the races.

After 1960 gambling became a UK growth industry but its growth rate was not spectacular. It lagged behind other leisure industries such as tourism, the media, and out-of-home eating and drinking. Gambling became common, but not the norm, in most sections of the population. It is true that most people took part in charity raffles and had a flutter on the Derby and Grand National if only in an informal pool, but in the 1970s and 1980s only around a quarter of all adults were playing the football pools regularly, and no more than a third were visiting betting shops even occasionally. Bingo and the hard varieties of gambling – spending prolonged spells in betting shops, visiting casinos and playing gaming machines regularly – all involved less than 10 per cent of adults.

Nowadays roughly 70 per cent of all UK adults gamble at least occasionally (once a year or more). Gambling is like many other leisure activities – reading newspapers, watching television, and going to the cinema – in that it is fairly evenly

Table 12.1 Participation in gambling by gender, Great Britain 1999 (percentages taking part during the last year)

	Men	Women
National lottery	68	62
Scratchcards	22	22
Fruit machines	20	8
Horse races	18	9
Private bets	17	6
Football pools	13	5
Another lottery	9	8
Dog races	6	2
Bingo	5	10
Other betting with a bookmaker	5	1
Casino table games	4	1
Any gambling	76	68

Source: British Gambling Prevalence Survey, National Centre for Social Research.

Table 12.2 Participation in gambling by age, Great Britain, 1999 (percentages taking part during the past year)

	16–24	25–34	35–44	45–54	55–64	65–74	Older	All
National lottery	52	71	72	72	69	61	45	65
Scratchcards	36	32	23	17	16	11	6	22
Fruit machines	32	22	15	8	6	3	1	14
Horse races	12	19	15	14	11	9	5	13
Private bets	21	18	11	10	6	5	3	11
Football pools	4	9	8	11	13	10	6	9
Another lottery	8	9	8	9	9	8	6	8
Bingo	7	7	7	6	7	9	10	7
Dog races	6	7	7	6	7	9	10	7
Other betting with a bookmaker	5	5	3	2	2	1	–	3
Table games in a casino	4	5	3	2	1	–	–	3
Any gambling	66	78	77	78	74	66	52	72

Source: as Table 12.1.

spread among all social groups. One needs to explore finer detail – which newspapers, which TV channel and so on – before clear differences appear. Men are slightly more likely to gamble than women (see Table 12.1). The latter play more bingo while most other kinds of gambling are done mainly by men. Women are actually the better gamblers: they tend to stake less, place less outrageous bets, and lose less (Bruce and Johnson, 1996). People in all social classes gamble, but the poorer groups stake the higher proportions of their incomes (see Table 2.1, p. 19). All age groups gamble: there is a sharp drop only among the over-75s (see Table 12.2). The main age differences are in how people gamble. The young tend to favour scratchcards, fruit machines and casinos, and they place more private bets. Football pools have an ageing clientele and have suffered since the introduction of Britain's National Lottery (see below). Bingo is really the only form of gambling in which participation increases with age. Why do so many people gamble? It is partly for excitement and sociability, but also, for the majority, it is their best chance of becoming rich. It is a hope that people can hang onto; something that is reliable in an otherwise uncertain world (Reith, 1999).

Britain's National Lottery

Faced with a modest growth rate the UK gambling industry, as might be expected, favoured liberalisation of the gaming laws. The industry has never advocated complete deregulation: all-out competition could force operators further into the shade. However, the industry always seems to favour less regulation, which is expected to expand the market. The National Lottery, which began in 1994, has proved to be a huge liberalising measure. Why was it introduced? The stated purpose was to raise money for good causes which the public expected the government to support while objecting to tax hikes. In practice the National Lottery has led to a massive expansion of the gambling industry. Most adults do gamble regularly nowadays: they play the National Lottery (see Table 12.1, p. 174). This is despite the 'take' per game having declined since the mid-1990s. The National Lottery has all the features that gambling 'science' associates with success. There is the prospect of a huge cash prize. The percentage of stake money that is returned to players in prizes is just 50 per cent, which is pathetically low by industry standards (at least 80 per cent of stake money is usually returned). But the National Lottery channels 28 per cent of its take to good causes (see Box 12.2). The takes by the organisers and the government are in line with long-established industry norms. Players seem to pay less attention to these figures than to the size of the top prizes despite knowing that the odds are millions against. Ticket sales always rise when there is a roll-over and the chance of a really huge prize. This is the big attraction of the National Lottery – the prospect of real wealth. After purchasing a ticket everyone can daydream for a few hours about becoming a millionaire. However, the National Lottery has other features that draw and retain punters. There are lots of smaller 'reinforcer' prizes. Variable amounts can be staked and the entire business is linked to good causes. The National Lottery itself has led to a substantial increase in the proportion of the population that gambles regularly and, mainly indirectly, in the total gambling spend. More people in Britain play the National Lottery than participate regularly in any other form of gambling, but the National Lottery accounts for only 20 per cent of all stakes. This is because visitors to casinos, race courses, betting shops and so on tend to stake more per occasion. However, the really big effect of the National Lottery has probably been to change the culture. There have been short-term repercussions and there will be longer-term consequences.

From the beginning the National Lottery was allowed to advertise. Television adverts told the public that 'it could be you'. This lottery, although operated by a commercial business (Camelot up to now), has government approval. Maybe premium bonds were the first step, but they were a small step towards government support. The National Lottery has been a giant stride towards giving gambling the seal of government support. The National Lottery is now the largest single gambling operation in the UK. Sales amounted to roughly £5 billion in 2001, and approximately £1.5 billion a year was being distributed to 'good causes'. It is said, by government ministers, to be just fun, a harmless flutter.

Since the National Lottery was introduced, the rest of the UK gambling industry has demanded a level playing field. Pools companies, betting shops, bingo halls and casinos have demanded and have been given the right to advertise. Membership rules have been relaxed. In-house facilities, especially in betting shops, have become less spartan. Only the football pools and charity scratchcards appear to have lost business due to the National Lottery. Betting shops have increased their trade, and casinos likewise. Indeed, they appear to have benefitted from the liberalised gambling culture. They have also been able to deploy additional arguments.

BOX 12.2 THE UK NATIONAL LOTTERY: WHERE THE MONEY GOES

Total

1. Prizes	50%
2. Retailer	5%
3. Operating costs and profit	5%
4. Treasury duty	12%
5. Good causes	28%

Good causes

1994	2002	
Millennium fund	New opportunities	33.33%
Arts	Arts	16.66%
Sport	Sport	16.66%
Heritage	Heritage	16.66%
Charities	Community fund	16.66%

Sources: www.national-lottery.co.uk, www.camelotgroup.co.uk, Department for Culture, Media and Sport (2003), National Lottery Funding: Decision Document, London.

Tourists in Britain are said to expect the same facilities that are available abroad. A similar argument is presented in towns and cities that compete in the same regional leisure markets. None want to be denied an attraction like a casino that is available to competitors. As explained above, some gambling businesses are now able to operate off-shore if the tax or other regimes are more hospitable elsewhere. Bets can be placed by telephone or via the internet to companies that are based abroad. It is now possible to play casino games on the internet. Online gambling companies are not allowed to set up shop in the USA but Americans can still place bets online. How can any country prevent this if some countries are prepared to host the businesses? The same considerations now apply to tobacco and alcohol. If taxes in Britain exceed the rates in neighbouring countries, then, it appears, contraband will flood in no matter what the law says. Certainly no country, unless much larger than Britain, wishes to take a moral stand when this runs against the grain of today's leisure markets.

Cause for concern or celebration?

In 2002 the UK government announced its intention to make further changes in the gambling regime, amounting to a massive further liberalisation (see Box 12.3). It is likely that before long Blackpool and some other tourist meccas will become UK versions of Las Vegas. The UK is emulating the gambling regime that, for some years now, has operated in most parts of the USA where it has resulted in a huge expansion of the industry. Nowadays, in the USA, six out of every seven adults gamble compared with just two out of every three in the 1970s (National Opinion

Research Center, 1999). In 2001 in the UK two-thirds of all adults were gambling regularly (as in the USA in the 1970s). Unlike in Britain up to now, in the USA the heaviest gamblers nowadays are the over-45s, and lotteries and casinos are the main forms of gambling. Bingo and horse-race betting have been in decline in the USA for some years. This may happen in Britain if and when casinos become sufficiently numerous and appealing. However, it is possible in Britain that other gambling businesses will demand a level playing field. If casinos can serve alcohol, why not betting shops? And why should gaming machines in pubs be restricted to lower prizes than those in casinos?

Understandably, given the historically-laid view of gambling as a problem – maybe a necessary evil – concerns have been raised over the long-term effects of the liberalisation of gambling and the circumstances that have been responsible. Instead of articulating moral and aesthetic standards, national governments are now under pressure to assist all their domestic businesses, not just including but especially their leisure businesses because these are such an important growth sector. Leisure businesses include gambling firms. Governments want such home-based enterprises to claim as large as possible a share of their market. This matters. There is an economic upside. Who wants to forgo this? But what about the social and cultural aspects? If not by virtue of the uses of time and money that are approved of and deplored, how is any moral order to be proclaimed and upheld? 'Anything goes' may seem to have become the rule. Where will it end? Sex tourism is now a significant segment of the tourist trade. Must all countries offer the full range of services which international tourists and business travellers have come to expect? Can we anticipate NVQs in sex work so as to ensure that our own professionals are up to scratch? There are now hundreds of lottery millionaires in Britain. All major towns and cities must have at least one. Most people will be more likely to know someone, or to know of someone, who has become a millionaire by lottery than by any other method. What will be the long-term effects on our culture?

The National Lottery has become the UK's main national source of public funds for arts, sports and heritage projects. When the National Lottery began the

---

BOX 12.3 REFORM OF UK GAMBLING, 2002

- ■ Gambling Commission to become the single regulator of the National Lottery and all other forms of gambling
- ■ Online betting to be legalised, via the internet and interactive TV
- ■ 24-hour membership rule (for casinos and bingo halls) to be abolished
- ■ Use of credit cards to be permitted
- ■ Casinos to be allowed to offer:
  - – Any form of legal gambling including slot machines with unlimited stakes and prizes
  - – Live entertainment
  - – Alcohol on the gaming floor

Source: Department for Culture, Media and Sport (2002), *A Safe Bet for Success*, London.

government gave assurances that all this was new money and would not replace any existing public funds but in the longer term such assurances have proved to be meaningless. By 1998 the government had decided that some of the 'good causes' cash should go to health, education and environment projects (the New Opportunities Fund, see Box 12.2, p. 177). By 2002 this fund was taking more of the National Lottery's cash than any of the other 'good causes'. Again, of course, the same assurances were given when the New Opportunities Fund was created, that no existing public funds (for health, education or the environment) were to be withdrawn. In 2003 the government decided to merge the New Opportunities Fund and the Community Fund (which distributed to charities) thereby creating a super-fund with control of 50 per cent of the good causes budget. A fact of this matter is that it proves easier for a government to raise money through gambling than by direct (or indirect) taxation. In 2003 the UK government decided to skim the lottery fund to help to bid for and, if successful, to stage a London Olympics. At the outset the National Lottery was one game per week. It is now twice-weekly with more than one game per occasion. There are also National Lottery scratchcards. Bids to operate the Lottery are judged primarily against how much cash they are likely to raise. Will there come a time when schools and hospitals depend on a thriving and expanding gambling industry? Maybe this time has already arrived.

Another issue is the manner in which lottery money is distributed to good causes, which has encouraged further commercialisation of leisure provisions, even those that are under voluntary and public sector management. Graeme Evans (1995) has observed that the National Lottery was brought into existence without much thought having been given to the policies which should guide the disbursements to good causes except that these should be charities, the arts, sport, heritage and a millennium fund (wound down after 2000) to which the 'new opportunities' fund was added in 1998. Understandably, the panels that judge bids and distribute these monies have preferred to fund capital projects rather than cover running expenses. They have wanted to ensure that recipients have business plans which show, plausibly, that revenue will cover running costs. Some 'mistakes' have been made. Some museums have foundered like Sheffield's National Centre for Popular Music which closed in 2000 after just one year. It had cost £16.9 million including £10.9 million from the Arts Council's share of lottery proceeds. The centre had attracted just 66,000 visitors in its first six months. It needed more than 400,000 a year to break even (Gibbons, 2003). The Millennium Dome was a far bigger flop. However, a larger question that these examples raise is whether public leisure provisions should be judged against commercial criteria. If we want to protect and bequeath the country's pop music heritage for later generations, should the viability of the project depend on the number of visitors attracted during the first six months? Should visiting members of the public be charged commercial rates? This practice undermines the citizenship-enhancing potential of public leisure provisions. All that said, thanks partly to the National Lottery, the UK now has a batch of impressive new leisure facilities: the Millennium Stadium in Cardiff, the revamped Hampden Park in Glasgow, and a new Wembley to follow. The Royal Opera House has been rebuilt and new buildings include the British Museum, the Tate Modern and the Lowry in Salford, In other areas, lottery funding has created the UK Sports Institute, the World Class Performance Programmes, an emergent National Cycle Network and so on.

Who benefits? Everyone, but it must be admitted that the lion's share of the benefits goes to the better-off who have the tastes, inclination and money to travel to use the facilities. The propensity to play the National Lottery is not class-related but poor people tend to stake the larger proportions of their incomes. As a pseudo-tax, the Lottery is regressive. It is an amazingly successful method of persuading the poor to pay for the rich's good causes and pleasures (see Fitzherbert, 1995). This remains the case despite the creation in 2002 of a 'Fair Share' fund totalling £169 million, drawn from the National Lottery's New Opportunities and Community Funds. The 'Fair Share' money is targeted at just 56 of Britain's most deprived communities which it hopes to regenerate through investment, mainly in local voluntary associations.

Another loser from the latest liberalisation of UK gambling is likely to be the National Lottery itself. It will be difficult to sustain the Lottery's ticket sales against fiercer competition. Government income will not suffer – any gambling can be a source of revenue for the state – but there is no guarantee (in fact it is beyond the bounds of credibility) that 28 per cent of other gambling stakes will be channelled to 'good causes'.

The main answer to the tirade of criticism against the gambling boom has to be 'Yes, but, but, but . . .'. First, there are costs attached to any change. Someone always objects. Second, as in sport and broadcasting (see Chapters 7 and 10), the changes in gambling have been possible only because enough people have been prepared to pay. They obviously find the financial and other costs bearable. Gambling offers excitement and fuels daydreams. Those who pay clearly feel that these returns are worth the money. Third, people's leisure options have been widened. Nothing has been withdrawn. The expansion of commercial gambling has not prevented other commercial enterprises, voluntary associations or public bodies, doing the things that they do best. Fourth, governments can proclaim moral and aesthetic standards more effectively through what they support than through what they merely permit. The fact that cigarette smoking remains legal and a source of state revenue does not give it the seal of government approval. Fifth, gambling delivers public benefits, principally economic benefits, through the business that is attracted and the boost to public funds and spending on 'good causes'. Sixth, the development of a clear and coherent leisure policy should lead to better distribution of the good causes budget, but it must be borne in mind here that redressing socio-economic inequalities is not among the capabilities of state interventions in leisure (see Chapter 4, pp. 50–3). Seventh, and finally, commerce is an effective regulator. Legitimate businesses are sensitive to both the benefits of gambling (which promoters seek to maximise) and any damage which might drive customers away or, via public opinion, lead to a government clamp-down. With alcohol and gambling, commerce has demonstrated its capacity to act as a powerful, albeit, in these instances, a still controversial civilising force.

CONCLUSIONS

This chapter began by explaining gambling's shady reputation. The shadiness is partly a product of earlier heavy regulation but it is partly inherent in the activity. We then saw how Britain and other countries liberalised their gambling regimes during the second half of the twentieth century. By then governments throughout the world had become aware that gambling had turned Las Vegas and Monte Carlo into boom cities. Britain's National Lottery, introduced in 1994, has been a further liberalising measure. It has helped to change the culture – people's attitudes towards gambling – and it has led to a substantial expansion of the industry. Online gambling is sure to lead to yet more growth.

We have seen why alarm bells have rung in some quarters. However, we have also seen that there are benefits, and that the public costs of gambling may well be best controlled by regulations which reflect the inclinations of legitimate gambling businesses. Controlling the social costs of gambling is in these businesses' own interests: they want to remain legitimate and to avoid the re-imposition of heavier regulations.

13 The Arts

Introduction

This is the only leisure industry where the state is a principal provider. We saw in Chapter 4 that in Britain (which is typical of all countries in this respect) the central government department with responsibility for leisure is a pygmy in terms of staff numbers and the size of its budget. In most areas of leisure governments provide amenities and otherwise assist in some while regulating all, but, in totalitarian countries, state broadcasting and the arts aside, the public sector has never been the main direct provider. The state provides infrastructure and co-ordination for tourism, sport and events. The state always sets the legal framework within which leisure providers operate, and this is virtually all government does *vis-à-vis* shopping and out-of-home eating and drinking. Elsewhere the state is a minor provider – more minor than in the past in the case of the media, but more active in gambling in countries such as Britain where national lotteries have been introduced. The arts, as defined in this chapter, are different because the state is a crucial if not the principal provider. Major art galleries, museums, libraries and much of the heritage are owned and managed by government departments. Opera, ballet, the 'serious' theatre and classical music are usually provided by non-profit organisations but the leading companies are so dependent on state subsidies that they are best treated as quangos (see Chapter 3, p. 23). The amateur layers of the arts, like the amateur layers of sport, are run primarily by voluntary associations and their crucial fuel is enthusiasm. Much of the elite end of sport is also under voluntary management. The top levels in some sports – like the base levels in all of them – depend primarily on voluntary effort. A few sports (at elite levels) depend primarily on money raised from spectators, the media, various forms of sponsorship and commercial spin-offs. There is a serious (professional) segment of arts production which operates commercially. This branch of the leisure industries has been dealt with in Chapters 9 and 10 on the media and popular culture. The arts, as defined in this chapter, are the non-commercial serious segment, and they could not exist on anything like their present scale or in their present shape without state support.

The big question, then, is why the arts are privileged in this way. There are three contending answers. There is a 'class' answer, delivered most persuasively by the French sociologist, Pierre Bourdieu. This explains state support in terms of the role that the arts perform in legitimising and consolidating the wider class structure. Second, there is a diametrically opposed answer given by most spokespersons for the arts themselves. They have always claimed that state support is needed so that the arts can be made accessible to everyone (a right of citizenship). Third, there are the public sector's other special capabilities in leisure that were identified in Chapter 4 – investing to trigger an economic multiplier, setting standards, and enhancing the host's prestige and identity.

This chapter opens by noting the importance of cultural icons in creating public identities for their host places. It then tackles the thorny question, 'What is art?'. The class explanation of state support for high culture is then outlined, interrogated and rejected. The most frequently cited official rationale for state support – arts for all – is then considered and found to be less ludicrous than is often supposed. The chapter then examines the arts' contributions as economic investment, in setting standards, and in boosting a host's identity and prestige. We shall see that the arts are unusual and merit unusual levels of state support because they mesh with all the public sector's distinctive capabilities. The chapter concludes with a critical interrogation of state arts policy and indicates where fine tuning (or even something stronger) is needed. This raises broader questions which are taken up in the book's final chapter.

Places and images

What do people know about Sydney? Unless they have lived there, their most likely image will be the Sydney Opera House (Box 13.1). Here is an instant clue to the importance of the arts and one reason why, in most countries, they receive government support. People's images of places are often set by their theatres, art galleries, museums and concert halls. Greece was the site of the ancient Olympics and the first host in the modern series of Olympic Games. Even so, you are more likely to be able to picture Athens' acropolis than the restored 1896 stadium.

What is art?

The arts considered in this chapter are those that are recognised and supported by the UK Arts Councils and by the equivalent government bodies that have been created in most other modern societies. This is an instance where opting for a 'realist' definition is not blatant buck-passing. Most human behaviour has a cultural, symbolic, artistic dimension. It is not implied here that only arts which are state sponsored can have any, or exceptional, artistic merit in an absolute sense. However, state sponsorship clearly indicates that some important people, those who wield political power, believe that the relevant arts are especially worthy. The

---

BOX 13.1 SYDNEY OPERA HOUSE

This must be one of the most recognised images in the modern world. Yet the building was opened only in 1973. It is situated on Bennelong Point, which reaches out into Sydney harbour.

In the late-1950s the New South Wales government launched an appeal for funds to construct an opera house and a competition for its design. The Danish architect, Jorn Utzon, won the competition. As is often the case, his design and his victory were extremely controversial. The opera house cost Aus$102 million (approximately US$50 million) which was a massive amount of money at that time.

The building contains a main auditorium (2679 seats), a separate opera house, a drama theatre, a smaller playhouse, and an even smaller studio. It also has an impressive reception hall and forecourt.

Nowadays the opera house provides guided tours for approximately 200,000 visitors each year and has a total annual audience of around 2 million at its performances.

Sources: www.sydneyoperahouse.com,
www.cultureandrecreation.gov.au/articles/sydneyoperahouse/

---

sociological questions, then, are how it comes about that the relevant arts are singled out, and what are the wider economic, social, cultural and political implications. These are both public provision issues on the one hand, and priority issues for the arts on the other, because without government subsidies the main opera and ballet companies, symphony orchestras, and much of the 'serious' theatre would cease to exist in their present forms or on their present scale. Likewise the high culture segment of 'the heritage' (see Chapter 5, pp. 72–3) – the British Museum and the UK's national art galleries, for example – would struggle.

We can stay agnostic toward claims that there are objective criteria which enable some paintings, musical compositions and literary works to be identified as 'art', and, among these, some as 'high culture'. It remains a hard social fact that some objects are generally regarded as possessing exceptional artistic merit. Even unrepentant philistines who prefer beer, football and easy listening to ballet and symphony, who refuse to feel culturally deprived, and who would prefer to believe that the so-called arts are just one among many sets of minority tastes, have to admit that, in our wider society, attitudes towards the traditional arts are reverential. The arts are a high status field of academic enquiry. Most people treat them more seriously than bingo. The levels of government support granted to particular projects such as the refurbishment of London's main opera house – £78 million (see Box 13.2) – may provoke debate, but not the principle of government support for high culture. The UK's Labour Party, most of whose supporters have always been working class and relatively 'uncultured', has treated the arts as generously as Conservative governments. In 1997–98 (when New Labour was voted into office) the Arts Council's government grant was £186 million. By 2003–04 it had been raised to £337 million. We may all know that our best authors are the likes of Catherine Cookson (now deceased) and Jeffrey Archer, but the Booker and other committees are treated seriously when they select their books of

---

BOX 13.2 ROYAL OPERA HOUSE

London's Royal Opera House is the home of three international performing arts companies: The Royal Opera, The Royal Ballet, and the Orchestra of the Royal Opera House.

The first theatre on the site (the Theatre Royal) opened in 1739. It was primarily a playhouse. The first serious music to be performed there were the operas of Handel who personally gave regular performances up to 1759. The original building was destroyed by fire in 1808 but a replacement opened in 1809 with a performance of *Macbeth*. There was another fire in 1851 and the third and present building opened in 1858. It became known as the Royal Opera House in 1892 but continued to present a mixed programme until 1946 (when the Arts Council was established). Since then it has been devoted to opera and ballet.

In 1975 the House was given adjacent land to enable it to extend, but the extension, accompanied by a thorough refurbishment and modernisation, had to await National Lottery funds (£78 million) becoming available in the 1990s.

Sources: www.royaloperahouse.org, www.fsz.bme.hu/opera/roh.html

---

the year and award small monetary prizes, insignificant compared with best-seller royalties. The 'great and the good' have their deliberations and verdicts covered in the national media. Central government created the Arts Council of Great Britain in 1946, years ahead of the Sports Council (1965), and the former has always received the larger grant. It is only fair to point out here that most public subsidy to sport is by local, not national, government, but this itself is revealing. National government backing places high culture clearly on the bright side of leisure. It signifies that some arts are of national importance. Other art forms (and other uses of leisure time and money) are thereby defined as somehow less worthy.

The higher arts are distinguished from those that are purely commercial, popular, lowbrow. The popular arts could be produced only by commerce (see Chapter 9, p. 126). This culture is commercially viable because it can be made popular on a sufficient scale and in the necessary (commercial) sense. Most people are consumers and are willing to pay cost-plus for the products. The popular arts earn money for the UK in exports and for the government in tax revenues. These arts have no need of state support. Any public benefits are purely incidental. This is why politicians who try to align themselves with 'cool Britannia' and such like succeed only in turning themselves into figures of fun.

The higher arts are just as capable of selling seats as any other live performances. Many people are prepared to pay handsomely for the experience of symphony concerts, Shakespeare plays, and opera and ballet performances. The arts which are government-supported in the UK obtain just 37 per cent of their total income from central and local governments: 57 per cent is from consumers who spent a total of £768 million on the performing arts alone in 1997. However, state largesse is crucial for those arts, and for many of the individual arts companies that receive public subsidies. In 2000–01 London's Royal Opera House (see Box 13.2) had a box office take of £18.2 million and government subsidies totalling £20 million. Clearly, something would change – the character of the productions, the number of productions, or the composition of the audiences – if state support was withdrawn. The position in the USA is somewhat different. US opera companies generate around 40 per cent of their revenue through the box office (roughly the same proportion as in the UK). However, in the USA government bodies contribute only around 20 per cent: the shortfall (*vis-à-vis* the UK) is made up by private (mainly charitable) donations (Operaam, 2002).

Some claim that the old division between high and popular culture is now breaking down and everyone is becoming middle-brow. Pop stars are now welcomed in Downing Street; they are applauded as major exporters. Government ministers try to link themselves with 'cool Britannia'. Rock music receives serious reviews in the broadsheets. It has been played in the grounds of Buckingham Palace. Nigel Kennedy looks like a pop star. Paul McCartney dabbles in classical composing. Classical music is played at football grounds. Opera stars stage popular concerts. Some classical records sell to a much wider public than just the people who attend symphony concerts (see Box 13.3).

However, the so-called classical pops are short clips rather than full-length symphonies. As explained below, there is still a distinct section of the population, no more than 5 per cent, that consumes full-strength high culture on a regular basis. In all countries there is still a division between a cluster of highbrow tastes on the one hand, and lowbrow tastes on the other. The content of the former cluster has changed little over time except that in Europe, though not in North America, jazz has migrated from the lowbrow towards the highbrow cluster (Katz-Gerro, 1998). Finally, certain tastes (arts), but not others, still receive extraordinarily generous government support. There are crossovers and various mixtures, but the distinction between 'the arts' and popular culture is as alive as ever.

BOX 13.3 CLASSICAL POPS

In 2001 the volume of recorded classical music sales in the UK rose by 2 per cent to 15.8 million units, 7 per cent of the overall recorded music market.
  What are the classical pops? The top 10 were:

1. *Encore*, Russell Watson.
2. *Classical Chillout*, Various.
3. *Classics 2002*, Various.
4. *The Voice*, Russell Watson.
5. *Time to Relax*, Various.
6. *The Opera Album 2002*, Various.
7. *Gladiator Soundtrack*, Hans Zimmer, Lisa Gerrard.
8. *Harry Potter Soundtrack*, John Williams.
9. *Utopia Chilled Classics*, Various.
10. *The Classical Album 2001*, Various.

Sources: Charlotte Higgins, 'Music, maestro, please', *The Guardian*, 28.2.02. p. 19.

State support for certain arts obviously has sufficient support within the political system, plus public acquiescence if not enthusiasm. These facts are not at issue. The 'problems' are why this support exists, the wider ramifications, whether the publicly stated aims of public subsidies are the key actors' true intentions, whether these correspond with the results being achieved and, if not, exactly what is going on.

High culture and the class structure

The really controversial issue is not how many people benefit directly, or exactly who they are (these facts are well known), so much as why the arts receive such extremely generous state support. However, according to one school of thought, this is intimately bound up with the generally privileged character of the arts constituency. Pierre Bourdieu, a French sociologist, contends that the arts can be properly understood only when set in the context of the surrounding class structure. He draws attention to how cultural tastes and behaviour signify membership of particular social groups: they help to define the boundaries between insiders and outsiders. This occurs at all social levels, and Bourdieu contends that high culture plays a crucial role in forming and cementing mutually beneficial relationships between economic, political and cultural elites (see Bourdieu, 1984; Bourdieu and Darbel, 1997). Cultural elites are those who define themselves as such, and whose opinions of themselves are endorsed, initially by the economically wealthy and politically powerful. Political, economic and cultural elites are not exactly the same people playing different roles, but their memberships overlap: the core audience for high culture is generally well-educated and employed mostly in intellectual professions, and there are important exchanges between all the elites. Bourdieu argues that, by supporting the arts, political elites are able to establish themselves as guardians of a nation's cultural heritage. By patronising and consuming high culture, economic elites are able to present themselves simultaneously as benefactors, and as exceptionally cultured, refined people rather than simply privileged and wealthy. In return, cultural elites are given resources and influence – their views are heard by people with economic and political power. The *quid pro quo* is that they share their esteem with politicians and the business class. The outcome, Bourdieu contends, is a set of relationships which serves the interests of all the elites, and which is extremely difficult to break. He claims that high culture has played a crucial role in consolidating and sustaining the wider systems of economic and political stratification in the Western world.

There are several qualifications, if not outright objections, to this thesis. The arguments exaggerate, on the one hand, the extent to which the arts audience is privileged (see below), and, on the other, the extent to which the privileged are united in their love of art. Maybe France is different, but elsewhere nowadays there is not a neat split between highbrow upper and middle classes on the one side, and lowbrow workers on the other. The present-day middle classes are known to be cultural omnivores (they like most things) (van Eijck, 1999; Erikson, 1996; Peterson and Kern, 1996). The well-to-do do not spend most of their leisure time and money on opera and fine art even though high culture is more likely to be among the diverse tastes of the privileged than it is among the masses. Furthermore, there are other processes – like education, interlocking company directorships and inter-marriage – that serve to unite elites and consolidate the class structure. Correspondingly, there are non-class reasons for people developing a love of art, and why governments may wish to offer support.

Arts for all?

Minority tastes?

Most of the arts, as defined here, are minority passions, although everything depends on exactly which arts are being considered and the yardsticks that are used. Sixty per cent of UK adults belong to a library (Skelton *et al.*, 2002). There are more library visits than trips to the cinema. More people go to museums than to theme parks or pop concerts. Nearly a quarter of all adults go to the theatre to see a play at least once a year (see Table 13.1). It is true that 'only' just over 12 per cent of people go to classical concerts, and less than 7 per cent to the opera and/or ballet. However, 45 per cent of adults attend a theatrical performance or concert of some type, or visit an art gallery or exhibition, in any year. By way of comparison, less than half of all adults play any sport. Most specific sports have participation rates that lag behind attendances at opera and ballet (Table 3.2, p. 33 and Table 4.1, p. 51). Well under a half of the adult population belong to a leisure-related voluntary association (Table 3.1, p. 27). The arts also have widespread support among people who are not direct consumers. Ninety-seven per cent of people agree that all children should be able to learn to play a musical instrument, to learn poetry, and

Table 13.1 Consumption of selected arts

	Percentages of adults who attended at least once, last year (2000–01)
Plays	23.4
Opera	6.6
Ballet	6.4
Contemporary dance	4.4
Classical music	12.3
Jazz	6.1
Art galleries/art exhibitions	21.4
Any performance in a theatre	36.0
Any of the above	45.8

Source: BMRB International Target Group Index/Arts Council, London

to take part in a play (Skelton *et al.*, 2002). It is possible for non-participants to support public provision for minority arts just as those who do not personally take part can approve of publicly provided sport facilities and access to the countryside for all.

Popularising high culture

The Arts Council's declared mission is to develop, sustain and promote the arts. Its aims are to increase awareness, education and access. One of its top priorities is to take art to a wider audience. 'Arts for all' is the ideal, but, like 'sport for all', this is probably best treated as an inspirational but unattainable goal. In a market economy where so many uses of time and money are on offer, engaging everyone in anything is hardly realistic. It is true that virtually everyone watches television and listens to the radio, but not to any single kind of programme. The arts audience was probably larger than has ever been achieved elsewhere in the major cities in communist Eastern Europe. There was plenty on offer, for example, Prague had five opera houses. Admission was cheap: less than a dollar a seat at the time when communism ended in 1989. Perhaps most crucially, under communism the market and commercial popular culture were not allowed to compete.

It may be impossible to actually engage everyone, but creating universal opportunity, access, can be realistic, and the UK's state arts agencies have treated this objective seriously. Free admission to museums and art galleries, and free use of public libraries, have been regarded by many as matters of public service principle. Free admission has practical and symbolic aspects. During the seven months immediately following the abolition of entrance charges to the UK's national art galleries and museums in December 2001, visitor numbers rose by 62 per cent. The symbolic aspect is that people do not pay to enter buildings and to look at exhibits which already belong to them. Free access acknowledges that the provisions belong to all citizens. Access to the arts has also been promoted via state education where all children have been introduced to 'good' music, literature and art. Subsidised orchestras and theatre groups have visited schools, or have performed especially for school parties, with a view to kindling children's interest. In its early years the BBC's government-approved aim was to gradually raise the level of popular taste. This aim has now been abandoned, but the arts are still given generous space on the BBC's radio and (digital) television schedules.

Despite these efforts, Britain's arts establishment has become accustomed to fielding accusations of elitism (see Braden, 1978; Clark, 1980; Kahn, 1976). The charge may well have been encouraged by the Arts Council's determination not to sacrifice quality. When choices have been necessary, the Council has always opted for 'few but roses' (Hutchinson, 1975). The Arts Council has been accused of catering not just for a cultural, but also for a socio-economic, elite. Is this charge justified? It is true that consumption of the arts is class-related, but this applies to most uses of leisure. Generally, the middle classes do more whatever the activity, the main exception being TV viewing. Public providers usually have no alternative but to flow with this tide (see Chapter 4, pp. 50–3). The social class skew in arts consumption is not as marked as is sometimes implied. The ABs (upper middle class) are responsible for 41 per cent of all purchases of classical long-playing records compared with just 16 per cent of pop music purchases (Longhurst, 1995). The upper middle class is far more likely than the working class to attend classical concerts, opera, ballet and drama productions, to visit art galleries and museums, and to use libraries. However, 34 per cent of classical album purchases are by C2s and DEs (the working class). It is true that the social class skew becomes more pronounced when we separate out the people who go regularly to classical concerts and so on (rather than just buy the occasional chill-out recording). The core audience (regular consumers of several varieties of art) for high culture appears to comprise no more than 5 per cent of the population in any country, and its members everywhere tend to be exceptionally well-educated and to work in the intellectual professions (Hantrais and Kamphorst, 1987). In the USA just under 5 per cent of the adult population attends opera at least once a year (slightly fewer than in the UK). The US opera audience differs from the general population in the same ways as arts goers in general, only more so. Compared with all arts goers, the opera audience is wealthier, older and more highly educated (Operaam, 2002)

Despite the efforts of the UK Arts Councils and their overseas counterparts, the size and social composition of the core arts audience does not appear to have changed or expanded from beginning to end of the twentieth century (Evans, 1999; Zuzanek, 1977). Linda Hantrais and Teus Kamphorst (1987) have noted that the core audience for the arts comprises mainly people who were reared in arts-loving families and thereby acquired the relevant tastes early in life. Such appears to be the importance of early arts socialisation that Hantrais and Kamphorst express pessimism towards any prospect of the size of the core audience ever being enlarged substantially. Maybe, but even so, the proportion of adults who take part in sport with sufficient regularity to improve their health-related fitness is less than 10 per cent (see Cox et al., 1993; Roberts and Brodie, 1992). The size of the arts' core audience is not embarrassingly small. Far more than 5 per cent of the population has some contact with the arts (see Table 13.1, p. 188), and even non-participants may gain some share in the public benefits. They know that they could go to art galleries and so on, if they were so inclined, and that they are among the owners of the buildings and their contents.

It is the state supported performing arts that challenge whether access for all is really being achieved or can ever be achieved. Theatres and concert halls impose entrance charges. One can argue that the charges would necessarily be higher, and that access would be less open, in the absence of state subsidies, but it remains the case that opportunities are rationed partly by price. Some seats at London's Royal Opera House cost as little as £3 but there is no way in which the entire UK population could be crammed into these seats even if everyone was rationed to just one admission per year. Other seats cost over £150. These seats are clearly not intended for everyone. Symphony concerts – and ballet and opera even more so – are expensive to stage. In a sense, these art forms are inherently and inevitably elitist. There is no prospect of state funding ever being inflated to a level that would provide enough halls and performing companies to enable everyone to attend regularly (although this did happen under communism). Nor is there any hope of everyone paying for admission regularly under a regime of full cost pricing.

Top level performing arts are really best compared with top level sport. It is necessary for there to be peaks in order for there to be broader bases. Most boxing fans are unable to attend world championship heavyweight contests regularly. The same applies to performances by the world's top orchestras, and opera and ballet companies. Access for all is not realistic but, as we shall see below, there are other public benefits that can accrue from public subsidies.

Cultural democracy

This has been a sometimes complementary and sometimes an alternative aim in the arts policy community. Some protagonists claim that traditional high culture is inherently bourgeois (and sometimes masculine and white Anglo-Saxon also). They claim that it is not just the surrounds – the dress conventions in concert halls, for example – but the arts themselves whose aesthetics are alien to the bulk of the population. Hence, it can be argued, the popularisation of the elite's arts is simply not on. The aim can be condemned as an attempted cultural colonisation of the masses (Braden, 1978). Supporters of cultural democracy have been persistent critics of the extent to which state support in the UK is skewed in favour of the London-based, traditional arts. They have sought to re-direct much of the largesse to the provinces, and then to women's, ethnic and other community organisations (Braden, 1978; Dixon, 1991; Kahn, 1976). This was in fact the cultural policy of the Greater London Council, then led by Ken Livingstone, in the 1980s. It was among the policies that led to the 'loony left' charge, followed by the Council's abolition. However, to a large extent the supporters of spreading state largesse around have campaigned successfully. It is true that the Arts Council still makes some whopping awards to the main national companies: £13 million each to English National Opera and the National Theatre in 2002, £11 million to the Royal Opera, and £9 million to the Royal Ballet. However, out of its total 2001–02 government grant of £252 million, the Arts Council delegated £104 million to its regional offices. And some substantial awards have been made outside London, especially since the Arts Council's income was enlarged by National Lottery funds in the mid-1990s: £40 million to the Baltic Flour Mills, a contemporary arts venue in Gateshead (see Box 13.5, p. 193); in 2002 £40 million was spent on 'creative partnerships' which enable arts organisations to link with young people, usually via schools; £70million was ploughed into regional theatres; and in 2001 £29 million was ring-fenced for black, Asian and Chinese arts organisations. At any time, several hundred painters and sculptors have work in process that is funded by the Arts Council. So do some individual authors (around 17 per year) so that they can work full-time on their writing. The biggest arts organisations tend to receive the biggest awards, and likewise the relatively expensive arts, but even so, in practice the Arts Council's funds are scattered widely.

The anger displayed by supporters of cultural democracy probably owes more to their own over-optimistic view of the masses' artistic inclinations than biases in state arts funding. They believe (or appear to believe) that there is a huge reservoir of creative artistic potential waiting to be unblocked (Hoggart, 1957; Williams, 1963; Willis, 1990). France's state-funded animateurs have been a source of inspiration (Baldry, 1976; Kingsbury, 1976). Advocates of cultural democracy seek state recognition of ordinary people's arts, and assistance to enable them to develop their own music, painting, poetry and forms of dance. It must be said, however, that neither France's animateurs nor exponents of community arts in Britain have ever been able to involve even a substantial minority of any socio-demographic group in artistic production. Sara Cohen (1991) was able to identify scores of teenage rock groups on Merseyside, but the ESRC 16–19 Initiative which was being conducted simultaneously, and which questioned a representative sample of the age group, found that no more than 10 per cent played any musical instrument (Banks *et al.*, 1992). Ruth Finnegan (1989) was able to uncover a dense network of 'hidden' amateur musicians in Milton Keynes but she estimates that they amounted to no more than 6 per cent of the population. The brutal fact of this matter is that at present most citizens choose to be consumers, albeit often active consumers, rather than producers, of culture, and the types of culture that are consumed most widely are produced commercially, not with state subsidies to national companies or by local community organisations.

The arts as economic investment

There is a powerful business case for state support of the arts, albeit some arts more than others. Top culture attracts visitors. Some people go to Paris just to visit the Louvre (Box 13.4). More often the attraction is the overall package and the image of a place that is projected. Particular elements in the package may not, in themselves, exist primarily for overseas visitors. London's West End commercial theatre seats plenty of tourists. The Royal Opera House does not have the capacity that would be necessary to be a normal option on tourist itineraries, and all seats at the more popular performances can sell out to locals well in advance. Yet the buildings and the general environment of Covent Garden are part of the London that attracts visitors. They can visit the opera house building itself and its precincts.

The economic case for investment in culture has been strengthened, like the economic rationale for many other kinds of leisure investment, by the growth of tourism. Quantification is difficult, but there are now sufficient cases to endorse the conviction that culture can work (see Box 13.5, and also Bianchini and Parkinson, 1993). Chapter 8 explained how events have flourished as the tourist market has both grown and matured. More and more people are taking multiple breaks, and are seeking alternatives to the sea, sand and sun package. Cultural tourism has become a distinct tourist market segment, hence the enthusiasm with which Barcelona, then Glasgow, then Dublin were crowned as European cities of culture and Liverpool's celebrations on being chosen for the title in 2008. The city looks forward to an additional 1.7 million visitors, 14,000 extra jobs, and £2 billion of extra investment (see www.liverpoolculture.com). London's heritage buildings and

BOX 13.4 LE GRAND LOUVRE

This is another of the world's most famous buildings, and one of the more easily recognised since the pyramids were added in the late 1980s. The Louvre has been among the world's greatest public museums since 1793. Its present exhibits include the Mona Lisa and the Venus de Milo.

The original building on the site was a fortress, which was replaced during the sixteenth and seventeenth centuries by an elegant palace suitable to serve as a residence for the kings of France. During this period Paris became an artistic capital of the world, and hundreds of artists and craftsmen lived at the Louvre as guests of the king. By the early 1700s the royal collection contained over 2400 objects of art.

Since the French Revolution the art has ceased to be available only to the upper classes and has been accessible by everyone.

Sources: http://home.speedfactory.net/psmith/louvre/, www.louvre.fr

BOX 13.5 ART AND URBAN REGENERATION

The Tate Gallery, which houses the UK's main collection of modern art, is in London, but to display its expanding collection the Tate has created two offshoots, both in formerly run-down districts.

Tate Liverpool opened in 1988. It houses the UK's largest gallery outside London of modern and contemporary art. It is in a converted warehouse which is part of Liverpool's Albert Dock. This dock was opened in 1846 (by Prince Albert) and closed in 1972. Tate Liverpool is part of a development scheme which also includes the Merseyside Maritime Museum as well as shops, offices, apartments, bars and restaurants.

Tate Modern opened in 2000. It is in the former Bankside Power Station (which closed in 1981). The site is on the south bank of the River Thames, and is now linked to St Paul's Cathedral by the millennium footbridge. Tate Modern displays the Tate's collection of international modern art including works by Dali, Picasso, Matisse, Rothko and Warhol. The Tate Modern and the adjacent rebuilt Globe Theatre are helping to regenerate a formerly derelict area. The gallery attracted 5.25 million visitors during its first 12 months, four times the volume recorded by Bilbao's Guggenheim in its debut year (see Box 5.2, p. 71).

The Baltic opened in 2002. It is located in Gateshead, on the south bank of the River Tyne. Baltic Flour Mills opened in 1950 to produce flour and animal feed, and closed in 1982. Since then the entire area has been characterised by industrial decline, deprived housing estates, poverty and crime. The new Baltic is part of a larger redevelopment project on Gateshead Quays which also includes the £60 million Music Centre Gateshead, a multi-screen cinema, restaurants, bars, a nightclub, an international hotel, loft style apartments, and the Gateshead Millennium Bridge (for pedestrians and cyclists) which connects with another rejuvenating area in Newcastle. The Baltic featured prominently in the Newcastle/Gateshead bid (unsuccessful – Liverpool won) to become European Capital of Culture in 2008.

Sources: www.tate.org.uk, www.balticmill.com

ceremonies are among the city's principal tourist assets. Most European cities have historical buildings which can be presented to the 'tourist gaze'. Add art galleries and museums, and surround these with theatres, concert halls, and restaurants, then it appears that a place becomes more likely to feature on holiday itineraries and as a venue for business conferences.

Traditional culture has an edge over rock venues: the former pulls in people with money who are likely to stay for days. Culture has an edge on sport megas: culture is not one-off and can pull constantly flowing streams of visitors whereas sport megas are isolated peaks. The promotion of tourism was not an original reason for modern governments supporting the arts. Nor may it be the main concern of present-day cultural elites. But in our present age it has become an argument that is highly likely to loosen government purse strings. However, the 'business case' is stronger for some types of culture than for others. The business argument works only for provisions which attract outsiders (to a country, region or city) rather than just or mainly locals. The business case is fundamental for most festivals and other events, but not necessarily so with round-the-year provisions, and never when use is overwhelmingly by locals. And as explained in Chapters 5 and 8, one problem with all business cases is that countries, cities and regions become locked into beggar-my-neighbour competition. The global size of the tourist market cannot be enlarged. The business case proves sound only for winners.

Image, standards, prestige and identity

There are additional public interest grounds for governments to support the arts. Culture gives a place an image. We have seen that arts and heritage buildings are among many places' best recognised images. Culture attracts (cultured) visitors, and a place's image may make it admired more widely. Nowadays people are more likely to link Bilbao with its Guggenheim building (see Chapter 5, p. 71) than its run-down shipyards. In so far as it leads to admiration, culture boosts the prestige of a city, region or country. Even when it had a drab communist government, Moscow also had the Bolshoi, and even while Berlin was ruled by Nazis and destroyed by fighting, the city had its Philharmoniker (Box 13.6). Admiration of a city by others may (but will not necessarily, see below) encourage locals to feel a pride in, and to identify with, their home place. The arts, along with the heritage and sport, can play a role in nation building. French governments have adopted, and the French people have expected their governments to adopt, cultural policies with this explicit aim. The French have no qualms about appointing a government minister for culture. Nor have the Russians.

There is a similar justification for state sponsorship of elite sport, but this becomes difficult when sport is run commercially for profit, when teams are not owned by the local population, and when the players and coaches may be from all over the world. There are rarely such objections to state sponsorship of culture. The British feel that the treasures held in the country's museums are theirs even though most of the objects have been acquired, sometimes by force and sometimes by

---

BOX 13.6 PRESTIGE EARNERS

The Bolshoi Theatre

After the Kremlin and St Basil's, the Bolshoi Theatre is probably Moscow's best-known building. It is situated in the square which is at the very centre of the radial-circular network of Moscow streets. The theatre, with its monumental colonnade and quadriga of bronze horses, stands in the northern part of the square. It was built in 1820–24 and was meant to be the finest theatre building in the world. The original building was partly destroyed by fire in 1855 but was rebuilt preserving the original lay-out while increasing the height of the theatre with an additional third storey. The five-tier auditorium is famous for its excellent acoustics and rich ornamentation.

Many outstanding artists have performed at the Bolshoi. Fyodor Chaliapin sang there, and Galina Ulanova and Maya Plisetskaya danced on its boards. Today a new generation of young Russian performers is maintaining the Bolshoi's fame.

Sources: www.bolshoi.ru, http://glasssteelandstone.com/RU/BolshoiTheatre.html

Berliner Philharmoniker (symphony orchestra)

This world famous orchestra has been a continuing presence in Berlin through two world wars, the era of national socialism, and the cold war.

The orchestra was formed in 1882 by 54 ambitious musicians who rebelled against the autocratic rule of Benjamin Bilse in whose ensemble they played. Ever since then the Berliner Philharmoniker has preserved, and prided itself on, its democratic character.

The young orchestra was saved from dissolution by the engagement of director/ conductor Hans von Bulow in 1887 who laid the lasting foundations of the orchestra's technically brilliant manner of playing.

The orchestra gave its last concert under national socialism in April 1945 and was playing again before the end of May (Germany had capitulated in the meantime). Herbert von Karajan became the orchestra's principal conductor and artistic director in 1955 and remained until 1989. Since 1963 the orchestra's home has been the Philharmonic Hall at Kemperplatz.

The musicians are now employed by the 'state' of Berlin but still operate as a 'free orchestral republic'. They decided to hire Simon Rattle who became artistic director and principal conductor in 2002.

Source: www.bach-cantatas.com/Bio/Berliner-Philharmoniker.htm

---

purchase, from all over the world. The galleries and museums themselves are nearly always non-commercial and are securely attached to their home place. Likewise the orchestras and other performing arts companies may tour from their home cities and countries but they are securely based in, and associated with, them.

It has been suggested that when city councils, national governments and cultural elites present images that are attractive to 'cultured' outsiders, and when places are designed primarily for such visitors, local people may feel alienated and dispossessed. For example, there is little place for Red Clydeside in Glasgow's new image as a European city of culture. Nor, it appears, is the city's working class well catered for in the revamped Glasgow city centre (see Hughes and Boyle, 1992). If the working class was to identify with the new Glasgow, then, it could be argued, this would amount to its colonisation and the destruction of its own authentic culture. There are certainly potential pitfalls in using culture to boost a place's prestige and to strengthen locals' identification with a city, region or country. Internal social divisions may be exacerbated while concealed beneath 'sticking plaster'. Culture can work well only when all sections of a population associate themselves with the standards and tastes in question (which they may do even if they themselves are not regular 'consumers'), and when they warm whenever other societies' representatives, whether ordinary people or elites, admire their own places' cultural assets.

Interrogating arts policy

Public funding for the arts creates more hullabaloo than state intervention in any other area of leisure. This is not just on account of the large amounts of money that are involved. The reasons are straightforward. First, in addition to conserving and presenting the heritage, artistic production itself is funded, and there is far more scope for argument over what to produce than what to preserve. Second, unlike with sport, arts professionals are funded. In sport the 'rule' has always been that if players are paid and/or spectators are paying then the clubs and sports are on their own. There has been no such rule in the arts. This means that people's livelihoods depend on state funding which is never secure because in the arts public money does not go solely to a limited number of state companies such as the BBC. Anyone can apply and be rejected. An outcome is that there are always hordes of unsuccessful applicants and successful ones who are awarded less than they feel they need and deserve. The victims are articulate, skilled communicators, with access to the media. Third, state largesse is distributed on the basis of artistic merit, as judged by experts, and the experts are never in total agreement. Which art is best is less clear-cut than who is the fastest runner. The hullabaloo is useful because it forces, or should force, all concerned to search for leisure policy criteria against which to assess government decisions. To begin with, one might ask why, in so far as public funds are at stake, should artistic criteria be paramount? Why not social and economic criteria derived from the public sector's special capabilities in leisure?

Citizenship is enlarged mainly by making the heritage, and the acquisition of artistic tastes and skills, accessible to all. Free admission and use of libraries, art galleries and so on is a sound principle. But why is so much of the UK's heritage hidden from the public? The government's own art collection (11,500 works from Gainsborough to contemporary artists) is available for loan to other public institutions such as libraries as well as for use in government buildings, including overseas embassies, whereas this does not apply to the buildings and treasures which the crown holds for the nation but which are treated as if they were the monarch's personal property.

National prestige and identity are enhanced only by world-class collections and performances. The national galleries and museums, and the major performing arts companies, are the crucial players here. These 'jewels' are the arts' most (actually or potentially) powerful tourist attractions. The leading performing arts companies, galleries and museums are quangos, quasi-autonomous government organisations rather than genuine voluntary associations. They are, in effect, state companies, and on leisure policy grounds they need to be expanded. Access/citizenship requires their presence in all regions. The leading performers, companies and exhibitions need to tour routinely, and to function as the country's advanced training schools in their particular branches of the arts. There are no economic, prestige or identity grounds for long-term state funding of anything that is less than top notch.

If the arts are deemed particularly worthwhile uses of leisure then, maybe, as with sport, there should be more attention to feeding the grassroots with suitable buildings, teachers, animateurs and other facilitators. We should probably be less concerned over how many or how few people attend performances than, for example, that less than 10 per cent of Britain's young people are able to play a musical instrument. How many become competent in acting, drawing and writing – capable of writing for the printed media, TV, radio and film? Arts education supplies talent to the popular, commercial arts as well as the state supported arts. All countries have an interest in nurturing such talent if they are to compete effectively for global market shares in the culture-based leisure industries. Computing is not the sole core skill required in today's labour markets. There will be additional spin-off benefits from arts education; in the design of manufactured products, public buildings and transport, and urban spaces. Moreover, we know that children who become involved in the arts do better in education, achieve higher earnings and are more likely to be involved in civic activities as adults than their social class teenage peers who use their leisure in other ways (Robson, 2003). As in other areas, but especially clearly in the arts, at present state interventions are insufficiently focused, and too weak in exploiting the public sector's special capabilities.

CONCLUSIONS

We have seen that the arts are an exceptional leisure industry in depending mainly on state support, and we have also seen that this special state dependence does not require an arts-specific explanation. There is no need to postulate a special explanation in terms of legitimising and solidifying the class structure. We have also seen that equalising all-round access, irrespective of socio-economic status, is no more within the state's capabilities in the arts than in other areas of leisure. The manifest political consensus that the state should be the basic funder of the arts is explained most parsimoniously in terms of the arts yielding all the public benefits that the public sector is able to deliver via leisure. The arts can be effective in triggering the economic multiplier. They can express standards with which people in all socio-demographic groups wish to identify. Public sector arts provisions can extend citizenship and can boost national, local or regional identities and prestige. Of course, realising these benefits depends on exactly which arts are supported, and on the form and the extent of this support. The messages from this chapter are, first, that the relatively generous state support that the arts receive is not a mistake or a distortion due to the effective lobbying of powerful lobbyists, and, second, that deriving best value will require much fine tuning and sometimes more rigorous adjustments in arts policy so as to achieve the closest possible match between what is provided and the public sector's special leisure capabilities.

Part

III

POLICIES

14 Leisure Policies

Introduction

This chapter does not try to summarise or even to draw every possible conclusion from everything that has gone before. Rather, it extracts and draws together the lessons for leisure policy. As acknowledged in Chapter 1, there is little point in preaching to commerce or the voluntary sector. Commerce will always seek profit – in fact market-based enterprises must seek profit – whatever the arguments against. Happily for all concerned, we have seen that there is rarely a sound case for obstructing the commercial leisure industries' pursuit of profit. Businesses can thrive only by giving people what they manifestly want and in leisure there are no captive markets – consumers always have alternatives. The public interest is usually better served by state support for commerce rather than imposing restrictions, because investing in loss leaders is likely to yield tax revenues which exceed the investment. The market place, and the self-interest of legitimate businesses, are usually the best policemen. Voluntary associations can survive and grow only by responding to their members' enthusiasms. Again, the public interest is usually best served by allowing the voluntary sector to follow activists' enthusiasms and offering support when there is a public interest in enabling the associations to expand or strengthen their efforts. Politics is different: arguments can count. Chapter 4 identified the public sector's special capabilities in leisure. The subsequent chapters have examined how the state intervenes in the various leisure industries. Now is the time to judge the closeness of the match.

This chapter begins by explaining why leisure is a mixed blessing for society, and why government ministers with leisure responsibilities are unlikely to be able to satisfy everyone. Explicit leisure policies will make life easier for the ministers, and the subsequent section draws conclusions about the ways in which existing UK state interventions need to be overhauled in some cases and fine-tuned in others. The two final sections present broader issues – policy issues – raised by the growth of leisure and the leisure industries. These arise from the growth of employment in leisure on the one hand, and the sustainability problem on the other.

Mixed blessings

Leisure sounds good. The word creates all the right vibes: fun, laughter, pleasure, excitement. The leisure industries may appear to be purveyors of unmitigated blessings: enjoyment, business, jobs. What more could anyone ask? The more these industries can do, then so much the better, or so it might appear. Ministers for leisure must surely have a ball! This is not how things have worked out since the UK's 'ministry of free time', renamed the Department for Culture, Media and Sport (DCMS) in 1997 (see Chapter 4, p. 46), was created in 1992. Up to now the department has been a graveyard for political careers: David Mellor, Peter Brookes, Virginia Bottomley and Chris Smith. In 2001 the chalice passed to Tessa Jowell. In 2002 she took over as chair of UK Sport so as to gain a stronger steer on how some of her department's money was being spent and also, presumably, on her own political career.

Leisure scholars used to envisage a not too distant society of leisure in which everyone would bask in free time and have plenty of money to indulge their whims (Dumazedier, 1974). Some continue to link leisure (by definition) to self-expression and fulfilment (for example, Wearing, 1998). Government ministers soon become aware that their territory has a dark side. We have seen that people spend far more time and money on drink, tobacco, drugs, gambling and television than on taking exercise. Leisure can damage our health, our finances and family relationships. The public sector's special capabilities in leisure may have contradictory implications. What is good for business may not be in accord with standards that politicians otherwise wish, and which people expect their governments, to uphold.

Government ministers also find that the leisure industries are riven with conflicts and rivalries. Leisure matters to a lot of people who are easily upset. It matters to those whose jobs and investments are at stake. Then there are all the people who take their own leisure seriously, or who are otherwise passionate about football, the theatre or whatever. All these people are easily offended by governments that intervene or fail to intervene in leisure, or that make the 'wrong' interventions. Ministers are likely to get the blame when things go wrong for anyone but not the praise when people enjoy their sports, television and holidays. Actors and athletes milk all the applause. Politicians are accused of behaving badly if and when they try to bask in the glory.

Part of the answer for politicians will lie in proper explicit leisure policies, based squarely on the public sector's special capabilities in leisure (see Chapter 4, pp. 54–7), and linked via political parties to public opinion. Such policies will protect politicians from unreasonable demands, reduce the incidence of bloomers, and lead to more public benefits per pound invested. Proper policies *in* leisure will help. Developing such policies is not easy but it is the easiest part. Politicians with an oversight across leisure soon realise that their problems run deeper. They quickly become aware that the growth of leisure, in the forms that this has taken up to now, is not sustainable indefinitely. They also realise that for substantial and growing sections of people the growth of leisure is not delivering the good life but degraded jobs. They are sure to conclude that the current situation cannot continue indefinitely but realise that they will earn no gongs for delivering this message to either fellow politicians or the wider public. Addressing the policy issues posed by the expansion of the leisure industries is a mammoth task which as yet has hardly begun.

Policies in leisure

How do governments' performances measure up to the public sector's special capabilities in leisure (triggering economic growth by drawing-in spending, enlarging and strengthening citizenship, enhancing a political entity's and the population's prestige and identity, and defining and strengthening shared standards)? There is, of course, a rough match; inevitably so because virtually any action by governments can be justified with reference to at least one of the special capabilities

That said, governments could do even better. Sometimes governments do completely the wrong things but they are more likely to do what are basically the right things the wrong way (Britain's Millennium Dome, for instance) or to miss opportunities. This certainly applies to the UK government. Social science will never do politics' basic work. Governments need to establish their own leisure priorities and decide how any contradictions between their several capabilities are to be resolved. This is a political task. Social science's contribution is, first, to identify the aims that are in fact within the public sector's capabilities. Largely because of the absence of clear leisure policies which would justify public expenditure, governments are so hesitant about investing in high quality, national prestige facilities: art galleries and museums; sport stadiums and arenas suitable for top-level cycling, ice hockey, athletics and basketball; and concert halls and theatres suitable for staging drama, musicals and full-scale opera and ballet. Local authorities could be expanding and upgrading their playing fields and indoor sport facilities, not commercialising or closing them. Urban parks really need upgrading and updating constantly. Why are we not creating outdoor arenas for car, motorcycle and horse riding and racing, and open air venues for 'raves' and other warm weather events? All neighbourhoods need meeting rooms. Neighbourhood, city centre and out-of-town shopping precincts could be designed for public relaxation and enjoyment rather than solely to yield maximum cash returns per square metre. UK governments have surely been too cautious – too wary of opposition from farmers and other landowners – when considering how to widen access to the countryside. They have surely been too slow to inform the royal household that the nation's palaces and treasures should be managed as if they really did – if indeed they do – belong to the nation. Overall, successive governments have been too nervous about spending public money. They need to be clearer about the kinds of public service broadcasting that will be maintained indefinitely, and not necessarily by the BBC as we have known it up to now. Our leisure capital is being squandered by 'cold feet'. The Millennium Dome has been virtually given away. The 2002 Commonwealth Games stadium (see Box 4.5, p. 57) has been, in effect, given away to a privately-owned company, Manchester City AFC. As soon as the Commonwealth Games ended the UK was once again without an athletics stadium suitable for major international events. Explicit leisure policies based on the public sector's genuine capabilities, for which broad-based political and public support can be won, will increase politicians' confidence when considering projects and committing tax-payers' money.

In other ways governments currently do too much. Money is still being frittered away on token schemes to redress socio-economic disadvantages – to combat social exclusion, as they say nowadays. Meanwhile, inequalities remain as wide as ever or become even wider. Governments are too nervous about standing back. There are still far too many restrictions on commercial leisure providers. Further liberalisation is needed in gambling, alcohol, entertainment and shopping. Governments normally need to do no more than enforce legitimate businesses' own preferences. Aesthetic and moral standards are better defined and maintained by what the public sector actually does than by what governments merely permit. The golden rules for the public sector to follow are fourfold.

- Invest for economic reasons only when spending will be drawn into a territory. There is no reason whatsoever why national governments should fund developments which are likely to stimulate only or mainly domestic trips and tourism.
- Regional and local authorities should bear in mind that the economic benefits of investments in leisure will ripple through most sections of their populations only in places where tourism is a major industry.
- Prestige and identity will only be strengthened by prestige projects. The Arts Council's old maxim, 'few but roses', is worthy of emulation.
- Standards are defined and strengthened, and citizenship is extended and strengthened, only when provisions are appreciated and accessible by all socio-demographic groups. Free admission, at times and on terms to suit the public, is a sound principle. People need to be reminded, and to feel, that the land, buildings and contents (where relevant) are not just for them but are theirs, having been acquired with their money. Admission charges for exhibitions and performances to which only some of the public can gain or will seek access are justified, but not inflated charges which reflect the value of the public assets, be these concert halls or sport stadiums.

There is much that can be stripped away apart from petty restrictions on commerce:

- Programmes intended to compensate for economic disadvantages. This task should be left to economic and social services ministries.
- Programmes and provisions intended to cure 'bad' behaviour.
- Scattergun 'something different for everyone' funding (of voluntary associations, for example). Rather than a little for every taste and section of the public, we need provisions – prestige provisions – that are valued by all sections.

The sums of money to be invested in leisure by the public sector will never be large compared with other claims on state budgets (defence, health care and education, for example) whereas the benefits from leisure spending can be considerable. The condition for reaping these benefits is the development of clear leisure policies which have informed, and therefore solid, support, not mere acquiescence, among political actors and the public at large. Frittering away resources on ill-conceived projects will then be less likely and, when it happens (as it always will), it will not damn the entire field. Politics really needs to catch up with the historical upward shift in the economic, social and cultural role of leisure. And this means considering some wider policy issues raised by the growth of leisure and its industries, and developing policies that address these matters.

Work in leisure

Before long, politicians who take on leisure can rely on meeting the moneymen – investors and executives. The politicians know that businesses licensed to broadcast and to operate gambling, for example, are likely to make a good deal of money. They know, too, that someone will profit handsomely, maybe via hospitality deals or media links, when they plough public money into sports stadiums and concert halls. The also know that the bank accounts of top concert artists, top players in some sports, and TV stars will benefit from the state's investments. Maybe the politicians can be relaxed about this, secure in the knowledge that there are overwhelming public benefits, but they cannot escape the fact that most of the benefits of leisure activity, and the investment that makes these benefits possible, are reaped by the better-off. We are back once again to Table 2.1 (see p. 19). Leisure spending and the related activities are very unequally distributed. There are some relatively 'democratic' uses of leisure in terms of gender and age groups as well as social class; television viewing, reading, gambling and hobbies. Across the rest of leisure the bulk of any benefits from public spending enrich the leisure of the relatively well-off. Other people may get jobs. As the proportion of consumer spending devoted to leisure goods and services rises, so does the proportion of all employment that is in the leisure industries. The creation of these jobs is among present-day governments' objectives when developing buoyant leisure sectors. But just what kinds of jobs do the leisure industries offer?

Poor work

There are many different leisure industries offering a variety of jobs at all levels. Yet most leisure services (the main exceptions are the media) share a bottom-heavy employment profile. Cinema chains, professional football clubs, hotels, restaurants and holiday-package companies all have plenty of 'donkey work'. McDonald's and other fast food chains are typical (see Reiter, 1991). The leisure industries have lots of low-level, low-paid, temporary, seasonal, casual and part-time jobs, and much of the work is at unsocial hours. Leisure work has to be done when other people –

those with money to spend – are at leisure. If leisure demand is seasonal, then so are the jobs. If leisure demand is fickle, workers must be flexible. Over half of all jobs in sport, health and well-being, tourism, hotels and catering, cultural recreation, amenities and horticulture, are part-time, twice the proportion in the UK workforce as a whole (M Lowe, 2002). It is not true that low-level jobs are being wiped out and that today all employees need to be well-educated, highly-skilled and well-qualified in order to stand any chance in the labour market. It is skilled manual jobs that have been decimated by de-industrialisation. They have been replaced by new working class jobs, mostly semi-skilled at best, in leisure and other consumer services including the expanding call-centres.

Gender and sexuality

Women get a particularly raw deal in the leisure industries. What applies in other types of work applies in leisure, only more so. Local authority leisure services departments have plenty of women on the bottom rungs while men are usually in control of policy and decision-making (Aitchison, 1997). Business as usual? Not quite. Gendering is especially harsh in the leisure industries' front-line service roles. In addition to delivering the basic service, women who want to get on in public contact roles need to market their sexuality. Female sport players are unlikely to attract much media attention, or to be offered lucrative product endorsements, unless they look good, and it is their looks rather than their technical skills that are likely to receive the most media coverage. Female hotel staff have to learn how to decline politely requests for a type of service that they do not provide; they are expected to regard all this as just part of the job (Guerrier and Adib, 2000). Researchers have confirmed what everyone else already knew: female betting office staff are expected to look and act sexy (Filby, 1992); airlines expect female counter and cabin staff to be sexy and slim (Tyler and Abbott, 1998). Women who simply want to get in, let alone to get on, in the leisure industries, have no option but to comply. Richards and Milestone (2000) interviewed 27 women who were working in Manchester's music industry in retail, as journalists, promoters, disc jockeys, venue managers and musicians. The majority of those interviewed had been through higher education yet only three were earning in excess of £25,000 a year. The women explained how difficult it was for them to get on in a boundary-less business where work and leisure were normally intermingled. They knew that it would be impossible for them to operate alone at night in a strictly professional capacity, and that their line of work was incompatible with motherhood. They also knew that their credibility and effectiveness were based partly on performing a beauty function and that when their looks faded their time in the industry would expire.

Men may sometimes envy women's ability to trade on their sexuality, and it is true that some women's careers benefit from this, but only some women are able and willing to operate in this way. It is different for men. Male footballers do not need to be good looking, let alone sexually enticing, in order to become stars. However, there are exceptional cases where gendering works to women's advantage.

Top women tennis players earn more than the top men. This is because the women's matches are shorter in the important grand slam tournaments (3 sets rather than 5). There is no physiological justification for this, but women are supposed to be the weaker sex. In practice their shorter matches enable women players to enter more competitions (doubles as well as singles) and, as a result, even though men's and women's prize money sometimes remains unequal (to the men's advantage), the women who win consistently earn more in total than the top males (Macbeth, 2000).

Recruitment and careers

Despite the poor quality of employment that they offer, many of the leisure industries find it very easy to recruit staff. This applies wherever some (never all) of the jobs are tinged with glamour. For young people in particular, this can make even mundane work attractive. It sounds good, and it can feel good, to be part of the music or football industry. Vocational courses in sport, tourism, journalism, artistic production (so-called fame schools), and hotels and catering, recruit strongly when offered in schools, further and higher education. Entrants to the industries usually find that proximity to glamour supplants decent pay and career prospects. The gloss is spread around very unequally even in the real glamour occupations. Few actors are stars; the occupation is grotesquely over-crowded. The same applies in music and sport. And as well as glamour jobs, all these industries involve a lot of backstage work; fetching and carrying, sorting and filing. The players are a minority among the employees at professional football clubs. They are vastly outnumbered by all the turnstile staff, ticket office staff, ground staff, programme sellers and so on. There is plenty of vacuous, mind-numbing work at holiday resorts, and in restaurants and casinos (see Seabrook, 1988). The work is often tiring. This is invariably the case when the work involves dealing with streams of leisure-seekers. In consumer services front-line staff are expected to perform aesthetic labour. The appearance and personalities of the staff are part of the service, the consumer experience. So staff are expected to look smart even though they are low-paid, and they may be expected to act and appear as if they felt bright and bubbly even if in reality they are bored stiff. Some hotels require their staff to attend grooming and deportment sessions led by external consultants (Nickson et al., 1998).

The leisure industries' glamour radiates from stars who are recognised and acclaimed by the wider public. This applies not only in sport and the performing arts but also, in a more modest way, among hairdressers, chefs, journalists etc. These occupations also share an absence of standard routes to the top. Recruits to the occupations join pools from which stars somehow emerge (Elliott, 1977). No-one seems to know exactly how this happens but it can happen very quickly, literally overnight in some cases. Even experienced journalists are unable to spot the trainees who will become broadsheet leader writers and tabloid editors. Football club managers cannot tell which, from a group of 16-year-old trainees, will become professional players let alone stars. Nor can the players themselves always understand why they succeed or fail to make the grade. Is it physique, skill or character? The majority who do not succeed (and some of those who do) are likely to be genuinely puzzled. Television channel controllers cannot tell which actors will become popular game-show hosts. No one seems able to predict, or to explain 'scientifically', who will sparkle when under the spotlight. It is exciting to be rising but frustrating to be sinking without knowing exactly why.

So there are no structured routes to stardom. Buggins' turn does not apply. There are no elite training programmes or qualifications which guarantee a glittering future. Yet despite this, the normal predictors of career success (those that 'work' in other occupations) appear to operate in sport, the arts and all the other branches of the leisure industries about which we have the relevant information. One might have thought that artistic and sporting talent would be distributed at random among young people from all social classes, but this does not appear to be the case. Whether as a gift of nature or a product of nurture, the stars who emerge tend to be educational achievers from middle-class families. Since the 1960s this has applied among rock musicians. In the 1950s the first wave were often from modest backgrounds, but subsequent pop performers have been better musicians in a technical sense, and usually from art schools or other types of tertiary education (Frith, 1978, 1988). The young people who make it into the national sports squads from which Olympic teams are drawn have a similar social profile to their counterparts in the performing arts. Twenty per cent are from private schools compared with just 6 per cent of the entire age group, and 38 per cent are from AB (upper middle class) families compared with 19 per cent in the population in general (English Sports Council, 1999). We still lack an evidence-based explanation of this skew, but it appears that recruitment to the elite ranks in sport and the arts is governed by the same social mobility (and immobility) flows that operate throughout the rest of the occupational structure.

Stars never feel secure. They know that their appeal can fade for no apparent reason. Professional footballers know that at any time their careers can be destroyed by injury, a mysterious loss of form or falling out with a manager. Film stars have to deliver whenever they are on set. They know that most releases flop. Sometimes the experience is repeated. Demand for their services can then evaporate. Pop stars are in an identical situation. There is no proven formula for staying at the summit. Even the glamorous jobs can be a hard grind while they last. Film acting itself is not glamorous. Casts spend hours waiting for their scenes to be called. There may be numerous retakes. Amateur drama can be fun whereas professional theatre is real work. The same applies in gardening and sport. Alan Roadburg (1977) interviewed 98 amateur and professional gardeners and footballers. All the professionals regarded their activities as work. They did not feel that they were being paid for leisure activities. They had to work at specified times, and to perform in ways, and with other people, chosen by someone else. Remuneration became a constraint. Being paid made negative features of the work unavoidable. For amateurs the activities are different; they are leisure. In leisure there is an absence of constraint, and each individual can decide for how long, exactly when, where and with whom to do something. Becoming a professional means sacrificing all this.

Despite this, some leisure industries, especially sports and the arts, are inundated with would-be entrants. The glamour attracts far more young people than can ever rise above the very bottom rungs. UK schoolboys who are good at soccer flock to the 'academies' that are managed by the top professional clubs. Any who are 'signed-up' dream of future stardom. Very few are ever offered professional contracts. Parents and coaches encourage children with talent at swimming, skating, music, ballet and so on to practise and train daily. There is simply no way in which most of these keen and committed young people can achieve international stardom let alone make long-term livings in their fields. Remarkably, despite their normal reservations about premature vocational specialisation, governments sometimes encourage the congestion on the leisure industries' bottom rungs by funding sports, drama, art and music schools. The UK has its World Class Performance Programmes, which, in effect, allow talented athletes to become (temporary) full-time professionals. The USA's colleges act as nurseries for future professional sports players and the country's national amateur squads (see Box 7.2, p. 98). Some of the leisure industries' cast-offs find that they have gained skills which are transferable to other careers. The self-presentation and communication skills of drama students make them formidable job applicants and can be used in many other occupations. Young people with highly developed skills in music and sport are less fortunate.

It is sometimes argued that countries need 'hothouses' to develop talented young people if the nations are to compete internationally in sports and the performing arts, but there is another way. The enthusiasm of young players and performers, their parents and coaches, can be sufficient in itself. They will practise and develop their abilities as leisure activities, which is what they will always be for the majority. The amateur segments of sports and the performing arts are able to develop talent if allowed to do so, that is, if there is no 'creaming off' by professional schools. The most talented amateurs then rise to the top and, if they wish, into the professional ranks. This works just as well as nurturing excess numbers to within sight of the summits, then obliging most to make rapid and long-range descents back into the amateur ranks, often without the skills and qualifications needed for successful careers in other fields. It is noteworthy that many of the migrant professional footballers who play in the top European leagues are from countries where there are no 'academies' or other hothouses.

Professionalisation: a failed project

Behind the front-stage stars, all the leisure industries – commercial, voluntary and public – employ managers and a variety of professional staff – accountants, marketing specialists and so on. In the commercial and voluntary sectors they necessarily work under pressures which arise ultimately from the public's leisure tastes being fickle and markets being intensely competitive. Since the 1980s the UK government has invited these pressures into the public sector (see Box 4.3, p. 49), where, as a result, managers now complain of being stressed-out and unable to relax (see Bacon and Pitchford, 1992).

As Chapter 4 explained (see pp. 45–6), efforts to professionalise public sector leisure management began in the 1970s. The trigger was local government reorganisation which created omnibus leisure services departments. It proved to be the wrong time to embark on professionalisation (see Roberts, 1999b). Local authority leisure staff embarked on professionalisation when, although unforeseen, their departments were on the threshold of unprecedented exposure to market forces. Market-disciplined leisure work is simply not a suitable base for traditional professional organisation in which courses are accredited, then churn out graduates, whose practice is based on skills and knowledge already certified, and where a professional association enforces standards. This model is far too slow for market-based leisure industries and also for public sector providers who nowadays must, in a sense, compete with commercial enterprises, because the public will inevitably compare them. The occupations need entrepreneurial staff who are sensitive to, and capable of responding rapidly to, shifts in taste (see Godbey, 1997). Theme pubs and restaurants rarely last for more than five years before needing a make-over. Public leisure services that aim to maximise their market share need to be equally flexible, and these demands are inevitably conveyed into the workforces.

Consumer power

Ultimately it is consumer power which inflicts all the horrors on leisure workers: the pressure on managers, the low-paid and temporary jobs, often at unsocial hours, and the exposure of female staff to sexual propositions. Over time consumers have become more and more demanding. The expansion of the commercial sector with its consumer culture has not merely tolerated but encouraged consumers to become unpredictable and opportunistic (Gabriel and Lang, 1995). Consumers now believe that they are entitled to expect providers to be flexible. They want to be served at their convenience. They also want bargains. Even then they expect staff to be polite, attentive and maybe sexually attractive. Consumers expect to be made to feel important. Sex discrimination at work may be unlawful nowadays but this does not apply when people are at leisure. What happens when one person's leisure is someone else's job? No-one has really resolved this conundrum but commercial providers know that, if they expect consumers to concede, their own businesses will suffer. As television has become a more competitive industry (see Chapter 10, pp. 144–5), pressure on its employees has mounted. Broadcasters now outsource more programme-making. The programme-makers need to be competitive, and flexible, and a result is that over half of the UK industry's creative workforce is now freelance or on temporary contracts (see Dex et al., 2000; Patterson et al., 2002). The public services have become more like commercial businesses where computers and telecommunications feed information about consumer preferences straight back from supermarket and other retailers' tills, all the way down the production lines (Miller, 1995). The pressure that we experience as workers, whether this means working long hours, or at odd times, or for minimal wages, is generated by the demands that we make as consumers, except that those making and those responding to these demands are not exactly the same bodies of people.

Class relations

In the closing decades of the twentieth century economic inequalities widened in many countries, including Britain. The highest earners enjoyed the greatest gains in income. There has been an expansion – a doubling in size during the second half of the twentieth century – of a new middle class whose core members are salaried managers and professionals. More of these people than in the past live in households where at least two, and sometimes more, adults have middle-class jobs. Some work in the leisure industries but the majority earn their livings elsewhere – in manufacturing, law, medicine, financial services, education and other public services. These people have not been experiencing any increase in their leisure time in recent years. Rather, they have been lengthening their hours of work either under pressure from their employers or as a result of their own desire to advance their careers and maximise their incomes, and to enjoy high-spending leisure (see Roberts, 1999a). Roughly one-third of the population belongs to this new middle class. Others, including higher-paid members of the working class, can hope to join them and/or share features of their lifestyles. The upper echelons of the new middle class are extremely well-off. They are very few in number but they are responsible for a much higher proportion of leisure spending. The middle class as a whole supplies most of the leisure spenders who have stimulated the expansion of the commercial leisure industries in recent years (see Table 2.1, p. 19).

For the working class, recent trends have been much harsher. There are fewer working class jobs. Much skilled employment has been lost in successive waves of de-industrialisation. The risk of unemployment has risen. Those without jobs have faced a tougher welfare regime as benefits have become less generous. The unemployed have come under stronger pressure to take whatever work is available. They have been told that they need to be flexible. Trade unions, formerly the working class's first line of defence, have been weakened. The Labour Party has been transformed at the top from a working class movement into a party of business. So the working class has become disorganised and unrepresented (see Roberts, 2001). At the beginning of the twenty-first century over one-sixth of Britain's households which contained adults of working age had no-one in employment. The unemployment figures had been hauled down from the peak of earlier years, but the real level had been, and remains, concealed by early retirements, young people sheltering from the labour market by prolonging their education and training, and people without jobs having themselves classified as medically unfit for work. At the end of the twentieth century almost one-third of all Britain's children were being born into, then reared in, poverty. Above the long-term unemployed and impoverished groups, there are those who get by, in and out of poor quality jobs, many in consumer services, including leisure services. Roughly one-quarter of all households are part of this new disorganised working class. In an initially unequal society, the growth of the leisure industries divides the population into those whose encounters with these industries are always as consumers, and those whose encounters are first and foremost as workers.

Poor quality jobs may be acceptable to marginal workers – students, people who have retired from their main careers, housewives and others who regard their own employment as a secondary role and a secondary source of household income – but in recent years many members of the working class have found themselves confined to poor quality jobs (the so-called McJobs or Mickey Mouse jobs) not through choice but through lack of alternatives. This is what the expansion of the leisure industries has meant for a substantial section of the population. On a global scale the schism is even starker between the rich countries that produce most of the high spending consumer-tourists who find that they obtain best value by spending their leisure in countries where labour is cheaper. Hence the volume and direction of tourism flows – generally out of rich and into poor countries. The growth of leisure and its industries is currently dividing the world into countries which supply consumers, and countries which service their leisure.

These are consequences of the growth of the leisure industries in unequal societies. The kind of leisure industries which exist today are possible only amid, then add a new dimension to, wide economic inequalities both within and between countries. The growth of leisure will have similar implications for everyone, and will lead to everyone enjoying more free time, and more money to spend on leisure, only in an initially equal society, and such a society will not come about through leisure programmes targeted at the disadvantaged. In societies, and in a world, divided by wide inequalities, the growth of leisure is structured by these inequalities. The long-standing middle–working class schism, and the interdependencies between rich and poor countries, now pivot around relationships of consumption as well as relationships of production. The continued growth of the leisure industries will not lessen these divisions. Current trends will not be towards more and more and more people becoming prosperous consumers until everyone joins this category. This is partly because consumers need workers to service their tastes, but also because crucial commodities will have to be more and more tightly rationed.

Seeking sustainability

Some leisure industries could grow and grow and grow. Maybe at some point demand will be satiated, but at present there appears to be infinite scope for expanding the number of radio and TV programmes and channels, sales of CDs, videos and DVDs. Likewise there is still plenty of room for expansion in the hospitality trades. People can eat more and more of their meals out of the home, and go out for a drink more frequently. They can take more exercise in swimming pools and gyms, and lose more of their money to the gambling industry. At some point pain will set in, but even in the richer countries, not to mention globally, there is still plenty of room for growth. Likewise it may well be possible to stimulate demand for more and more visits to theatres, concerts, art galleries, theme parks, heritage sites, events and other attractions. No doubt people would like to take more holidays. More places can probably find ways of making themselves more attractive as tourist destinations. The problem is that these uses of leisure involve travel. Indeed, governments at city, regional and national levels invest in facilities precisely because they are likely to pull in visitors. There are some astonishing developments in today's busy world of leisure. More and more people are travelling between continents to ski, to play golf, and to experience white water and mountains. More and more people are travelling between countries to watch football matches and concerts (pop and classical). Tourist destinations are all into sustainability nowadays. They are all trying to ensure that visitors do not degrade whatever attracts them. The destinations may well achieve sustainability on their own beaches, in the mountains and in forest areas. The travel is the big problem. It is the environment again – boring ecology, but it's true. At some point the fossil fuels will be depleted. At some point the congestion and pollution from air and road travel will become unbearable. 'Low cost' airlines are not going to turn international travel into a regular feature of everyone's lives. The low costs are most likely to prove temporary and/or exceptional. We can add runways and terminals to existing airports, but this is unlikely to make much impression on the 95 per cent of the global population who are not already international travellers (see Chapter 5, p. 61). Can we create the extra road space to enable car journeys in Europe and North America to triple or even double?

In their rational moments, when in public forums, most people will agree that some kind of rationing is inevitable. Privately they are likely to regard it as desirable that other people should leave their cars garaged thereby creating more road space for 'essential' users such as themselves. In market economies the most likely rationing is by price, which means that it will be the better-off who fly and drive frequently. We can invest in public transport but market pricing of rail and road travel (by bus and taxi) will have the same consequence as the market pricing of air travel: it will be the better-off who have the most access. Martin and Mason (1998) have argued that sustainable leisure must mean local leisure: developing neighbourhood facilities and getting people to spend more of their time and money close to their homes. No politician would wish to convey this message to voters. Actually Martin and Mason are wrong. Allowing a relatively rich minority to consume scarce resources while excluding the rest is also sustainable and, it appears, far easier to sell to voters by creating an impression that, in time, the good life will be brought within everyone's reach.

∗   ∗   ∗

Politicians do not want to tell talented aspirants that there is no public interest in assisting them, let alone try to persuade them that it is not in their own interests, to dedicate their young lives to hopes of fame and fortune in some branch of the leisure industries. They do not want to confront leisure workers with the news that their interests must be sacrificed to those of consumers. Nor do they want to tell consumers that their preferred leisure experiences must be restricted or made more expensive in order to enhance the terms and conditions of employment of leisure workers. Politicians certainly do not want to tell everyone that they must cut back on their travel and all the associated leisure activities. Developing policies in leisure may be difficult. Addressing all the policy issues raised by the growth of the leisure industries may be deemed essential at some time, but not necessarily now.

If present-day commercial leisure not merely reflects but adds an additional dimension to inequalities, and if it will never be possible to extend this version of the good life to everyone, why advocate the further liberation of commerce and more public investment to expand the commercial leisure industries and create more poor jobs? The alternative at present for countries, regions, towns and cities is far less palatable. The leisure business would simply go elsewhere, including much of the leisure business based on the spending of wealthier residents in the relevant territory. There would be less demand for labour, which, all other things remaining equal, would lead to even poorer labour market prospects for those who would otherwise have been offered jobs in leisure. Yet the necessary companion points which have now been made are that the expansion of the leisure industries is not of equal benefit to everyone, and that it will be impossible, even in the long term, for all the people of the world to live in the manner of the present-day Western upper middle classes. Maybe it is not happening now, but somewhere, sometime, some excluded groups will mobilise support for another way and ecology will be on their side.

In the meantime, all strata, not just the rich, still seem to want more of the commercial leisure experience. People are unlikely to vote for politicians who say 'no'. They want to be mobile, to travel widely, to feel free from cares, to demand what they want, when they want, at bargain prices, and on their own socio-cultural terms. This love affair is still alive even though people know – certainly leisure scholars and politicians who head leisure departments ought to know – that this version of the good life will never be for everyone. This book has been about the leisure industries that developed in first world countries during the nineteenth and twentieth centuries. The conditions that hosted these developments will not last for ever. The conditions and trends have not yet been exhausted. Even so, it is most unlikely that we have now reached the end of history.

Bibliography

Adorno, T (1996) *The Culture Industry: Selected Essays on Mass Culture*, Routledge, London.

Adorno, T and M Horkheimer (1977) 'The Culture Industry: enlightenment as mass deception', in J Curran, M Gurevitch and J Woollacott (eds), *Mass Communication and Society*, Edward Arnold, London.

Airola, J with S Craig (2000) *The Projected Economic Impact on Houston of Hosting the 2012 Summer Olympic Games*, Department of Economics, University of Houston, Houston.

Aitchison, C (1997) 'A decade of compulsory competitive tendering in UK sport and leisure services: some feminist reflections', *Leisure Studies*, **16**, 85–105.

Aitchison, C, N E Macleod and S J Shaw (2000) *Leisure and Tourism Landscapes: Social and Cultural Geographies*, Routledge, London.

Albemarle Report (1960) *The Youth Service in England and Wales*, HMSO, London.

Alcohol Concern (2002) *The State of the Nation: Britain's True Alcohol Bill*, www.alcoholconcern.org.uk, 12 February.

Allan, G and G Crow (1991) 'Privatisation, home-centredness and leisure', *Leisure Studies*, **10**, 19–32.

Appadurai, A (1986) *The Social Life of Things: Commodities in Cultural Perspective*, Cambridge University Press, Cambridge.

Appadurai, A (1996) *Modernity at Large: Cultural Dimensions of Globalization*, University of Minnesota Press, Minneapolis.

Audit Commission (1989) *Sport for Whom?*, HMSO, London.

Audit Commission (2002) *Sport and Recreation*, Audit Commission, London.

Bacon, W (1990) 'Gatekeepers of public leisure: a case study of executive managers in the UK', *Leisure Studies*, **9**, 71–87.

Bacon, W (1997) 'The rise of the German and the demise of the English spa industry: a critical analysis of business success and failure', *Leisure Studies*, **16**, 173–87.

Bacon, W and A Pitchford (1992) 'Managerial work in leisure: a deconstruction', in J Sugden and C Knox (eds), *Leisure in the 1990s*, Leisure Studies Association, Eastbourne.

Bailey, P (1978) *Leisure and Class in Victorian England*, Routledge, London.

Baldry, H C (1976) 'Community arts', in J Haworth and A J Veal (eds), *Leisure and the Community*, Leisure Studies Association, University of Birmingham.

Bandyopadhyay, P (1973) 'The holiday camp', in M A Smith *et al.* (eds), *Leisure and Society in Britain*, Allen Lane, London.

Banks, M, I Bates, G Breakwell, J Bynner, N Emler, L Jamieson and K Roberts (1992) *Careers and Identities*, Open University Press, Milton Keynes.

Batan, C M (2002) 'A sociological account of young cellular phone and text users in the Philippines: the case of Metro-Manila', paper presented at International Sociological Association Congress, Brisbane.

Batty, D (2002) 'Caught in the net', *The Guardian*, 18 July, 21.

Baudrillard, J (1998) *The Consumer Society*, Sage, London.

BBC (2002) 'Newspapers reading survey', http://news.bbc.co.uk.

Beck, P J (1999) *Scoring for Britain: International Football and International Politics*, Frank Cass, London.

Bennett, A (2000) *Popular Music and Youth Culture*, Macmillan – now Palgrave Macmillan, Basingstoke.

Bennett, A (2001) *Cultures of Popular Music*, Open University Press, Buckingham.

Berrett, T, T L Burton and T Slack (1993) 'Quality products, quality service: factors leading to entrepreneurial success in the sport and leisure industry', *Leisure Studies*, **12**, 93–106.

Bianchini, F and M Parkinson (eds) (1993) *Cultural Policy and Urban Regeneration*, Manchester University Press, Manchester.

Bishop, J and P Hoggett (1986) *Organising Around Enthusiasms*, Comedia, London.

Bourdieu, P (1984) *Distinction: A Social Critique of the Judgement of Taste*, Routledge, London.

Bourdieu, P and A Darbel (1997) *The Love of Art*, Polity Press, Oxford.

Bowden, S (1994) 'The new consumerism', in P Johnson (ed.), *Twentieth Century Britain*, Longman, London.

Boyd-Barrett, O (1977) 'Media imperialism', in J Curran, M Gurevitch and J Woollacott (eds), *Mass Communication and Society*, Edward Arnold, London.

Braden, S (1978) *Artists and People*, Routledge, London.

Brooks-Buck, J and E L Anderson (2001) 'African American access to higher education through sports: following a dream or perpetuating a stereotype?', *Widening Participation and Lifelong Learning*, **3**, 26–31.

Brown, T J (2002) 'Access to culture: resolving tourism conflicts through visitor research and management', paper presented at Leisure Studies Association Conference, Preston.

Bruce, A C and J E V Johnson (1992) 'Toward an explanation of betting as a leisure activity', *Leisure Studies*, **11**, 201–18.

Bruce, A C and J E V Johnson (1995) 'Costing excitement in leisure betting', *Leisure Studies*, **14**, 48–63.

Bruce, A C and J E V Johnson (1996) 'Gender based differences in leisure behaviour: performance, risk taking and confidence in off-course betting', *Leisure Studies*, **15**, 65–78.

Bryman, A (1995) *Disney and his Worlds*, Routledge, London.

Bulkley, K (2003) 'Everything to play for', *Media Guardian*, 10 March, 2–3.

Burns, T (1977) *The BBC*, Macmillan, London.

Butler, K N (1978) 'Roles of the commercial provider in leisure', in M A Talbot and R W Vickerman (eds), *Social and Economic Costs and Benefits of Leisure*, Leisure Studies Association, Leeds.

Callender, C and M Kemp (2000) *Changing Student Finances: Income, Expenditure and the Take-Up of Student Loans Among Full-Time and Part-Time Higher Education Students in 1998/99*, Research Report 213, Department for Education and Employment, Sheffield.

Campbell, C (1997) 'Shopping, pleasure and the sex war', in P Falk and C Campbell (eds), *The Shopping Experience*, Sage, London.

Campbell, D (2003) 'With pot and porn outstripping corn, America's black economy is flying high', *The Guardian*, 2 May, 3.

Carroll, R (2003) 'What Zola did next', *The Guardian, Guardian 2*, 24 February, 7.

Cashmore, E (1982) *Black Sportsmen*, Routledge, London.

Cassy, J (2002) 'New breed talks a good game', *Guardian*, 30 March, 12.

Cavill, A (2002) 'Repositioning Blackpool to become Las Vegas of the UK', presentation at Leisure Studies Association Conference, Preston.

Centre for Leisure and Sport Research (2002) *Count Me In: The Dimensions of Social Inclusion Through Culture and Sport*, Leeds Metropolitan University, Leeds.

Chatterton, P and R Hollands (2001) *Changing Our 'Toon': Youth Nightlife and Urban Change in Newcastle*, Department of Sociology and Social Policy, University of Newcastle.

Clapson, M (1990) *A Bit of a Flutter*, Manchester University Press, Manchester.

Clark, R R (1980) *The Arts Council*, Centre for Leisure Studies and Research, University of Salford, Salford.

Clarke, A and L Madden (1988) 'The limitations of economic analysis – the case of professional football', *Leisure Studies*, 7, 59–74.

Clarke, J and C Critcher (1985) *The Devil Makes Work*, Macmillan – now Palgrave Macmillan, London.

Coalter, F (1990) 'The politics of professionalism: consumers or citizens', *Leisure Studies*, 9, 107–19.

Coalter, F (1995) 'Compulsory competitive tendering for sport and leisure management', *Managing Leisure*, 1, 3–15.

Coalter, F (1998) 'Leisure studies, leisure policy and social citizenship: the future of welfare or the limits of welfare?', *Leisure Studies*, 17, 21–36.

Coalter, F (2000) 'Public and commercial leisure provision: active citizens and passive consumers', *Leisure Studies*, 19, 163–81.

Coalter, F, M Allison and J Taylor (2000) *The Role of Sport in Regenerating Deprived Urban Areas*, HMSO, Edinburgh.

Coalter, F, J Long and B Duffield (1988) *Recreational Welfare*, Avebury, Aldershot.

Cohen, E (1979) 'A phenomenology of tourist experiences', *Sociology*, 13, 179–201.

Cohen, S (1991) *Rock Culture in Liverpool*, Oxford University Press, Oxford.

Collins, R (1999) 'European Union media and communication', in J Stokes and A Reading (eds), *The Media in Britain: Current Debates and Developments*, Macmillan – now Palgrave Macmillan, Basingstoke.

Cox, B D, F A Huppert and M J Wichelow (1993) *The Health and Lifestyle Survey: Seven Years On*, Dartmouth, Aldershot.

Crisell, A (1999) 'Broadcasting, television and radio', in J Stokes and J Reading (eds), *The Media in Britain: Current Debates and Developments*, Macmillan – now Palgrave Macmillan, Basingstoke.

Critcher, C (1992) 'Sporting civic pride: Sheffield and the World Student Games of 1991', in J Sugden and C Knox (eds), *Leisure in the 1990s*, Leisure Studies Association, Eastbourne.

Critcher, C (2000) 'Still raving: social reaction to ecstasy', *Leisure Studies*, 19, 145–62.

Crompton, J L (2000) 'Repositioning leisure services', *Managing Leisure*, 5, 65–75.

Crompton, J L (2001) 'Public subsidies to professional sport team facilities in the USA', in C Gratton and I Henry (eds), *Sport in the City: The Role of Sport in Economic and Social Regeneration*, Routledge, London, 15–34.

Cross, G (1993) *Time and Money: The Making of Consumer Culture*, Routledge, London.

Crouch, D (ed.) (1999) *Leisure/Tourism Geographies: Practices and Geographical Knowledge*, Routledge, London.

Crowhurst, A (2001) 'The portly grabbers of 75 per cent: capital investment in the British entertainment industry, 1885–1914', *Leisure Studies*, 20, 107–23.

Curran, J (1977) 'Capitalism and control of the press', in J Curran, M Gurevitch and J Woollacott (eds), *Mass Communication and Society*, Edward Arnold, London.

Davidson, J O (1994) 'British sex tourists in Thailand', paper presented to Women's Studies Network Annual Conference, University of Portsmouth, Portsmouth.

Davis, D E (1978) 'Development and the tourist industry in third world countries', *Society and Leisure*, 1, 301–24.

Deckers, P and C Gratton (1995) 'Participation in sport and membership of traditional sports clubs: a case study of gymnastics in the Netherlands', *Leisure Studies*, 14, 117–31.

de Grazia, V (1992) 'Leisure and citizenship: historical perspectives', in *Leisure and New Citizenship*, Actas VIII Congreso ELRA, Bilbao.

DeNora, T (2003) *After Adorno: Rethinking Music Sociology*, Cambridge University Press, Cambridge.

DeNora, T and S Belcher (2000) 'When you're trying something on you picture yourself in a place where they are playing this kind of music – musically sponsored agency in the British retail sector', *Sociological Review*, 48, 80–101.

Department for Culture, Media and Sport, Policy Action Team 10 (1999) *Arts and Sport: A Report to the Social Exclusion Unit*, London.

Department of National Heritage (1995) *Sport: Raising the Game*, Department of National Heritage, London.

Devine, F (1992) *Affluent Workers Revisited: Privatism and the Working Class*, Edinburgh University Press, Edinburgh.

Dex, S, J Willis, R Patterson and E Sheppard (2000) 'Freelance workers and contract uncertainty: the effects of contractual changes in the television industry', *Work, Employment and Society*, **14**, 283–305.

Dixey, R (1987) 'It's a great feeling when you win: women and bingo', *Leisure Studies*, **6**, 199–214.

Dixon, D (1992) *From Prohibition to Regulation*, Clarendon Press, Oxford.

Dixon, R M (1991) *Black Arts, Policy and the Issue of Equity*, Race and Social Policy Unit, University of Liverpool, Liverpool.

Driver, B L, P Brown and G Peterson (1991) *Benefits of Leisure*, Venture Publishing, Pennsylvania.

Dumazedier, J (1974) *Sociology of Leisure*, Elsevier, Amsterdam.

Edwards, A E (2000) *The Impact of Compulsory Competitive Tendering on the Role of the Local Authority Leisure Professional*, PhD thesis, University of Loughborough.

Egerton, M (2002) 'Family transmission of social capital: differences by social class, education and public sector employment', *Sociological Research Online*, **7**, 3.

Elliot, P (1977) 'Media organisations and occupations', in J Curran, M Gurevitch and J Woollacott (eds), *Mass Communication and Society*, Edward Arnold, London.

English Sports Council (1999) *The Development of Sporting Talent 1997*, English Sports Council, London.

Erikson, B H (1996) 'Culture, class and connections', *American Journal of Sociology*, **102**, 217–25.

Eurescom (2002) *e-Living: A Cross Sectional and Comparative Analysis*, www.eurescom.de/e-living/.

European Commission, Directorate-General for Employment and Social Affairs (2001) *Exploitation and Development of the Job Potential in the Cultural Sector*, European Commission, Brussels.

European Commission, Directorate-General for Employment and Social Affairs (2003) *The New Actors of Employment*, Office for Official Publications of the European Communities, Luxembourg.

Evans, G (1995) 'The National Lottery: planning for leisure or pay up and play the game?', *Leisure Studies*, **14**, 225–44.

Evans, G L (1999) 'The economics of the national performing arts – exploring consumer surplus and willingness to pay: a case of cultural policy failure', *Leisure Studies*, **18**, 97–118.

Eysenck, H J and D K D Nias (1978) *Sex, Violence and the Media*, Maurice Temple Smith, London.

Featherstone, M (1991) *Consumer Culture and Post-Modernism*, Sage, London.

Filby, M P (1992) 'The figures, the personality and the bums: service work and sexuality', *Work, Employment and Society*, **6**, 23–42.

Filby, M and L Harvey (1988) 'Recreational betting: everyday activity and strategies', *Leisure Studies*, **7**, 159–72.

Filby, M and L Harvey (1989) 'Recreational betting: individual betting profiles', *Leisure Studies*, **8**, 219–27.

Finnegan, R (1989) *The Hidden Musicians*, Cambridge University Press, Cambridge.

Fisher, S (1993) 'The pull of the fruit machine: a sociological typology of young players', *Sociological Review*, **41**, 446–74.

Fitzherbert, L (1995) *Winners and Losers: The Impact of the National Lottery*, Joseph Rowntree Foundation, York.

Flyvbjerg, B, N Bruzelius and W Rothengatter (2003) *Megaprojects and Risk: An Anatomy of Ambition*, Cambridge University Press, Cambridge.

Football Foundation (2003) *Register of English Football Facilities*, Football Foundation, London.

Franzen, A (2000) 'Does the internet make us lonely?', *European Sociological Review*, **16**, 427–38.

Frith, S (1978) *The Sociology of Rock*, Constable, London.

Frith, S (1988) *Music for Pleasure*, Polity Press, Cambridge.

Gabriel, Y and T Lang (1995) *The Unmanageable Consumer*, Sage, London.

Gaming Board for Great Britain (2000) *Internet Gambling*, www.gbgb.org.uk.

Gardner, P (1974) *Nice Guys Finish Last: Sport and American Life*, Allen Lane, London.

Garland, J, D Malcolm and M Rowe (eds) (2000) *Future of Football*, Frank Cass, London.

Gershuny, J (1978) *After Industrial Society*, Macmillan, London.

Gershuny, J (2000) *Changing Times: Work and Leisure in Postindustrial Society*, Oxford University Press, Oxford.

Gibbons, F (2003) 'Get a grip on lottery projects, arts council told', *The Guardian*, 2 May, 7.

Giddens, A (1998) *The Third Way: The Renewal of Social Democracy*, Polity Press, Cambridge.

Giddens, A (2001) *Sociology*, 4th edn, Polity Press, Cambridge.

Gillespie, D L, A Leffler and E Lerner (2002) 'If it weren't for my hobby, I'd have a life: dog sports, serious leisure and boundary negotiations', *Leisure Studies*, 21, 285–304.

Glyptis, S (1989) *Leisure and Unemployment*, Open University Press, Milton Keynes.

Godbey, G (1997) *Leisure and Leisure Services in the 21st Century*, Venture Publishing, Pennsylvania.

Gratton, C, N Dobson and S Shibli (2001) 'The role of major sports events in the economic regeneration of cities: lessons from six World or European championships', in C Gratton and I Henry (eds), *Sport in the City: The Role of Sport in Economic and Social Regeneration*, Routledge, London, 35–45.

Gratton, C and I Henry (2001) 'Sport in the city: where do we go from here?', in C Gratton and I Henry (eds), *Sport in the City: The Role of Sport in Economic and Social Regeneration*, Routledge, London, 309–14.

Gratton, C and P Taylor (2000) *Economics of Sport and Recreation*, Spon, London.

Green, M and B Oakley (2001) 'Elite sport development systems and playing to win: uniformity and diversity in international approaches', *Leisure Studies*, 20, 247–67.

Grunewald, R de A (2002) 'Tourism and cultural revival', *Annals of Tourism Research*, 29, 4, 1004–21.

Guerrier, Y and A S Adib (2000) 'No, we don't provide that service: the harassment of hotel employees by customers', *Work, Employment and Society*, 14, 689–705.

Hall, C M (2001) 'Imaging, tourism and sports events fever: the Sydney Olympics and the need for a social charter for mega-events', in C Gratton and I Henry (eds), *Sport in the City: The Role of Sport in Economic and Social Regeneration*, Routledge, London, 166–83.

Hall, S and T Jefferson (eds) (1976) *Resistance Through Rituals*, Hutchinson, London.

Hanson, D (1982) *The Professionalisation of Fun*, Centre for Leisure Studies and Research, University of Salford, Salford.

Hantrais, L and T J Kamphorst (eds) (1987) *Trends in the Arts: A Multinational Perspective*, Giordano Bruno, Amersfoort.

Hargreaves, J (1975) 'The political economy of mass sport', in S Parker *et al.* (eds), *Sport and Leisure in Contemporary Society*, Leisure Studies Association, London.

Hargreaves, J (1985) 'From social democracy to authoritarian populism: state intervention in sport and physical recreation in contemporary Britain', *Leisure Studies*, 4, 219–26.

Harker, D (1978) *One for the Money*, Hutchinson, London.

Harper, R (2001) *Social Capital: A Review of the Literature*, Office for National Statistics, London.

Harper, W J (1997) 'The future of leisure: making leisure work', *Leisure Studies*, 16, 189–98.

Heeley, J (1986) 'Leisure and moral reform', *Leisure Studies*, 5, 57–67.

Henley Centre (1993) *Inbound Tourism – A Packaged Future*, London.

Henry, I P (2001) *The Politics of Leisure Policy*, Palgrave – now Palgrave Macmillan, Basingstoke.

Henry, I and P Bramham (1986) 'Leisure, the local state and social order', *Leisure Studies*, 5, 189–209.

Henry, I and C Gratton (2001) 'Sport in the city: research issues', in C Gratton and I Henry (eds), *Sport in the City: The Role of Sport in Economic and Social Regeneration*, Routledge, London, 3–11.

Hesmondhalgh, D (1998) 'The British dance music industry: a case study of independent cultural production', *British Journal of Sociology*, 49, 234–51.

Hesmondhalgh, D (2002) *The Cultural Industries*, Sage, London.

Hill, J (2002) *Sport, Leisure and Culture in Twentieth Century Britain*, Palgrave – now Palgrave Macmillan, Basingstoke.

Hodgson, P (1988) 'Why leisure research is different', 41st ESOMAR Market Research Conference, Lisbon.

Hoggart, R (1957) *The Uses of Literacy*, Chatto & Windus, London.

Hollands, R G (1995) *Friday Night, Saturday Night*, Department of Social Policy, University of Newcastle.

Hollands, R (2002) 'Divisions in the dark: youth cultures, transitions and segmented consumption spaces in the night-time economy', *Journal of Youth Studies*, **5**, 153–71.

Hollands, R and P Chatterton (2002) 'Producing nightlife in the new entertainment urban economy: corporatisation, branding and market segmentation', paper presented at International Sociological Association Congress, Brisbane.

Houlihan, B (1990) 'The politics of sports policy in Britain', *Leisure Studies*, **9**, 55–69.

Houlihan, B (1997) *Sport, Policy and Politics*, Spon, London.

Houlihan, B and A White (2002) *The Politics of Sports Development: Development of Sport or Development Through Sport?*, Routledge, London.

Hughes, G and M Boyle (1992) 'Place boosterism: political contention, leisure and culture in Glasgow', in J Sugden and C Knox (eds), *Leisure in the 1990s*, Leisure Studies Association, Eastbourne.

Hutchinson, R (1975) 'Provision for the performing arts', in S Parker and J Haworth (eds), *Leisure and Public Policy*, Leisure Studies Association, Birmingham.

Hutson, S (1979) *A Review of the Role of Clubs and Voluntary Associations Based on a Study of Two Areas of Swansea*, Sports Council/Social Science Research Council, London.

Ingham, A G (1985) 'From public issue to personal trouble: well-being and the fiscal crisis of the state', *Sociology of Sport Journal*, **2**, 43–55.

Jam Feng-chien Lee (2002) 'The exploratory study of youth's behaviour in the internet chat room in Taiwan', paper presented at International Sociological Association Congress, Brisbane.

Jeffreys, S (1999) 'Globalising sexual exploitation: sex tourism and the traffic in women', *Leisure Studies*, **18**, 179–96.

Kahn, N (1976) *The Arts Britain Ignores*, Community Relations Commission, London.

Katz-Gerro, T (1998) 'Leisure activities and cultural tastes as lifestyle indicators: a comparative analysis of Germany, Sweden, Italy, and the USA', in F Lobo (ed.), *Social Knowledge: Heritage, Challenges, Perspectives*. Proceedings of Research Committee 13, 14th World Congress of Sociology, Edith Cowan University, Perth.

Kay, T A (1987) *Leisure in the Life-Styles of Unemployed People: A Case Study in Leicester*, PhD thesis, Loughborough University of Technology, Loughborough.

King, A (1998) *The End of the Terraces*, Leicester University Press, London.

King, P, S Town and S Warner (1985) 'Leisure provision and ethnic minorities in Bradford', in I Henry (ed.), *Leisure Policy and Recreation Disadvantage*, Newsletter Supplement, Leisure Studies Association, Bradford.

Kingsbury, A (1976) 'Animation', in J Haworth and A J Veal (eds), *Leisure and the Community*, Leisure Studies Association, University of Birmingham.

Kraut, R, V Lundmark, M Patterson, S Kiesler, T Mukopadhyay and W Scherlis (1998) 'Internet paradox: a social technology that reduces social involvement and psychological well-being', *American Psychologist*, **53**, 1017–31.

Lancaster, B (1996) *The Department Store: A Social History*, Leicester University Press, Leicester.

Lee, A J (1976) *The Origins of the Popular Press, 1855–1914*, Croom Helm, London.

Lengkeek, J (2000) 'Imagination and differences in tourist experience', *World Leisure Journal*, **42**, 3, 11–17.

Li, Y, M Savage, G Tampubolon, A Warde and M Tomlinson, 'Dynamics of social capital: trends and turnover in associational membership in England and Wales, 1972–1999', *Sociological Research Online*, **7**, 3.

London, J and J Hearder (1997) *Youth and Music in Australia: Part I – A Review*, Australian Broadcasting Authority, Sydney.

Longhurst, B (1995) *Popular Music and Society*, Polity Press, Cambridge.

Lowe, G (2002) 'Teenagers and the mall: findings from a survey of teenagers at Royal Randwick Shopping Centre', paper presented at *International Sociological Association Congress*, Brisbane.

Lowe, M (2002) 'Working in leisure – a part-time career', *Leisure Studies Association Newsletter*, **61**, March, 10–13.

Macbeth, J (2000) *Are Women Players Discriminated Against in Professional Tennis? A Critical Economic Analysis of Prize Money Differentials and Relative Earnings at Grand Slam Tournaments*, Stirling Research Papers in Sports Studies, 1, 1, University of Stirling, Stirling.

MacCannell, D (1976) *The Tourist: A New Theory of the Leisure Class*, Macmillan – now Palgrave Macmillan, London.

McCrone, D, A Morris and R Kiely (1995) *Scotland – The Brand: The Making of Scottish Heritage*, Edinburgh University Press, Edinburgh.

McCullagh, C (2002) *Media Power: A Sociological Introduction*, Palgrave – now Palgrave Macmillan, Basingstoke.

McDonald, P (1999) 'The music industry', in J Stokes and A Reading (eds), *The Media in Britain: Current Debates and Developments*, Macmillan – now Palgrave Macmillan, Basingstoke.

McGovern, P (2002) 'Globalization or internationalization? Foreign footballers in the English leagues, 1946–95', *Sociology*, **26**, 23–42.

McNamee, M J, H Sheridan and J Buswell (2000) 'Paternalism, professionalism and public sector leisure provisions: the boundaries of a leisure profession', *Leisure Studies*, **19**, 199–209.

McNamee, M J, H Sheridan and J Buswell (2001) 'The limits of utilitarianism as a professional ethic in public sector leisure policy and provision', *Leisure Studies*, **20**, 173–97.

Magee, J (2002) 'Shifting balances of power in the new football economy', in J Sugden and A Tomlinson (eds), *Power Games: A Critical Sociology of Sport*, Routledge, London, 216–39.

Malbon, B (1999) *Clubbing, Dancing, Ecstasy and Vitality*, Routledge, London.

Malcolmson, R W (1973) *Popular Recreations in English Society, 1700–1850*, Cambridge University Press, London.

Manchester City Council (2003) *The Impact of the Manchester 2002 Commonwealth Games*, www.manchester.gov.uk/corporate/games/impact.htm accessed February 2003.

Markovits, A S and S L Hellerman (2001) *Offside: Soccer and American Exceptionalism*, Princeton University Press, Princeton.

Martin, B and S Mason (1988) 'The role of tourism in urban regeneration', *Leisure Studies*, **7**, 75–80.

Martin, W B and S Mason (1998) *Transforming the Future: Rethinking Free Time and Work*, Leisure Consultants, Sudbury.

Meethan, K (2001) *Tourism in Global Society: Place, Culture, Consumption*, Palgrave – now Palgrave Macmillan, Basingstoke.

Meller, H E (1976) *Leisure and the Changing City, 1870–1914*, Routledge, London.

Miah, A (2000) 'Virtually nothing: re-evaluating the significance of cyberspace', *Leisure Studies*, **19**, 211–25.

Miles, S (2000) *Youth Lifestyles in a Changing World*, Open University Press, Buckingham.

Miller, D (1995) 'Consumption in the vanguard of history', in D Miller (ed.), *Acknowledging Consumption*, Routledge, London.

Moore, K (2002) 'Football: our common culture?', presentation at Leisure Studies Association Conference, Preston.

Morgan, N and A Pritchard (1998) *Tourism Promotion and Power: Creating Images, Creating Identities*, Wiley, Chichester.

Morgan, N J and A Pritchard (1999) *Power and Politics at the Seaside*, University of Exeter Press, Exeter.

Morley, D (1986) *Family Television: Cultural Power and Domestic Leisure*, Comedia, London.

Mungham, D and G Pearson (eds) (1976) *Working Class Youth Culture*, Routledge, London.

Murdock, G and P Golding (1977) 'Capitalism, communication and class relations', in J Curran, M Gurevitch and J Woollacott (eds), *Mass Communication and Society*, Edward Arnold, London.

Murphy, P E (1985) *Tourism: A Community Approach*, Methuen, New York.

Myerscough, J (1988) *Economic Importance of the Arts in Britain*, Policy Studies Institute, London.

Nash, R and S Johnstone (2001) 'The case of Euro96: where did the party go?', in C Gratton and I Henry (eds), *Sport in the City: The Role of Sport in Economic and Social Regeneration*, Routledge, London, 109–23.

National Opinion Research Center (1999) *Gambling Impact and Behavior Study*, University of Chicago, Chicago.

Neal, N (1998) 'You lucky punters! A study of gambling in betting shops', *Sociology*, **32**, 581–600.

Negus, K (1999) *Music Genres and Corporate Cultures*, Routledge, London.

Nichols, T and J O Davidson (1993) 'Privatisation and economism: an investigation among producers in two privatised public utilities in Britain', *Sociological Review*, **41**, 705–30.

Nickson, D, C Warhurst, A Witz and A-M Cullen (1998) 'Aesthetic labour in the service economy: an overlooked development', paper presented to International Labour Markets Conference, Aberdeen.

Oldman, D (1974) 'Chance and skill: a study of roulette', *Sociology*, **8**, 407–26.

Oldman, D (1978) 'Compulsive gamblers', *Sociological Review*, **26**, 349–71.

Operaam (2002) 'Quick facts about opera', www.operam.org.

Parker, G and N Ravenscroft (1999) 'Benevolence, nationalism and hegemony: fifty years of the National Parks and Access to the Countryside Act 1949', *Leisure Studies*, **18**, 297–313.

Patterson, R, S Dex and J Willis (2002) *Working in Television*, Oxford University Press, Oxford.

Paxton, P (1999) 'Is social capital declining in the United States? A multiple indicator assessment', *American Journal of Sociology*, **105**, 88–127.

Peterson, R A and R M Kern (1996) 'Changing highbrow taste: from snob to omnivore', *American Sociological Review*, **61**, 900–7.

Pontinen, P (1996) 'Moral panics revisited', in H Helve and J Bynner (eds), *Youth and Life Management: Research Perspectives*, Helsinki University Press, Yliopistopaino.

Putnam, R D (1995) 'Bowling alone: America's declining social capital', *Journal of Democracy*, **6**, 65–78.

Putnam, R D (1996) 'The strange disappearance of civic America', *American Prospect*, **24**, 34–48.

Putnam, R D (2000) *Bowling Alone: The Collapse and Revival of American Community*, Simon & Schuster, New York.

Railton, D (2000) 'Somebody to love: the complex masculinities of boy band pop', *Leisure Studies Association Newsletter*, **56**, 30–4.

Ralston, R, P Downward and L Lumsdon (2003) 'The XVII Commonwealth Games – an initial overview of the expectations and experiences of volunteers', in G Nichols (ed.), *Volunteers in Sport*, Leisure Studies Association, Eastbourne, 43–54.

Rapoport, R (1977) 'Leisure and the urban society', in M A Smith (ed.), *Leisure and Urban Society*, Leisure Studies Association, Manchester.

Ravenscroft, N (1993) 'Public leisure provision and the good citizen', *Leisure Studies*, **12**, 33–44.

Ravenscroft, N (1998) 'The changing regulation of public leisure provision', *Leisure Studies*, **17**, 138–54.

Ravenscroft, N, S Chua and L K N Wee (2001) 'Going to the movies: cinema development in Singapore', *Leisure Studies*, **20**, 215–32.

Redhead, S (ed.) (1993) *Rave Off: Politics and Deviance in Contemporary Youth Culture*, Avebury, Aldershot.

Reiter, E (1991) *Making Fast Food*, McGill-Queens University Press, London.

Reith, G (1999) *The Age of Chance: Gambling in Western Culture*, Routledge, London.

Richards, N and K Milestone (2000) 'What difference does it make? Women's pop cultural production and consumption in Manchester', *Sociological Research Online*, **5**, 1.

Riordan, J (1982) 'Leisure, the state and the individual in the USSR', *Leisure Studies*, **1**, 65–79.

Ritzer, G (1993) *The McDonaldization of Society*, Pine Forge Press, Thousand Oaks.

Ritzer, G (1998) *The McDonaldization Thesis*, Sage, London.

Ritzer, G (1999) *Enchanting a Disenchanted World: Revolutionizing the Means of Consumption*, Pine Forge Press, Thousand Oaks.

Ritzer, G (2001) *Explorations in the Sociology of Consumption: Fast Food, Credit Cards and Casinos*, Sage, London.

Roadburg, A (1977) *An Enquiry into Meanings of Work and Leisure*, PhD thesis, University of Edinburgh, Edinburgh.

Roberts, K (1999a) *Leisure in Contemporary Society*, CAB International, Wallingford.

Roberts, K (1999b) 'Deprofessionalise or die: the end of century choice for the leisure professions', *World Leisure and Recreation*, **41**, 4, 20–5.

Roberts, K (2000) 'The impact of leisure on society', *World Leisure Journal*, **42**, 3, 3–10.

Roberts, K (2001) *Class in Modern Britain*, Palgrave – now Palgrave Macmillan, Basingstoke.

Roberts, K and D Brodie (1992) *Inner-City Sport: Who Plays and What are the Benefits?*, Giordano Bruno, Culemborg.

Roberts, K, S C Clark and C Wallace (1994) 'Flexibility and individualisation: a comparison of transitions into employment in England and Germany', *Sociology*, **28**, 31–54.

Roberts, K, S C Clark, C Fagan and J Tholen (2000) *Surviving Post-Communism: Young People in the Former Soviet Union*, Edward Elgar, Cheltenham.

Robins, D (1990) *Sport as Prevention*, Occasional Paper 12, Centre for Criminological Research, University of Oxford, Oxford.

Robinson, J P and G Godbey (1999) *Time For Life: The Surprising Ways Americans Use Their Time*, Pennsylvania State University Press, Pennsylvania.

Robson, K (2003) *Teenage Time Use as Investment in Cultural Capital*, Working Paper 2003–12, Working Papers of the Institute for Social and Economic Research, University of Essex, Colchester.

Roche, M (1992) 'Mega-events and micro-modernization: on the sociology of the new urban tourism', *British Journal of Sociology*, **43**, 563–600.

Roche, M (2000) *Mega-events and Modernity: Olympics and Expos in the Growth of Global Culture*, Routledge, London.

Rojek, C (1993) 'Disney culture', *Leisure Studies*, **12**, 121–35.

Rojek, C (1997) 'Leisure in the writings of Walter Benjamin', *Leisure Studies*, **16**, 155–71.

Rojek, C (2000) *Leisure and Culture*, Macmillan – now Palgrave Macmillan, Basingstoke.

Rowe, D (1995) *Popular Cultures: Rock Music, Sport and the Politics of Pleasure*, Sage, London.

Rushton, D (2003) *Volunteers, Helpers and Socialisers: Social Capital and Time Use*, Office for National Statistics, London.

Russell, N and N Drew (2001) *ICT Access and Use: Report on the Benchmark Survey*, Research Report 252, Department for Education and Employment, Sheffield.

Russell, N and N Stafford (2002) *Trends in ICT Access and Use*, Research Report 358, Department for Education and Skills, Sheffield.

Ryan, C (2002) 'Tourism and cultural proximity: examples from New Zealand', *Annals of Tourism Research*, **29**, 4, 952–71.

Sassatelli, R (1999) 'Fitness gyms and the local organisation of experience', *Sociological Research Online*, **4**, 3.

Sassen, S (2000) 'The city and the global entertainment industry', in E B Garcia and F Lobo (eds), *Leisure in a Globalized Society*, World Leisure/SESC, Sao Paulo, 423–30.

Saunders, D M and D E Turner (1987) 'Gambling and leisure: the case of racing', *Leisure Studies*, **6**, 281–99.

Scheerder, J, B Vanreusel, M Taks and R Renson (2002) 'Social sports stratification in Flanders 1969–1999', *International Review for the Sociology of Sport*, **37**, 219–45.

Schulz, S (2002) 'Selection processes in the culture industries: the case of the high street fashion industry', paper presented at British Sociological Association Conference, Leicester.

Seabrook, J (1988) *The Leisure Society*, Blackwell, Oxford.

Sharkey, A (1997) 'The land of the free', *Weekend Guardian*, 22 November, 14–25.

Sharp, C, L Kendall, S Bhabra, I Schagen and J Duff (2001) *Playing for Success: An Evaluation of the Second Year*, Research Report 291, Department for Education and Skills, Sheffield.

Sharp, C, C Mawson, K Pocklington, L Kendall and J Morrison (1999) *Playing for Success: An Evaluation of the First Year*, Research Report 167, Department for Education and Employment, Sheffield.

Sharp, D J, J M Greer and G Lowe (1988) 'The normalisation of under-age drinking', paper presented to British Psychological Society, Leeds.

Shaw, P (1999) *The Arts and Neighbourhood Renewal: A Literature Review to Inform the Work of Policy Action Team 10*, Loughborough University, Loughborough.

Shibli, S and C Gratton (2001) 'The economic impact of two major sporting events in two of the UK's national cities of sport', in C Gratton and I P Henry (eds), *Sport in the City: The Role of Sport in Economic and Social Regeneration*, Routledge, London, 78–89.

Shindler, C (2001) *Fathers, Sons and Football*, Headline, London.

Silcock, B (1977) 'Anatomy of the British boozer', *Sunday Times*, 18 December.

Skelton, A, A Bridgwood, K Duckworth, L Hutton, C Fenn, C Creaser and A Babbidge (2002) *Arts in England: Attendance, Participation and Attitudes in 2001*, Arts Council of England, London.

Skogen, K and L Wichstrom (1996) 'Delinquency in the wilderness: patterns of outdoor recreation activities and conduct problems in the general adolescent population', *Leisure Studies*, **15**, 151–69.

Smart, B (ed.) (1999) *Resisting McDonaldization*, Sage, London.

Smith, M A (1982) *Brewing Industry Policy, the Public House and Alcohol Consumption Patterns in the UK*, Centre for Leisure Studies and Research, University of Salford, Salford.

Smith, R and T Maughan (1997) *Youth Culture and the Making of the Post-Fordist Economy: Dance Music in Contemporary Britain*, Discussion Paper DP97/2, Royal Holloway College, London.

Smith, S L J (1995) *Tourism Analysis: A Handbook*, Longman, Harlow.

Snape, R (2002) 'The Co-operative Holiday Association: rambling, respectability and romance in Victorian Britain', paper presented to Leisure Studies Association Conference, Preston.

Somnez, S, K Shinew, L Marchese, C Veldkamp and G W Burnet (1993) 'Leisure corrupted: an artist's portrait of leisure in a changing society', *Leisure Studies*, **12**, 266–76.

South-West Economic Planning Council (1976) *Economic Survey of the Tourist Industry in the South-West*, HMSO, London.

Sports Council (1985) *Olympic Review: Preparing for '88*, Sports Council, London.

Sports Council (1989) *Solent Sports Counselling Project*, Sports Council, London.

Stabler, M and N Ravenscroft (1994) 'The economic evaluation of output in public leisure services', *Leisure Studies*, **13**, 111–32.

Stebbins, R A (1992) *Amateurs, Professionals and Serious Leisure*, McGill-Queens University Press, Montreal.

Street, J (1993) 'Global culture, local politics', *Leisure Studies*, **12**, 191–201.

Sugden, J and A Tomlinson (1998) *FIFA and the Contest for World Football*, Polity Press, Cambridge.

Talbot, M (1990) 'Being herself through sport', in J Long (ed.), *Leisure, Health and Wellbeing*, Leisure Studies Association Conference Papers 64, Brighton Polytechnic, Eastbourne.

Tan Ying and K Roberts (1995) 'Sports policy in the People's Republic of China', in S Fleming, M Talbot and A Tomlinson (eds), *Policy and Politics in Sport, Physical Education and Leisure*, Leisure Studies Association, Brighton.

Taylor, P (1992) 'Commercial leisure: exploiting consumer preferences', in J Sugden and C Knox (eds), *Leisure in the 1990s*, Leisure Studies Association, Eastbourne.

Taylor, P (2001) 'Sports facility development and the role of forecasting: a retrospective on swimming in Sheffield', in C Gratton and I Henry (eds), *Sport in the City: The Role of Sport in Economic and Social Regeneration*, Routledge, London, 214–26.

Thornton, S (1995) *Club Cultures: Music, Media and Subcultural Capital*, Polity Press, Cambridge.

Tomlinson, A (1979) *Leisure and the Role of Clubs and Voluntary Groups*, Social Science Research Council/Sports Council, London.

Tomlinson, A (ed.) (1990) *Consumption, Identity and Style*, Routledge, London.

Tomlinson, A (1999) *The Game's Up: Essays on the Cultural Analysis of Sport, Leisure and Popular Culture*, Ashgate, Oxford.

Toohey, K and A J Veal (1999) *The Olympic Games: A Social Science Perspective*, CAB International, Wallingford.

Town, S (1983) 'Recreation and the unemployed: experiments in Bradford', *Leisure Studies Association Newsletter*, **4**, 5–10.

Travis, A S (1979) *The State and Leisure Provision*, Social Science Research Council/Sports Council, London.

Turner, L and J Ash (1975) *The Golden Hordes*, Constable, London.

Tyler, M and P Abbott (1998) 'Chocs away: weight watching in the contemporary airline industry', *Sociology*, **32**, 433–50.

Urry, J (1990) *The Tourist Gaze*, Sage, London.

Urry, J (2001) 'Transports of delight', *Leisure Studies*, **20**, 237–45.

Urry (2002) 'Mobility and proximity', *Sociology*, **36**, 255–74.

van der Poel, H (1994) 'The modularisation of daily life', in I Henry (ed.), *Leisure, Modernity, Postmodernity and Lifestyles*, Leisure Studies Association, Eastbourne.

van Eijck, K (1999) 'Socialisation, education and lifestyle: how social mobility increases the cultural heterogeneity of status groups', *Poetics*, 26, 309–38.

van Moorst, H (1982) 'Leisure and social theory', *Leisure Studies*, **1**, 157–69.

van Ophem, J and K de Hoog (1998) 'Differences in leisure behaviour of the poor and the rich in the Netherlands at the beginning of the 1990s', in J W te Kloetze (ed.), *Family and Leisure in Poland and the Netherlands*, Garant, Leuven-Apeldoorn.

Waddington, I, E Dunning and P Murphy (1996) 'Research note: surveying the social composition of football crowds', *Leisure Studies*, **15**, 209–14.

Wagg, S (ed.) (1994) *Giving the Game Away*, Leicester University Press, London.

Walvin, J (1975) *The People's Game*, Allen Lane, London.

Walvin, J (1978) *Beside the Seaside*, Allen Lane, London.

Warde, A and L Martens (2000) *Eating Out: Social Differentiation, Consumption and Pleasure*, Cambridge University Press, Cambridge.

Wearing, B (1998) *Leisure and Feminist Theory*, Sage, London.

Wearing, B and S Wearing (1992) 'Identity and the commodification of leisure', *Leisure Studies*, **11**, 3–18.

Wearing, S and C Foley (2002) 'The mobile phone; a fashion accessory or blanket security? Conspicuous consumption, identity and adolescent women's leisure choices', paper presented at International Sociological Association Congress, Brisbane.

Weed, M (2003) 'Mediated and inebriated? The pub as a spectator sports venue during the 2002 Football World Cup', paper presented at Leisure Studies Association Conference, Roehampton.

Weisbrod, B A (1988) *The Non-Profit Economy*, Harvard University Press, Harvard.

Whannel, G (1986) 'The unholy alliance: notes on television and the remaking of British sport, 1965–85', *Leisure Studies*, **5**, 129–45.

Whitsun, D (1987) 'Leisure, the state and collective consumption', in J Horne, D Jary and A Tomlinson (eds), *Sport, Leisure and Social Relations*, Routledge, London.

Wilders, M G (1976) 'Some preliminary observations on the sociology of the public house', in S Parker *et al.* (eds), *Sport and Leisure in Contemporary Society*, Leisure Studies Association, London.

Williams, J (1996) 'Surveying the social composition of football crowds: a reply to Waddington, Dunning and Murphy', *Leisure Studies*, **15**, 215–19.

Williams, R (1963) *Culture and Society, 1780–1950*, Penguin, Harmondsworth.

Willis, P (1990) *Common Culture*, Open University Press, Milton Keynes.

Wilson, J (1988) *Politics and Leisure*, Unwin Hyman, London.

Witt, P A and J L Crompton (eds) (1996) *Recreation Programmes that Work for At-Risk Youth*, Venture Publishing, Pennsylvania.

Wright, K (2000) 'Charitable change – creating a new culture of giving for Britain', *LSE Magazine*, **12**, 2, 19–21.

Yule, J (1997) 'Engendered ideologies and leisure policy in the UK', *Leisure Studies*, **16**, 61–84 and 139–54.

Zuzanek, J (1977) 'Leisure trends and the economics of the arts', in M A Smith (ed.), *Leisure and Urban Society*, Leisure Studies Association, Manchester.

Index

226